Visual Programming
Technology

Other McGraw-Hill Books of Related Interest

ISBN	AUTHOR	TITLE
0-07-912986-2	Harms, Fiske	*Web Site Programming with Java*
0-07-709292-9	Manger	*Essential Java: Developing Interactive Applications for the World Wide Web*
0-07-912273-6	Muller	*The Webmaster's Guide to HTML*
0-07-912309-0	Nemzow	*Visual Basic Developer's Toolkit*
0-07-709167-1	Zetie	*Practical User Interface Design*

Visual Programming Technology

Dimitris N. Chorafas

McGraw-Hill

New York   San Francisco   Washington, D.C.   Auckland   Bogotá
Caracas   Lisbon   London   Madrid   Mexico City   Milan
Montreal   New Delhi   San Juan   Singapore
Sydney   Tokyo   Toronto

Library of Congress Cataloging-in-Publication Data

Chorafas, Dimitris N.
   Visual programming technology / Dimitris N. Chorafas.
       p.   cm.
   Includes index.
   ISBN 0-07-011685-7
    1. Visual programming (Computer science) 2. Visual programming
languages (Computer science) I. Title.
QA76.65.C47 1997
005.1—dc20
                                         96-9933
                                           CIP

McGraw-Hill

A Division of The McGraw·Hill Companies

1 2 3 4 5 6 7 8 9 0 DOC/DOC 9 0 1 0 9 8 7 6

ISBN 0-07-011685-7

*The sponsoring editor for this book was John Wyzalek, the editing supervisor was
Jane Palmieri, and the production supervisor was Suzanne W. B. Rapcavage. It
was set in Century Schoolbook by Ron Painter of McGraw-Hill's Professional
Publishing Group composition unit.*

Printed and bound by R. R. Donnelley & Sons Company.

McGraw-Hill books are available at special quantity discounts to use as premi-
ums and sales promotions, or for use in corporate training programs. For more
information, please write to the Director of Special Sales, McGraw-Hill, 11 West
19th Street, New York, NY 10011. Or contact your local bookstore.

This book is printed on recycled, acid-free paper containing a
minimum of 50% recycled, de-inked fiber.

Contents

Preface

Many technical innovations were expected to change basic tenets in information systems, such as computer programming. But they disappeared without trace. Some others were thought to be nonstarters or to have addressed themselves to niche markets. Yet, they had a profound impact on the state of the art.

Visual programming technology falls in this second category. Artifacts originally developed to address the needs of engineers working in computer-aided design (CAD) found their way into a much wider market. Tier 1 banks, for instance, are convinced users of three-dimensional graphics and other visualization tools.

Object-oriented solutions and simulation have given further thrust to visual programming, but perhaps the most important factor propelling interactive visual technology as a better means to program machines is the Internet. That's why the text you have in your hands pays so much attention to the World Wide Web, Virtual Reality Modeling Language (VRML), and Java.

This book is designed for the professional market. It is addressed to information technologists in business and industry—from computer vendors to user organizations—providing both advice and practical examples. The book can also serve colleges and universities in graduate-level courses and as a reference material.

The goal of this text is to ensure an up-to-date description of the most significant developments in the software industry, based on an extensive research project done from 1993 to 1996 in the United States, Japan, and Europe among communications, computer, and software vendors and among leading user organizations in manufacturing and in finance.

The research was done on three continents and in academic institutions. Leading technologists in computers, communications, and software contributed ideas and information on visual programming techniques as well as references to what they have delivered with the new tools in their own spheres of activity.

The input received in the course of the research meetings permits me to identify the new domains of visual programming applications. This text elaborates on the developing implementation perspectives, presents the breakthroughs which have been achieved, and discusses some of the most outstanding research projects. It also outlines the systems solutions necessary to fruitfully exploit new software technology.

To address the changing role of programming tools and at the same time the evolving structure of computer programming solutions, the book reviews the requirements for leadership in the coming years, doing so from different viewpoints. That's why equipment manufacturers, software developers, and academic institutions have an interest in its contents.

The book is divided into five parts. Part 1 acquaints the reader with the new perspectives. Chapter 1 stresses the point that with the wider and wider diffusion of computer technology, programming is an activity which should be accessible to everybody—and it should be done by everybody.

This is one of the basic reasons why the time for visual programming has come. It provides a user-friendly approach for what I call *programming in the large*. Chapter 2 explains what comes under this heading and why a main beneficiary of this discipline is the end user.

But even the most novel ideas supported by powerful tools are not enough. Very important in programming is the conceptual infrastructure which develops with experience. To help the reader accumulate this experience, Chap. 3 introduces the subject of perception and cognition. Three-dimensional graphics are instrumental in producing interactive metaphors that the user needs for a comprehensive view of the products and processes on which he or she is working.

Part 2 focuses on the cultural change necessary to put these tools to profitable use. If programming continues to be done in the vanilla ice cream way along Cobol and Fortran lines, the results will be minimal, if detectable at all. Chapter 4 introduces the new culture that should be underlying visual programming efforts.

There is a counterpart to visual programming, and that's program visualization, as Chap. 5 suggests. Both processes permit the handling of spatial and temporal relationships, while they also offer an effective feedback to the user, who can then do more with fewer resources.

The impact of the Internet on the old craft of programming computers, particularly in using them as communications devices, is explained in Part 3. Chapter 6 discusses the World Wide Web and the Hypertext Markup Language (HTML), underlining their role in enlarging Internet's implementation horizons. By extension, Chap. 6 also introduces the concept of the *intranet*.

The topic of Chap. 7 is the Virtual Reality Modeling Language (VRML) and its impact on visual programming. In fact, VRML has been chosen as the best example available today of visual programming—if for no other reason than the fact that it is platform-independent, it is good-quality, and its use by end users can be widespread.

Chapter 8 gives a contrarian view of Java. It is not that negative, but neither does this chapter suggest that it is the answer to all prayers, as its promoters advise. Because Java uses an interpreter, it uses processing cycles like a sponge. Hence, it can be more effective with desk-area networks than with network appliances.

The requirements posed by modern computers and communications technology will not necessarily be satisfied only by the visual programming tools available on the Internet. For this reason, Chap. 9 covers further, more sophisticated requirements and introduces some of the three-dimensional visualization and programming tools available today, which assist from program analysis to animation and debugging.

Many of the concepts and programming tools introduced in Parts 1, 2, and 3 are compute-intensive. They also need a substantial communications bandwidth. Part 4 addresses the hardware and software issues underpinning visual programming—from computer-related subjects to telecommunications.

Chapter 10 explains why network appliances will not fulfill the requirements for modern and effective solutions. Rather, there is a need for quite the opposite: desk-area networks (DANs) in computing and the Asynchronous Transfer Mode (ATM) in telecommunications.

If desk-area networks are the answer in regard to computing power for advanced visual programming requirements and ATM provides the communications channel, object-oriented solutions underpin modern software development approaches. Object technology and the benefits users can derive from it are explained in Chap. 11.

Chapter 12 speaks of frameworks and languages for parallel computers. The same chapter also covers the need for integration of software tools, reviews Microsoft's OLE (Active X) as an implementation example, and critically evaluates what frameworks can deliver. Emphasis is placed on parallel computation.

The goal of Part 5 is to provide readers what they need in implementation perspectives for new software technology. The tools which we use in business and industry are not chosen just because of their novelty. The main criterion for their choice is the competitive edge which they can provide—and case studies are the best way to documentation.

Chapter 13 focuses on the developing information technology needs of the virtual bank. It casts the financial institution as a network of autonomous nodes and services, and it examines how advanced visualization tools can provide a significant amount of value differentiation, from financial analysis to management reporting.

Programming in a virtual reality setting is the theme of Chap. 14. A practical example is taken in the virtual dome, a project at the University of Tokyo which has a significant impact on telerobotics. This case study provides a good background for evaluating the effects of visualization on programming in the large, which was introduced in Chap. 2.

Another interesting applications paradigm is News in the Future, an advanced project at MIT. This is discussed in Chap. 15, which also examines similarities and differences between management reports and newspapers as well as the semantics of image modeling. The chapter concludes with the advantages of cost-effective number crunching, which returns the discussion to the hardware and software underpinning visual programming, which has taken place in Part 4.

While this book covers practical visual programming examples from three continents, its real aim is to provide a much needed upgrade of knowledge and skills for experienced technology professionals. It is particularly addressed to people who are seeking new solutions beyond the confines of the more traditional type of software tools, and it emphasizes the benefits to be derived from distributed information systems applications.

The names of senior corporate executives; specialists in computers, communications, software, and multimedia; as well as faculty members who contributed to this research project are found in the Acknowledgments. To all of them I wish to express my appreciation for their advice and assistance.

I am particularly thankful to some of my colleagues for their imaginative ideas and the support they have contributed to the research which led to this book. Particular mention should be made of Dr. Bernard Pedrazzini, whose contribution has been important in connection with Chaps. 7, 8, and 9.

Let me close by presenting my thanks to everyone else who has given a helping hand in making this book successful: most particularly to John Wyzalek for his role in the development of the manuscript and publication of the book; to Jane Palmieri for the excellent editing and production work; and to Eva-Maria Binder for the artwork, the typing of the manuscript, and the index.

Dr. Dimitris N. Chorafas
Valmer and Vitznau
October 1996

A Practical Approach to Visual Programming Solutions

Just as object databases and object programming are indivisible, the concepts of visual programming (VP) and data visualization and modeling cannot and should not be separated from each other. But there are differences in the approaches we take between stand-alone and networked solutions, as well as in the benefits we can derive from them. Part 1 focuses on networking approaches because these are by far the more promising.

Programming Is an Activity
Open to Everybody

1.1 Introduction

In spite of over 40 years of computer use in business and industry as well as in mathematics, engineering, and science, the development of software is still little more than a cottage industry. The techniques that are applied during the design, coding, and testing of computer programs have made no huge strides comparable to those of microprocessors and memory devices.

- Programmer productivity is dismal in spite of the different computer-assisted system engineering (CASE) tools—or because of them.
- Even where new formal tools have been explicitly adopted, the methodology is applied in a disengaged manner.

While programmers may be able to recognize some of the notations of formal methods, they often learn little of the intricacies characterizing the actual application. Therefore, they cannot apply the benefits of CASE tools in a practical, applications-oriented sense.

Besides this, the careful analyst is flabbergasted by the heterogeneity of the different tools and network. There is still no generally accepted discipline in the software engineering process. Over the years, there have been some evolutionary aspects to computer programming, as we will see in Secs. 1.4 and 1.5, but their impact has been fairly limited.

Concepts characterizing programming processes today date back to the 1950s, and they are particularly addressed to the coding aspects of the job. The Codasyl effort, in the late 1950s, introduced data design awareness. Twenty years later, in the late 1970s, fourth-generation languages introduced the notion of functional description and the need for rigorous testing as well as the automation of documentation.

But none of the currently popular languages—including the reincarnations of Fortran and Cobol—really provide the necessary formalisms for a user-friendly requirements analysis. Neither is there support of the necessary continuity, from the evolution of systems description to the automation of maintenance. Those in computer-assisted software engineering have made many promises which, by and large, have not been kept.

New methods and new approaches come and go, and we can never be sure how successful a different solution will be. Yet, there are reasons to believe that with *visual programming* the *software culture* may change, because graphics can effectively assist in the on-line specification of requirements. Graphics is a formal language which

- Can be linked in a seamless manner to the functional specifications
- Can help to define exactly what is to be done in programming terms, including program sustenance

This is now being achieved through the visual programming languages available on Internet, such as the Virtual Reality Modeling Language (VRML) and Java,* which are explained in Part 2. Sections 1.2 to 1.4 are introductory; Secs. 1.5 to 1.7 are a sort of demolition squad, called in to destroy the old programming images; and Secs. 1.8 and 1.9 address Internet, its software, and its languages.

1.2   Computer Programming in a Service Economy

It is an ironic fact, but also a real one, that most programmers and their managers do not yet fully understand that in a globalized economy every product depends for its success on *low costs,* fast *time to market,* and *high-quality* results. Programming is so important because a growing number of manufactured products are software-intensive—and this trend speeds up.

Not only are manufactured products being enhanced through microprocessors and software, but also today's service economy is based on properly functioning global information systems. The companies best positioned to succeed are the ones with first-class software which they roll out at a quick pace.

Another prerequisite for industrial competitiveness is focused data analysis, which must come in at the design level, as the programmer moves from specifying *what* is to be done to *how* it is to be done. Therefore seamless linkages to databases become much more important than ever before, with the program laying down how data is to be represented and in what order. The issues of visual programming and data visualization and modeling are so closely linked that they should be treated as indivisible. This has been true since the 1930s when technology developed scale models—from dams and

---

*Java, which we study in Chap. 6, was originally developed for appliances such as refrigerators—not for personal computers.

Figure 1.1 A fractal diagram is a good example of data visualization and at the same time reflects the programming which takes place in nature.

harbors to wind tunnels. This duality characterizes the way nature is programming itself. The fractal picture in Fig. 1.1 is a good example of dynamic visual programming, but at the same time it is the visualization of information flow from a Mandelbrot model.

In 1953, as a graduate at the University of California at Los Angeles (UCLA) working on von Neumann's standard western automatic calculator (SWAC), I had some colleagues who were able to read on the fly the binary string passing through a Williams tube. This was a fast stream of data and instructions, and it could be seen as a very early example of program visualization, which constitutes the other side of visual programming (see Chap. 5).

- Visual data analysis has many characteristics, and we must think in terms of all of them.
- The special feature of digital computers is that we do not distinguish between data and commands.

Because, however, for about four decades these twin subjects have been treated separately, almost distinct from each other, this chapter refocuses on the nature of human-machine communications. This is a deliberate choice. At the end of this book, Chap. 14 reintegrates visual data analysis and programming as two closely linked concepts. It does so by discussing the why, what, and when of visual programming approaches. To gain perspective, the reader who is versatile in programming may wish to go from Chap. 1 to Chap. 14, prior to reading Chap. 2. Chapter 14 presents an integrative example with the virtual dome.

Providing for seamless linkages to distributed databases is not easy. Programs require, and react to, all possible inputs, while classically specifications usually cover only inputs relevant to the intended context of immediate use. Hence, programmers tend to leave some cases ambiguous or undetermined. This is one of the challenges associated with software artifacts, as we will see through practical examples.

What is surprising is that, in spite of the overwhelming evidence pointing to the fact that business success increasingly depends on smart programs delivered on time and databases steadily sustained, the development and maintenance of software are still, to a very large extent, a manual job. Cognizant people with whom I met during my research made the projection that in the late 1990s

- Dramatic market advantages will go to companies whose systems analysts and programmers are an order of magnitude better than those of competitors.
- Conversely, a company whose software and systems people are laggards compared to those of competitors will be the loser in the toughening-up competition.

In the course of my work, I often come to comparisons between first-class software organizations and the laggards. The results indicate that rapid development timetables, low development budgets, and high-quality standards make the difference. These factors also correlate.

Figure 1.2 relates these fundamental factors to the software effort. From goals to work schedules, wise policies will emphasize not only development objectives but also testability and sustainability—doing so as a matter of life-cycle interest. The requirements implied by an intense software effort are in full evolution.

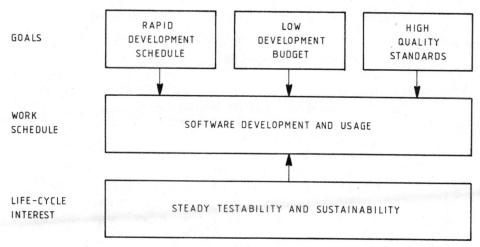

Figure 1.2 Software development and usage should be seen through a life-cycle perspective.

While hard work is always welcome, and quite often it provides worthy results, success in advanced software implementation and use is above all a matter of working more wisely—not just harder. That's what was done by

- Tim Berners-Lee who, while working at CERN, designed the World Wide Web

- Marc Pesce and Gavin Bell, when they created the Virtual Reality Modeling Language

- James Gosling and Arthur Van Hoff, designer and interpreter, respectively, of Java

- Bill Atkinson, in designing Apple's MacPaint and HyperCard software

- Stephen E. Deering, in codeveloping MBone and the Internet Protocol version 6 (IPv6)

- Vinton G. Cerf and Leonard Kleinrock, when they laid the original foundations of Arpanet-Internet and TCP/IP

In contrast to these developments which opened up new applications perspectives, the energy level of the average programmer in the vast majority of data processing shops and scientific installations is not impressive. Most have a difficult time remaining at par with what happens in the industry; some simply live in the dark ages of programming.

How intelligent people fail to appreciate the accelerated level of technological obsolescence, and act accordingly, is a great puzzle. Both the professional analyst-programmers and their management fail to understand that it does not do much good to write lots of software

- *If* it is delivered with delays and budget overruns

- *If* it does not work properly and has to be patched
- *If* it cannot be trusted, or even worse if it is obsolete by the time it is ready
- *If* it cannot be easily modified and sustained

In a service economy, the quality of software is much more important than the number of instructions being generated. Time to market and product quality are key issues for the late 1990s. This is an area where the old, slow, and ineffective methods of software production put a company at a terrible disadvantage.

Above all, the disadvantage is cultural, because the sloppy, slow, costly, and nondependable work done in programming shows throughout the performance of the company's products and processes. The reason why I give so much attention to this issue is that the lack of cultural change is today the number 1 problem.

- *Visual programming* technology is not producing miracles, and it may give poor results if the old culture is maintained.
- The contribution of visual programming is proportional to the prevailing systems methodology, organizational infrastructure, and management controls.

One cause of sloppy work and poor programmer quality is the value system that surrounds computer professionals every day of their working lives. It seems as if data processing managers and their bosses never heard that, to a significant measure, their company's survival depends on the work which they do.

In software production, among the worst mistakes being made is to depend on large numbers of people, rather than on the training, skill, and motivation of a *few highly qualified* individuals. Yet it is the few, not the many, who get the most noteworthy results.

- Big banks employ between 1000 and 2000 programmers each. How can these legions do anything other than step on one another's toes?
- Is it even possible for masses of people to understand the problem, let alone bring to bear imaginative, speedy, high-quality solutions?

Forty-three years of experience convince me that there is no better programmer of the problem on hand than "the person with the problem," that is, the professional R&D scientist, manufacturing engineer, treasurer, investment adviser, trader, or salesperson who needs *sophisticated* computer support and *needs it now.*

This is where *visual programming* can help. The lone programmer, or as a maximum a team of two to three persons, is able to compete effectively in the software marketplace, because the large majority of development projects are not intrinsically huge and complex. They became that way because of mismanagement.

1.3   Why Obsolete Software Tools and Processes Have No Place in the Modern Firm

In a large number of companies, the present methods of developing software are no different from those adopted four decades ago, when computers were expensive and the programmer's time was relatively cheap. Also programming tools were few and not that powerful, so much had to be done by hand.

With the huge changes in costs of machines versus the costs of programmers, the foremost companies readjusted their goals accordingly, but the majority stayed behind. Management is responsible for this failure in technology because, in the last analysis, management

- Elaborates goals
- Chooses tools
- Puts together teams
- Sets deadlines
- Establishes educational policies

Management also decides whether incompetence is allowed and whether the unable, unwilling, and unnecessary run the company. When they not only stay in the system but also are put in key positions, low-skill people impede the work of those who are able to produce high-quality software and are willing to deliver it on time.

Mismanagement sees to it that many software development projects are mundane and boring. I know of at least five different companies where software maintenance is currently done on 25-year-old Cobol programs by programmers who were born after these programs were written. To develop new software through Cobol, Fortran, and other obsolete languages is equally dull.

Because software projects are mismanaged, there exist plenty of ridiculous statistics regarding how programming projects are run—and what sort of queer results are obtained. Table 1.1 gives a glimpse at software mismanagement by emphasizing

- The time needed to complete a project (up to 4 years)
- The average number of people involved
- The total worker-days being invested
- The resulting cost of the project

Some years ago, Bankers Trust audited its software development projects and found out, to its surprise, that 80 percent of its ongoing projects were obsolete before they were completed. This happened because competitors had leapfrogged and took the best out of the market; the law had changed, but the project marched on; the financial products had an evolution which was not

TABLE 1.1   Project Sizes and Associated Costs as Reported in a Late 1995 Survey*

	Projects		
	Small	Average	Large
Days needed to complete project	107	355	876 (4 years)
Average people involved	2	6	21
Total worker-days invested	214	2.130	18.396
Cost of project ($000)	54	620	4800–8200

*Information and Software Technology, vol. 37, no. 11, 1995.

reflected in the software; and most importantly, the software project took years to reach completion.

This led to a cultural revolution at Bankers Trust and a very significant change in policies. But other companies continue on the same beaten path, throwing money at the problem. It is therefore not surprising that some startling statistics have been recently reported by *Information and Software Technology,*[1] of London.

Software delivered but never used	47%
Software paid for but never delivered	29%
Subtotal: Money down the drain	76%
Software used after extensive rework	19%
Software used after some changes	3%
Software used as delivered	2%

This 2 percent would have been a humorous statistic, if it were not published by a serious technical magazine.

Retrograde approaches simply attempt to improve quality, timeliness, and productivity by telling people to "do their best." These tactics always fail because rather than addressing the fundamentals, they just scrape the surface—and the results are pitiful, like the 2 percent rate of software used as delivered.

Yet, there exist today good possibilities for doing a first-class programming job, without waiting forever for *natural languages* to play the major role in computers, as so often promised but never delivered. Over the last 20 years we have heard plenty of hype about natural language programming. Only now *visual programming* offers the possibility to approximate a natural language solution.[2]

For this reason visual programming may well prove to be the missing link between machine language and the end user. I often hear the statement that "A VP in finance or a VP in marketing will not develop a program regardless of how easy the tool is to use," but I don't subscribe to it.

The reason for this response is that there is no great merit in insisting that applications development must still take professional programmers—or that it has to be so "because many organizations develop big programs." My answer to this argument is that user organizations should not develop big programs. If they do, they are at fault.

An example helps to demonstrate how severely that fault may be. A couple of years ago I was talking in Tokyo with the Dai-Ichi Kangyo Bank, one of the world's largest. The executive vice president of information technology said that because of nearly 100 percent terminalization, the bank had a programming backlog of 70,000 worker-years. Then he added: "The only way out is self-service programming."

This self-service programming is practiced in New York City among the top investment banks. They cannot afford to do otherwise. New financial products, like derivatives, have a shelf life measured in hours, days, or months. If the programmers take 2 years to develop software, the bank will not do any business and will go bankrupt.

The answer to another query which is sometimes posed—How can standards be enforced in an organization if everybody programs his own programs?—is also important. It is also straightforward. This must be done through software auditing by systems experts.

In Paris one of the major investment banks, Paribas, has been using self-service in programming for 20 years—well before visual programming arrived. The technology auditors check these programs and follow a three-way classification:

- Those programs which are of general interest and pass the test with honors are generalized.

- Those which are important to the person who developed them and which pass the test are stored locally.

- Those which don't pass the quality test or which present security problems are killed.

Visual programming does not bring to the user any miraculous solutions, but it does contribute to the establishment of a better human-machine programming interface through an interdisciplinary approach. This is shown in Fig. 1.3. Interactive programming tools should help in the analysis of the problem; in seamless database mining; and in the visual representation made to provide the end user with friendly and efficient interfaces.

1.4   What Are We Targeting through Visual Programming?

End-user computing, and therefore end-user programming, is the level for which formal notations need to be established and used, since formality allows an early control process. Effective human-machine communication through graphics helps to reduce errors in the subsequent levels of program development; therefore, it accelerates timetables, saves money, and improves software quality.

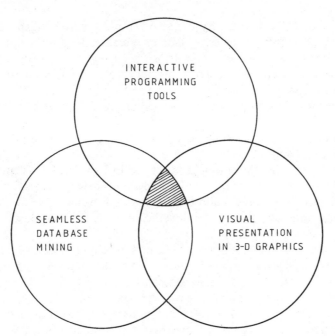

Figure 1.3 Visual programming requires an interdisciplinary approach.

- Visual programming approaches, as we study them in this book, help end-user computing by making programming skills accessible to many professionals and to consumers.

- Good managers have the knowledge to appreciate that numbers of programmers are less important than their skills; and visualization helps in perception and conception. (See also Chap. 3.)

The role of visual programming tools in the years ahead most likely will be more instrumental than any results produced so far by the different linear-type, procedural programming languages. It will also be more profound than the contribution of any of the existing CASE tools.

With the proliferation of multimedia and intelligent software, graphics tools and their natural language characteristics will become an increasingly reliable medium effectively linking people to communications systems through their computers. Visual programming tools will be used as a means of representing, storing, retrieving, converting, and transmitting. They will do so not only for information but also for knowledge. Once this is properly appreciated, the bulk of system software will be concerned with governing these five functions. Agile, knowledge-enriched software modules, or *agents,* and widely accessible electronic dictionaries will serve—the first as on-line assistants, the second as essential metaknowledge bases.

New technology will help not only in user applications but also in systems solutions. Cornell University has designed a binary neural network Java applet (for definitions, see Chap. 8) that works by calculating how much a node is in agreement with the nodes to which it is connected.

- Whether a node value should or should not be like that of a certain neighbor is determined by patterns.

- A distributed pattern agreement is embedded in the nodes, so no node has central control.

In a systems sense this provides fail-soft properties, including possibilities for load balancing. A similar concept can be instrumental in end-user applications, increasing by an order of magnitude the value of obtained results. These are benefits which escape the users of old programming technology.

Table 1.2 presents a projection of the transition currently taking place from Cobol and its precompilers (for instance, Delta), to C++ and graphics, leading to greater effectiveness with visual programming approaches. The type of main user, the associated development timetables, the flexibility of the resulting wares, and the most likely value of obtained results are identified.

In conclusion, the time has come to lay solid foundations for the advent of an era in which every computer contains network software, and every end user is able to explore a range of different scenarios in the research, development, trial, and use of programming artifacts.

- Together with multimedia solutions, language processing through intelligent artifacts will constitute the future infrastructure.

- This foundation will support, in an able manner, computers and communications solutions by the end of this century and beyond.

Understanding the major shift taking place in paradigms is practically synonymous with appreciating that important cultural and structural changes are underway in technology. The old order is giving way to the new, and the new requires powerful vehicles for programming, able to lead toward a state of sustained market competitiveness.

TABLE 1.2   Programming Timetables and Flexibility of the Application

Language	User	Development timetable	Flexibility	Value of obtained result
Cobol	Classical programmer	2 to 3 years	None	1
Delta	Classical programmer	6 months to 1 year	Minimal	10
C++	Designer, analyst	2 to 6 months	Fair	100
Classical Graphics	Designer, analyst	about 1 month	Good	1,000
Visual programming	End user (self-service)	3 to 5 days	Instantaneous change	10,000
Three-dimensional VP tools	End user (self-service)	1 hour to 1 day	Full interactivity	100,000

1.5 Explaining Fifty Years of Transition in Five Pages

The examples given in Sec. 1.4 are not the rule, but the exception. To understand how we have reached the state of ossification in programming practices in which most companies find themselves today, we should look back rapidly at the evolution of the last 50 years, in other words, since we started to use computers in business and industry for reasons other than military.

In the mid-1940s, the programming of accounting machines, certain analog computers, and even some of the then-available digital computers was done by plugging wires on a control board. These boards were read by a huge electromechanical machine. To a very substantial extent, this concept has found its way into the programming languages which are most popular today.[3]

Some of the tools have changed, but most of the concepts remain the same. While presently space balls and the mouse are used to manipulate visual images on machines as small as a notebook, this difference in media makes it easy to forget that software still revolves on a linear way of programming the computer—based on archaic concepts and awkward languages.

Not only has the plug board left its mark on programming, but also the punched card has had a deep impact on the foolish way in which we used disk memory. Serious studies document that because computer files are designed in the image of 80-column punched cards:

- On the average, only 5 percent of the available storage capacity is effectively used.

- Companies, however, pay 100 percent of the disk memory (they rent or buy) to their vendors, resulting in a 95 percent spoilage.

If the reader wants to know how far back these plug board and punched cards concepts go, they are more than 100 years old. Punched cards were invented by Herman Hollerith for use in the 1890 U.S. census. This approach had been suggested to Hollerith by his brother-in-law who worked in the textile industry and knew about an automatic weaving system involving sprung hooks pressed against a paper card with holes in it.

Where there was a hole, a hook passed through and picked up a thread. Hollerith replaced the hooks with electric wires and made each wire represent a piece of census data. Where a wire passed through a hole, it would make electrical contact and cause a dial to move forward by one number. For the size of the punched card, Hollerith took as a model the U.S. dollar at the turn of the century.

Plug boards serve a similar function in terms of electrical connection: pigeonhole A to pigeonhole B. Absolute (machine language) programming of the early 1950s and subsequently symbolic (assembly) programming did a similar job. They connected memory location A to memory location B. But they also added an important feature not existing with punched cards and plug boards: The stored program could *act upon itself.*

- As with plug boards, the programming of a computer is the process of mapping problems into the machine.

- The difference is that *digital computer programming* is proactive, therefore becoming a work of *translation.*

Information which is set in a form suitable to human users, who were the almost exclusive data processors up to the mid-1940s, must be written in a way acceptable to the computer. This process of writing the information in a form understandable by the machine is generally known as *coding.*

- The job of formulating the problem and of analyzing it, prior to coding, is usually referred to as *system analysis.*

- System analysis, coding, program testing, and documentation are activities within the overall programming effort.

Because every problem can and must be reduced to a series of elementary steps and transformed to computer instructions, any method which will increase the level of perception, speed up the timetable, and cut the cost of this process is important. Since their development in the mid-1950s, coding automation concepts have had multiple effects on the programming effort.

- In its earlier form, the *subroutine* consisted of supplying code by exploiting existing pieces of programs already tested and debugged, for use in the solution of other problems.

- The drive toward programming automation soon got beyond subroutines and involved assembler languages, in contrast to actual machine language used by early programmers.

Assembler and, subsequently, compiler languages, permitted intermingling of symbolic instructions with a group of *macroinstructions.* Whenever desirable and practical, logical records and fields within records were addressed symbolically, even where such fields are fractional, multiple, or multiple-plus-fractional words and where logical records did not correspond to physical records.

Another advance has been the conversion of information about desired tasks that address machine operations and/or fields and records to detailed machine coding through *generators.* This required the development of new techniques, since the strings of instructions vary in length and complexity and so does the size of the addressed fields and records.

Subsequently, some years later, fundamental operating methods were *multiprogrammed,* permitting the simultaneous processing of several programs. To make this technique feasible, the input/output and the supervisory control subsystems were redesigned to handle problems of relative priority, including buffer assignment. However,

- The fast-growing importance of distributed databases was not supported by appropriate tools, until object-oriented solutions became popular (see Chap. 11).

- The dichotomy between system analysis and coding remained unattended and often constituted a crevasse into which fell precious software efforts.

To solve the problems which underpin this spoilage of resources, it is necessary to look beyond system analysis at the bigger picture, which in Chap. 2 we call *programming in the large*. Today, this can be done, and must be done, visually by the person with the problem.

To the contrary, however, coding, that is, the writing of detailed machine instructions which carry out the intended operations, should be automated. *Computers should not be programmed* whether in actual machine language or in a symbolic form. We refer to this approach as *programming in the small*. The change in labels is not just a matter of cosmetics, but rather a necessity to dramatize the change in concepts. There were many problems in the old systems analysis/coding dichotomy which should definitely be avoided with the new procedures:

1. System analysis and coding have classically been taken as distinct processes with no easy or self-evident transition from the first to the second.

2. Traditional coding must be relearned to a large extent, in order to work with a new programming language—and that's irrational.

Neither problem has been solved with computer-assisted systems engineering tools, as we will see in Sec. 1.6. By and large, between systems analysis and coding there remains a large crevasse—a gap that visual programming technology helps to bridge. As for the need to learn different methods and tools, CASE worsened the situation because so many heterogeneous and incomplete CASE tools have been brought to the market.

1.6   Evolution in Programming Sophistication and in the Functionality of Visualization

From systems analysis to coding, the procedure discussed in Sec. 1.5 used to be the bible of programming. As this book will demonstrate, visual programming radically changes the process of human-machine communication—and of machine instruction. But to appropriately understand the nature of the change, we are well advised to contrast the old method to the new.

According to the old method, before a problem in mathematics, science, engineering, or business can be solved by a computer, a great deal of preliminary work must be done. The following steps have been classically necessary in connection with software development, and they have been executed in a linear manner.

1. *Problem formulation.*   This is common to the handling of all problems. Computers, however, require one to pay particular attention to the possibilities and limitations connected to a projected problem solution.

2. *Mathematical modeling.*   The problem formulated in step 1 must be modeled in a mathematical language, whether probabilistic or deterministic.

3. *Numerical analysis.*   The mathematical formulas must be subsequently reduced to a numerical form suitable for machine processing.

For all practical purposes, these three steps are part of system analysis, as discussed in Sec. 1.5. Traditionally, to a very large extent they have been done manually; this, however, radically changed with computer-aided design (CAD), and it changes further with visual programming, as we will see through practical examples in Chap. 2.

Since the 1950s, the results of step 1 in system analysis were expressed through block diagrams in a coarse manner. After numerical analysis, they were mapped into a flowchart, in a more detailed form. Flowcharts can be developed for sequencing the elements of any human activity, this, too, being a systems analysis phase.

4. *Flowcharting.*   The objective of this step is to develop the complete logical flow of operations leading to the solution of the problem by the computer.

This practically completes systems analysis and starts the coding procedures, a notion also introduced in Sec. 1.5. The coding reference is valid whether we talk of machine language, assembler coding, or compiler coding—and whether we handle step-by-step linear coding functions or follow a two-dimensional approach, as with the use of spreadsheets. Visual programming, however, falls outside the limited box of traditional approaches delineated in Fig. 1.4. In a classical solution,

5. *Coding* has the objective of establishing a detailed linear sequence of instructions in a selected programming language.

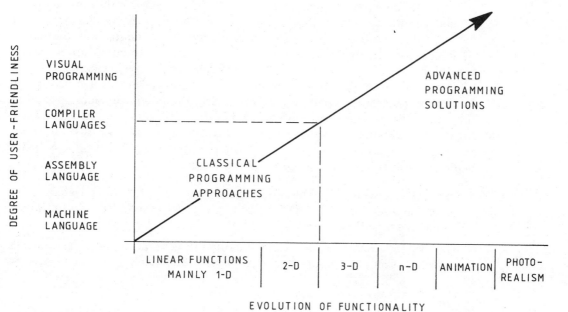

Figure 1.4 Evolution in programming sophistication and in the functionality of interactive visualization.

6. *Program test and system test* are subsequently necessary to ensure the correctness of the coding effort, respectively, at a program level and at a systems level.

Classical programming books state, and for good reason, that only when a whole range of these functions are performed in a suitable manner can an organization aim at effective computing operations. This statement changes significantly with visual programming solutions, as we will see in Chap. 2 when we discuss programming in the large.

With the old linear approach to programming, each step which has been outlined has those preceding it as prerequisites. In the bottom line, the responsibility for establishing a valid processing chain starts at the first building block and falls on the shoulders of the analyst.

- The analysis requires much detailed information about the problem itself and decisions of how it can best be handled.

- The problem, however, is that very few systems analysts are really versatile, or even versed in the specific domain they are analyzing for subsequent processing reasons.

This gap which classically exists between analyst-programmers and "the person with the problem" has many negative consequences in software development. Both timetables and costs increase exponentially when deviations have to be corrected and conceptual mistakes removed, way down the line from the programming.

Figure 1.5 helps one to appreciate the cost of changes when they are not made at the organizational specification and design levels*—hence during system analysis—but, for instance, after program testing or system testing. Because of its facilitation of perception and cognition, visual programming can be instrumental in the early fixing of conceptual errors, as we discuss in Chap. 3.

Supported through visual programming, end users are in a much better position to determine what they need to fulfill their requirements, and when they fail, they have only themselves to blame. This is a different way of saying that a much more advanced functionality is required for software development and implementation, making transparent to the end user successive layers, each lending to the programming task greater detail.

- One of the key objectives of an advanced visual programming system is the ability to adapt itself to the job (and to the machine) with a minimum of human intervention.

- The system should be, to a large extent, self-generating, with its routines capable of producing newer and better system functions.

---

*For a business problem, these correspond to the formulation, modeling, and numerical analysis levels, which we have seen in connection with scientific problems.

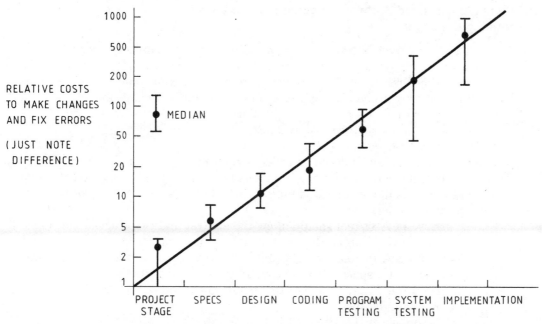

Figure 1.5 Cost of changes in function of the level in the development cycle at which they are done.

This concept is enhanced through visual programming, but it is not new. It originated in the late 1950s, and in programming jargon it has been known as *boot strapping*. What new technology adds in terms of programming tools is

- A graphical language
- Intelligent database mining
- Efficient network protocols
- Flexible real-time editors

There is as well a need for supporting systems software which enhances program visualization capabilities. This helps in not only software development but also its *sustenance* (which is a better term than *maintenance* in connection with on-line systems).

Because the products, market realities, laws, and user requirements change, one of the basic operations in software is *program upkeep*. But program maintenance has so far been a highly manual job that ends by consuming roughly three-quarters of the human resources of analysts, programmers, and other specialists. New solutions are necessary to remove this aberration from the system.

1.7   Computer-Assisted Software Engineering and Visual Programming Concepts

The last 20 years have seen a proliferation of computer-assisted software engineering development *methods* and *tools*. The advantages to be obtained from their use are widely discussed in meetings and conferences. The idea is that complex problems are broken down into more manageable units while at the same time the programming effort is enhanced through a development database and structured approaches.

In practice, however, there is quite a bit of hype associated with CASE tools. Critics say that the so-called structured programming is too inflexible and that its contribution has been widely overrated. In a way, structured programming is like evaporated milk. It may serve as a substitute for fresh milk, but it is tasteless.

Ideally, a CASE tool should allow the analyst and the programmer to modify flowcharts (or bubble charts) and reflect those modifications in the development database in real time. Also ideally, CASE tools should give the user a virtual drawing space with the capability of placing hundreds or thousands of objects on the diagram. When this is done, we find ourselves in a visual programming landscape.

Most importantly, the CASE tool should both reflect and underpin the method of the programmer. But two crucial questions are whether the now classical CASE solutions—as a methodology and as a tool kit—permit this to be done and whether it is feasible

- Without using different and incompatible CASE tools, whose heterogeneity complicates the programming effort
- By doing the intended job in a practical manner, which opens up the programming procedures to the person with the problem.

Whereas the generic nature of CASE methods suggests that computer-assisted programming should be relevant to a wide range of people and software projects, for many cases the method is only partially relevant, if applicable at all. This happens for a number of reasons.

User departments have preferences for particular documentation standards which are not supported by a given CASE tool. In some circumstances, a method is suitable for most of the problem domains, but additional techniques must be used to represent the other part(s).

More damaging to the use of such tools is the fact that there is a great deal of incompatibility between CASE methods, which affects their ability to describe the stages of an effective systems design. Many user organizations found that it is impossible to have different tools work in synergy. The implication is that

- While rigorous internal consistency and structure is one of the strengths advertised to be part and parcel of CASE, this advantage practically disappears because companies which consider structured methods are faced with a bewildering array of different, incompatible techniques.

Some of these techniques are, in fact, nothing more than a glorified Cobol solution by means of a precompiler, which starts at a higher level but ends with Cobol statements. This helps in no way to change the user organization's programming culture or to improve its human capital.

Classical CASE tools have also been hurt by the fact that some methods which have been aggressively marketed proved to be half-baked. One of the important theoretical considerations of CASE is that it analyzes the models created by a software engineer for *completeness* and *consistency*. But in reality few (and rather limited) error-checking features are provided by the different tools.

Another problem often discovered with CASE is that user organizations tend to the method, with the source of customization coming from their own experience and resulting in heterogeneous solutions. This is a cause for concern, since apart from the incompatibilities there is little indication that the customization being performed is always successful. Neither is CASE always reducing costs and cutting down timetables. Yet, as we have already seen, success in many sectors of business and industry is based upon fast time to market for new products and services.

Beyond this, methods become obsolete. Early CASE tools were often developed by companies that had little or no experience with building graphics programs, and the result shows up by complicating the actual work. Others have not been object-oriented; yet today object solutions are sought in business and industry. Still others have incorporated graphics approaches but with heterogeneous file descriptions.

What these examples suggest is that, quite often, CASE is part of the problem rather than part of the solution. A survey conducted by Andersen Consulting[4] in 1995 revealed three common motivations for pursuing newer methodologies such as object-oriented techniques:

- Improved quality
- Greater productivity
- Reduced systems maintenance

Better sustenance comes from the flexibility of extension. Therefore, object-oriented techniques attract attention because they promise to improve the software design and programming process. They do so by providing an application-oriented view while facilitating modification and reuse.

This statement is valid in regard to the strategy of building small, flexible programs. But it is just as true in connection with large-scale applications of significant complexity. The introduction of object languages provides new possibilities which tier 1 organizations are eager to employ, as we will see in Chap. 11.

In quite a similar way, visual programming approaches permit one to develop software with models more closely aligned to the business processes and structures. Visual programming solutions are capitalizing in an effective way on object notions such as abstract data types, metalayers, and encapsulation.

Last, but not least, visual programming can help to rejuvenate CASE and to cure one of its greater ills—file incompatibility. The Virtual Reality Modeling Language (see Chap. 5), for instance, provides a first-class graphics files standard which neither computer-assisted software engineering nor computer-aided design has featured over its more than 20 years of existence.

1.8   The Most Important Reference in Programming Today Is the Network, Not the Computer

The transition to a telecommunications-based economy, and the establishment of the corresponding infrastructure, has created a growing interdependence of basic investments. Each choice involves risk as a result of the evolving nature of competition, the rapid technological change, the deregulation characterizing most industries, and the impact of a globalized economy.

One of the key problems in this transition is that a new infrastructure resulting from technological developments has to be put in place in record time. This operation involves significant costs. The benefits, however, depend on the use to which we put the more sophisticated facilities we acquire. Applications are increasingly interdisciplinary:

■ The markets for telecommunications products and sophisticated software are mutually interlocking. They are also characterized by a critical mass.

■ Telecommunications is of value to its users and is profitable to its suppliers only when sufficiently large groups of people become part of the network— and they are willing and able to intercommunicate.

All the interest in building an *information superhighway* revolves on this simple notion. By the same token, the programming solutions we are after no longer concern a single computer or a system looked at in isolation, as the practice has been since the early 1950s, and by and large it still dominates the thinking of many companies.

By the middle to late 1990s and well into the 21st century, *the network is the computer.* Therefore, the best example today of a popular network where new programming concepts are born and used is *Internet.* Internet is a popular network; it is also the first incarnation of the information superhighway.

In connection with Internet, of particular interest in a text on virtual programming technology is the fact that network programming has taken over from computer programming. This changes to a very significant degree our concepts about what programming is and is not. As we will see in Part 3, when we talk of the World Wide Web (WWW), VRML, and Java:

- Computers are no longer made to be programmed.
- But networks need to be programmed through new strategic departures.

Developed in the late 1960s as the network of the Advanced Research Project Agency of the U.S. Department of Defense (DoD), and originally known as *Arpanet,* Internet was transferred to the National Science Foundation (NSF) to serve in interconnecting research laboratories and universities. Under both DoD and NSF, Internet was owned by the U.S. government; but in its global setting it is a cooperative effort overseen by the Internet Society (ISOC).

- Because Internet spent many years as largely a research-oriented network, commercial applications are fairly recent.
- Yet they are rapidly progressing, and the World Wide Web (see Chap. 6) now has a first-class graphical language, the Virtual Reality Modeling Language (discussed in Chap. 7).

What other networks such as IBM's and Sears' Prodigy,* General Electric's GEnie, AT&T's Interchange, NewsCorp's Delphi, and Microsoft's Microsoft Network have in common is that they are overtaken by Internet. The user community is abandoning proprietary networks for the World Wide Web.

The Internet was scarcely even mentioned at Telecom 91. At that time, it was widely dismissed as a playground for academics. Yet today it is appreciated that Internet may be the most important public service after voice telephony.

The change in concept and in culture is most important—and it will have wide repercussions as far as programming. Instead of telecommunications companies (telcos) offering services to users, it is customer applications that increasingly determine the type of service and the required bandwidth. But the ongoing intermediation by classical telcos poses dependability questions. At a debate at the September 1995 Networld + Interop event in Paris, a telecommunications manager at Paris-based Banque Nationale de Paris (BNP) asked a panel of experts whether Internet service providers today can guarantee quality of service, for example, by ensuring that a future BNP Web site would be accessible 24 hours per day, 7 days per week.

"On paper, yes. In reality, no," answered the managing director of EUnet France.[5] He then explained that a way to provide true redundancy is to use two Internet service providers, a process otherwise known as *dual-homing.* But dual-home networks exacerbate routing problems, because they require addresses to every router connected on the network.

Indeed, dual homing is a good example of programming in the large, which we discuss in Chap. 2. With the network being the computer, another example of programming in the large is the issue of how to ensure effective client-server

---

*Having cost $1 billion, Prodigy is now for sale for a fraction of that money.

handshake through the Web's Hypertext Transfer Protocol (HTTP). Also, how does one do document formatting for a user community of variable topology, through the Hypertext Markup Language (HTML)?

The Web is not the only platform on Internet, although it has become the most popular. Others include the File Transfer Protocol (FTP), Telnet, WAIS, and Gopher. But developers are increasingly focusing on the Web because building products for a very popular communications system can be a financially rewarding experience, which is also a self-feeding cycle.

1.9   The Expansion of Internet Will Mean a Booming Visual Programming Market

Although the notion of 30 to 35 million consumers jumping on line and exercising their communications needs or their purchase prerogatives is gross hyperbole, even the more conservative estimate of 5 to 10 million computers connected to Internet constitutes a solid community of users.* These are end users with on-line access to distributed databases—people who must, to a very substantial degree, depend on self-service programming related to their own work.

The boost that electronic mail has given to Internet is matched by the World Wide Web, which has transformed the text world of E-mail messages and other files. Companies, organizations, or individuals who want to publicize themselves on the Internet can now create Web pages that consist of words, graphics, and pictures.

- When these pages are designed, links to other Internet computers can be built, by using hypertext that highlights selected words, phrases, icons, or video clips.

- The Hypertext Markup Language is a relatively simple mechanism used to mark up information elements which could accommodate the more demanding needs of formal publishing.

Another approach is the Standard Generalized Markup Language, an ISO norm to be used as a framework, but it is not as popular as HTML. There are as well initiatives underway to standardize a security technology. At the current state of the art, security is indeed the Achilles heel of Internet—but this might change.

There are dozens of ways to connect to the Net, ranging from expensive, high-speed dedicated direct links over T1 lines to a shared dial-in link at 9.6 kilobits per second (kbits/s). The Internet addressing scheme is based on domain names combined with registered institutional addresses to provide a unique identifier for each host computer.

---

*Current statistics indicate that about 80 percent of Internet users are North American.

As industrial companies and financial institutions become eager to enter cyberspace through the Internet, the World Wide Web gains commercial importance. Corporations are spending millions of dollars to design Web sites, and the demand for site designers is outstripping supply.

- In their quest to master on-line interactive media, designers focus on visualization, resulting in a flood of graphics.

- Web animation is becoming a space-time phenomenon—an interactive, participatory virtual reality experience.

Browsers on the World Wide Web, as on Netscape's Navigator, Microsoft's Explorer, Sun's HotJava, Mosaic, and others, are presented with multimedia information through an easy surfing approach. Other applications, such as videoconferencing, call for the ability to capture live multimedia information, displaying it on local and remote screens; creating, transferring, and synchronizing real-time multimedia streams; and effectively handling delivery problems associated with on-line end-to-end services.

The progression from Internet to WWW, HTML and VRML is shown in Fig. 1.6. Another popular visual programming construct for networked computers,

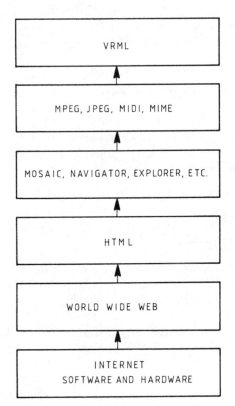

Figure 1.6 A layered view of the evolution from Internet infrastructure to VRML.

which we study in Chap. 8, is Java. It works on a virtual machine principle and utilizes paging applets.

All these terms sound as if they came from a different planet than the examples we have seen in Secs. 1.5 to 1.7. Communications, computers, and software are a domain full of conflicting interests—hence the crisis in which the profession now finds itself.

Advanced uses of the World Wide Web are proliferating. The same is true of business perspectives. *The Economist* reported 620 Web sites devoted to commercial television programs.[6] Most were just advertisements, but others included brief video samples that could be watched through a personal computer.

Because new technology sees to it that digital networks are dimensionless with respect to information transfer, *connectivity*—not location—is the key. Some experts think that this can lead to digital demographics as well as novel types of industrial, financial, and commercial applications—in addition to different interpersonal relations.

Channeled through Internet, community intelligence is becoming a watchdog, as the case of Pentium's fault demonstrates. The whole affair of the fault located in some Intel chips proves that there is no secrecy in terms of reliability, no matter how technical the subject may be. The most interesting aspect, however, has been the fact that much of the event played out on the Internet.

Internet-led discussions, including participation from Intel's CEO Andrew Grove, accelerated the publicity of the flaw, but they have also been instrumental in Intel's final decision to replace all affected chips.[7]

- Internet has become a force that cannot be ignored.

- This is increasingly true of most computer-based communications.

A strength and at the same time a weakness of Internet are the lack of a governing body. The nonprofit Internet Society serves as the umbrella for developing new technologies, standards, and applications for the global network. De facto standards hold the Net together.

- Many local networks are attached to it.

- Third-party software developers keep busy.

- Plenty of software is becoming available.

Equally important is the fact that, at least for the time being, there has been no serious attempt at control and regulation,* which is quite different from almost everything else. On the people's network no company or group has a monopoly on services or ideas.

A large majority of the user community believe that the lack of central control is the number 1 reason why Internet works. Nobody has to go through a

---

*Except some constraints imposed in Germany, Japan, and China, which so far just scratch the surface.

clearance point where bureaucrats pull the strings, and there is no place where one has to register a new node.

■ The Internet mode of networking benefits from a simple and open infrastructure.

■ This makes it feasible to build all applications on top of the transport layer.

Such flexibility and extensibility are in contrast to closed, proprietary architectures like SNA. Even CATV is a closed system. Precisely because it is an open architecture, the evolving global network will most likely change the business aspects of computers and communications from the way we have known them for 50 years—from operating systems to the way we develop programming artifacts, from terminal devices to the entire public telecommunications infrastructure.

Perhaps, the most important contribution of the open network, which is currently evolving, is its ability to generate new and powerful programming paradigms, as we will see in Part 2. Let's keep this in mind when we discuss the benefits that the end user can derive from visual programming and from the concepts underpinning programming in the large.

References

1. *Information and Software Technology,* vol. 37, no. 11, 1995.
2. See D. N. Chorafas and H. Steinmann, *Virtual Reality—Practical Applications in Business and Industry,* Prentice-Hall, Englewood Cliffs, N.J., 1995.
3. See D. N. Chorafas *Programming Systems for Electronic Computers,* Butterworths, London, 1962.
4. *Communications of the ACM,* vol. 38, no. 10, October 1995.
5. *CommunicationsWeek International,* Oct. 2, 1995.
6. January 20, 1996.
7. *Computer-Aided Engineering,* Feb. 4, 1995.

Chapter

2

What Is Meant by Programming in the Large?

2.1 Introduction

Programming in the large is a recent term coined to address high-level software design decisions.[1] In a strategic sense, high-level design decisions lead to policy commitments that should guide, inform, and constrain subsequent software design initiatives. In a tactical way, this process establishes the specifications for a systems solution, including its various subsystems and modules.

Visual programming approaches can be greatly assisted by programming in the large, in the sense that it helps set a framework. As explained in Chap. 1, if we turn back the technology calendar by 40 years, to the mid-1950s, when the programming effort in business and industry took off, we will see that

- The conceptual framework of a computer program was established by block diagrams which presented a systems view.[2]

- But as computer programs became big and their complexity significantly increased, there was a bifurcation between block diagramming expressing the grand design and detailed flowcharts.

Visual programming, the use of agents, and interactive, three-dimensional solutions permit the visualization of the software's grand design. Autonomous agents are intelligent software modules that operate in a dynamic environment. They are based on knowledge, reasoning, adaptation, and learning (see Chap. 3).[3]

A crucial role played by programming in the large is that of opening the programming profession to an exploding population of end users. It is doing so in a manner which is both comprehensive and comprehensible. But there are two other reasons why this type of solution has become important:

- The growing need for end-user self-service in computing
- The codesign of new products and processes

These two issues are related. As end users have become both computer-literate and knowledgeable about software, they find it simpler, more direct, and more rewarding to program their own applications. They do so by using visual approaches that technology puts at their disposal, with Internet being a first-class environment for this purpose, as Part 2 will document.

Broadband networks and the media see to it that remote research and development laboratories and software design boutiques, which may be separated by thousands of miles, can work together as if they were in the same building.

- Virtual corporations depend on *codesign.*
- Programming in the large offers a first-class solution in frameworking (see also Chap. 12).

In terms of their technical requirements, codesign and end-user computing call for a methodology able to monitor and coordinate the development of components and subsystems and to ensure that initiatives being taken are not in conflict with system-level design decisions. This is the context for examining programming in the large.

2.2   Programming in the Large and Its Impact on End-User Computing

It is no secret that the dynamic growth in end-user computing created serious problems for centralized information systems management. Fifteen years ago, when personal computers (PCs) came into the office over the head of the chief information officer, few companies were prepared for the changeover to distributed software development, in spite of

- Major technological advances which made mandatory a change in policy
- A growing end-user commitment to the PC which was there to stay

Most organizations have been slow to take seriously the impact of end-user computing on the way they choose and use their technological investment, particularly in terms of systems solutions and the software side. But tier 1 companies long ago laid out plans for a changeover to fully distributed information systems.

Figure 2.1 outlines what I call the ABC organizational model which now is standard in the United States. The responsibility for information technology resources, including software development, is shared at three levels. Each addresses well-defined user requirements:

- At end-user level A, programming in the large is done interactively on networked workstations, and the applications are highly competitive.
- Level B is the divisional level, which has inherited the mainframes and

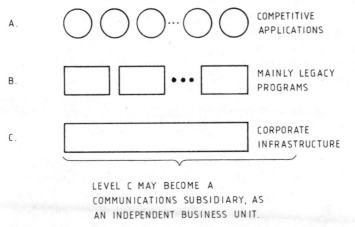

A. ○ ○ ○ ··· ○ ○   COMPETITIVE APPLICATIONS

B. ▢ ▢ ●●● ▢   MAINLY LEGACY PROGRAMS

C. ▭   CORPORATE INFRASTRUCTURE

LEVEL C MAY BECOME A
COMMUNICATIONS SUBSIDIARY, AS
AN INDEPENDENT BUSINESS UNIT.

Figure 2.1   The ABC organizational model for information technology.

legacy programs of formerly centralized operations, and it is now converting to client-servers.

- C is a logically integrated network which provides the corporate infrastructure covering wide-area network (WAN), metropolitan-area network (MAN), and local-area network (LAN) solutions.

What exactly is done at the end-user level? Some companies define end-user computing as simply giving PCs to everyone in the organization. That's not true. What the term essentially means is to change the way the work was done, revolutionizing the manner of looking at personal skills. A more accurate definition of *end-user computing* therefore is

- Getting the employees on line to the communications, computers, and software resources as a means to better their professional performance
- Providing appropriate training to make possible self-service by end users, from programming to interactive usage over the companies' private network(s) and public networks, including Internet

Self-assistance in programming has become a key element in any sound technology strategy, but it necessitates computer-literate people. On-line access to databases has accelerated this need; expert systems have offered smarter solutions than classical programming ever provided; and client-servers ensured the independence of the end users from an awfully centralized, costly, and slow-moving information technology.

After some hesitation on which way it is better to go, tier 1 companies divisionalized their data processing operations. Through client-server approaches they gave to their managers and professionals freedom of action. But the training of end users, as well as of system designers and analysts, so far has not included the ability to understand the consequence of a grand design when decisions are made in terms of functions and supports.

Yet, as the aggregate of the computers, communications, and software endowment grows, and given that its component parts are interconnected, we have to pay considerable attention to cooperating processes and to database accesses. While the systems specialists should be trained on a policy of software reuse, end users must learn not to develop system parts that are too tightly coupled to a specific application—or, alternatively, impossible to put together in a dynamic manner.

Figure 2.2 comes from a project in medicine, and it exemplifies a contribution of programming in the large. It is a conceptual schema to map applications and database resources. It presents an object-oriented approach (see also Chap. 11) which differentiates between clinical, how-to knowledge and operational knowledge, which states what is actually done. The aim of this block diagram is to provide a rich description of the medical record, and it is achieved by interactively programming in the large. This is how Fig. 2.2 was derived. It was

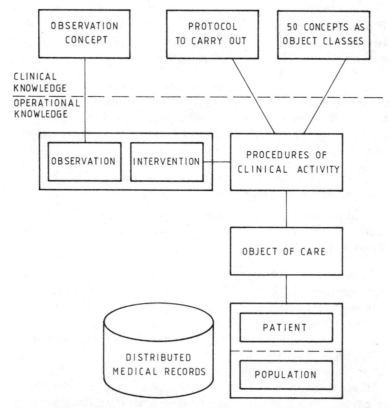

Figure 2.2 Programming in the large provides a conceptual schema useful for mapping databases and applications.

done exclusively by end users who did not have previous programming experience but who knew very well their medical jobs and what they needed to make them more proficient.

Another good example of programming in the large, in this case with tools provided on the Internet, is the Java Call Reporting and Analysis project by the British Telecom laboratories. Nicknamed *Jacaranda,** it aims to illustrate BT's vision of future developments in on-line services, by helping to deliver the results of ad hoc database queries through interactive visualization.

- The user can select the date and time of interest as well as initiate animation sequences on trends and patterns.

- As a geographic information system (GIS), Jacaranda links to graphical reporting. It also supports rotation and scaling of three-dimensional visual displays.

Jacaranda leads to a rather complex application, so the designers incorporated a guided tour which provides an overview of control panels. This process is user-actuated and is a good example of programming in the large. Four primary windows are supported: main visualization, pick information, display control panel, and data control panel.

- Animation commands are included in the data control panel.

- The user may choose to animate in an intraday setting (through the hours of the day) or interday time periods.

An overview of Jacaranda's commands is given in Fig. 2.3. With a few ingenious improvements, such as the addition of subsecond, second, and minute choices in data control, this type of solution can effectively handle *intraday financial time services*. This is an area of great competitive interest in the financial industry, as we will see in Chap. 13.

2.3 Identifying and Modeling Systems Components

Programming in the large can help correct past shortcomings in systems analysis and its largely manual chores. As the examples in Sec. 2.2 demonstrated, fundamentally it implies an advanced practice leading to the on-line solution of documentation problems—a sore point with computers.

Like any geographic information system, Jacaranda makes it feasible to effectively perform domain analysis. Applied in engineering practice, such an approach permits one to design parts that are reusable within a broader implementation domain. It assists in

---

*The E-mail address for Jacaranda is macro @ bt - sys.bt.co.uk

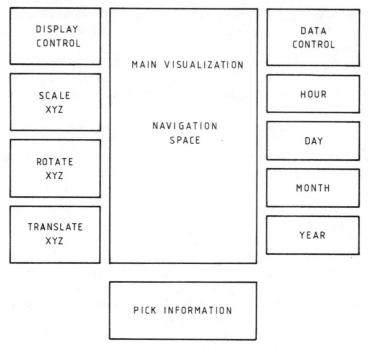

Figure 2.3 A guided tour through British Telecom's Jacaranda.

- Identifying system classes, common subsystems, and components to be used across classes, within the broader solution space

- Modeling these classes and components for supporting domain functions, and storing high-level system segment descriptions for further use.

Looking again into the medical application of programming in the large, the careful reader will notice that in the upper half of Fig. 2.2 are concepts which constitute object classes of clinical knowledge. The medical practitioners who developed this diagram also embedded "how to" procedures into each concept, which will need to be subsequently mapped into the database through software.

The examples given in Sec. 2.2 are no rare exceptions. For more than 10 years, and most particularly after the mid-1984 introduction of Macintosh, graphics-oriented software has provided standards for help and menus, universal commands (such as help, start, move, cancel, undo, end), and natural language interfaces. We are now talking of enhancing input/output capabilities through virtual reality—apart from the other developments we have already seen.

As both Jacaranda and the medical example help demonstrate, programming in the large is a necessary prerequisite to interactive software development. Many applications require multiple rounds of user input, and their requirements are difficult to project without a grand design. These, incidentally, are also excellent object technology targets (see Chap. 11) because of the opportunity to do iterative development.

- A prerequisite to programming in the large is (1) to understand present and future requirements and (2) either be able to predict the system's evolution or make the whole structure very flexible.

- One of the major problems with legacy programming has been that subsequent correlations, additions, and subtractions can invalidate allocation decisions.

Another sore point with classical programming is that it required widespread architectural changes which were costly and time-consuming. By contrast, programming in the large *is* the grand design—and it is done interactively through two- or three-dimensional visualization.

Decisions concerning programming in the large presuppose good knowledge of the professional functions to be executed as well as the evolution of the system itself. Attention must be paid to both current and future details, so that the grand design will not be invalidated as lower-level designs are carried out.

In sound practice, the grand design does not ignore the process of understanding emergent properties, which simply cannot be predicted in all details, but whose nature can be estimated. Therefore, emphasis must be placed on examining not only the whole but also its components. This needs

- A conceptual appreciation of the system's evolution
- Considerable knowledge of the professional requirements for new component parts

Programming in the large is a methodology which also requires tools able to store the experience of the different participants involved in the development process, including decisions associated with *modeling*. This enables a longer-term understanding of different methods and customization procedures used within the broader systems perspective.

- A *development database* is the answer in regard to the necessary interactive facility in the short, medium, and longer terms.

- *Visual programming* (*VP*) tools, and maybe *frameworks* (see Chap. 12), must cover not only visualization but also process integration.

This dual approach produces a working model of the company's business processes and databases. It also helps identify common sets of objects in an enterprise sense, facilitating reuse of common objects and thereby increasing software development productivity. It also results in higher-quality applications.

Mainframers might suggest that an enterprise model requires a centralized group to develop and maintain it. This is not a realistic requirement; nor is it a serious argument. In fact, a centralized group can easily become the *bottleneck*—and therefore counterproductive.

There is, however, a role for a central staff. Skilled systems professionals should act as consultants to end users who develop their own software through programming-in-the-large approaches. These professionals can also provide quality assurance and develop knowledge artifacts for more general use. As we will see in Sec. 2.8, agents play a key role in this process.

Three decades or more ago, discussion of software development by end users was couched in terms of the disparity between the ideal and the real; the promise and the product; the never-ever solution and a delayed, but doable computer program.

- During the last 10 years, this has most radically changed.

- In the course of the last 3 years, visual programming has opened far-reaching vistas.

In conclusion, interactive programming in the large permits the conception and development of enterprise models and associated applications modules. It provides a much clearer sense of direction for software projects and a basis for an integrative development approach. These are important considerations, particularly for organizations whose information technology is in full evolution.

2.4   Codesign in a Distributed Information Environment

Leading-edge companies either currently have or envision a networked information environment whose characteristics fit the description we saw in Sec. 2.3. Increasingly, attention is paid to the evolution of fully networked resources, which, cognizant designers were heard to comment, are partly clear and partly fuzzy in the sense that we do not yet fully understand them.

The principle with the new generation of interactive tools for software development is that solutions must transcend models. With this approach, user interfaces become an intrinsic part of networked computers and software modules.

- Able solutions require that systems designers learn the user's idiosyncracy in accessing the network and in manipulating database contents.

Interface design can benefit a great deal from facilities provided by programming in the large. An interactively done grand design is a requirement because multiple layers of software must be distributed across the network, adding value by integrating and refining information from heterogeneous sources.

Interfaces designed to be friendly to human users can become barriers when programs operate outside the context of a grand design. The end user is hurt by inconsistencies prevailing in these interfaces. This is one of many instances where *codesign* can aid in the development of new solutions, whose functions are characterized by polyvalence.

An example of polyvalence which needs to be supported in the business domain is given in Fig. 2.4. It describes the contents, linkages, and functions of a demand deposit account (DDA) agreement that the client signs with the bank.

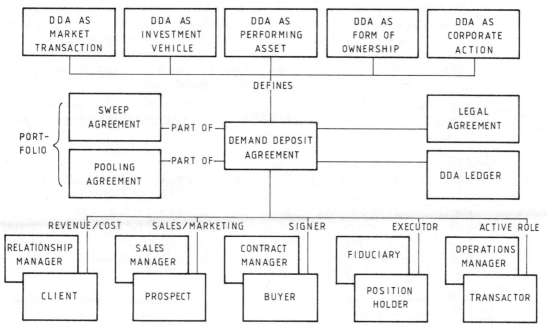

Figure 2.4 Business objects entering a demand deposit account (DDA) agreement.

- Several inputs define this current account agreement, which stands both on its own and as part of other banking functions.

- Typically, processes such as general ledger and portfolio management fall under the authority of other departments, hence the need for codesign.

Apart from the linkages shown in Fig. 2.4, a DDA agreement is part of a number of *terms* and *constraints*. Examples are transaction authority, deposit processing, currency restrictions, and overdraft restrictions. Special conditions may be applicable to the detail of a single client. In this graph there are no flow and direction arrows because during the project it was decided that every box should be multidirectional.

In a programming-in-the-large solution, each one of these terms can be effectively handled as an object. The principles are discussed in Chap. 11. All sorts of *fees* are also objects—including activity-based, check-connected, and deposit- and withdrawal-related. Other fees may be transfer costs, charges for advice and the mailing of statements, and position-based charges.

A golden horde of objects may be entering the grand design, for instance, check processing, cash payments, cash transfer in different currencies, and master agreement processing and its subsequent changes as well as financial charges such as interest on positive balances and negative interest on overdrafts. All these objects and their linkages can be effectively mapped through programming in the large.

The proper partitioning of codesign operations and their recombination affect not only conceptual issues but also the overall hardware and software solution and some of its details. Success depends on many factors. These include flexibility, functionality, performance, cost, and maintainability.

- An automated codesign approach would provide a variety of partitions projected as independent modules within the grand design.
- Through visual programming, system architects would be able to choose the best solution for their requirements, while sustaining a flexible, modular approach.

As every designer knows from experience, the choices to be made are never static, but change as the business environment evolves. Therefore, the design methodology should allow dynamic repartitioning and recombining of the objects being handled and of the functions that the system must perform.

Developers versatile in the practice of codesign look for a set of concurrently executing software modules that can be easily combined and recombined. They define nodes of *synchronization* and schedule them dynamically, using a schedule optimizer.

- Dynamic scheduling allows a data-driven approach to operations through real-time restructuring.
- A number of projects currently conducted tend to suggest that genetic algorithms can be instrumental in optimization work.

Since hardware and software rates of execution may differ, scheduling must ensure synchronized execution of individual modules, effectively projected to achieve an efficient but flexible systems solution.

Such an environment is fairly complex, and therefore anyone doing programming in the large should pay attention to the fact that different execution rates cause variations in the rates of communication across hardware and software modules. Furthermore, distributed computation requires the use of appropriate buffering and hand-shaking mechanisms.

Software graph models can be employed to minimize temporary register storage requirements. Design reviews should verify the correctness of what is being projected under different implementation scenarios.[4] This further stresses that a grand design needs to be kept up dynamically without process interruption.

2.5 Assisting Software Development through Visual Programming*

As we will have the opportunity to see in greater detail in the following chapters, with visual programming, what we see is what we get. As in the case of Jacaranda, the user defines a screen and associates it with an expression,

---

*As we will see in Chap. 7, the terms *visual programming* and *graphical programming* are not necessarily synonymous.

TABLE 2.1 **Principles and Features of Visual Thinking**

Principles	Features
Explicit end user's model	Desktop presentation, windows, icons, multimedia, animation
Seeing and pointing	Mouse, space ball, pop-up menus, graphical tablet
Universal commands	Insert, delete, copy, move, and show properties*

*Other universal commands include *help, search, change, exit, escape,* and *end.* Also necessary are arithmetic and logical operations, as well as cut and paste, clipping, and zooming. The principle is this: What we see is what we get.

without having to worry about file handling and the structure of the processing modules.

This can be achieved through programming in the large and a high-level interface, as discussed in Sec. 2.4. Processing is done by generators, based on the visual images developed by the end user. Table 2.1 explains the principles and features of visual thinking which, like the chicken and the egg, is both a prerequisite to and a result of visual programming.

Stating that objectlike visual thinking is both a prerequisite to and a result of the same process may seem to be a contradiction. But such duality is supported by a metaconcept and implemented through a metamodel, such as the one shown in Fig. 2.5.

- The old approach in software development employed the so-called waterfall model where, from analysis to coding and testing, one operation followed the other sequentially.

- The new model, shown in Fig. 2.5, is a virtual spiral: From conception to sustenance there is a steady cyclic procedure, with some of its components executed in parallel.

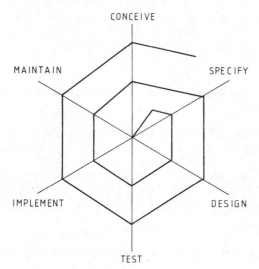

Figure 2.5 A metamodel framework for software evolution.

At the end-user level, visual thinking and visual programming are assisted by the fact that graphics is management's shorthand. Many companies started experimenting with graphs as part of a paper reduction program. The question of which reports to eliminate, shorten, or combine led ultimately to two issues:

- How much information can be put on one sheet of paper?
- Which is the most effective way to catch the end user's attention and lead to action?

With classical tabular presentation, when lots of numbers are crowded into a small space, the result is not legible. Worse, long tables hide rather than show the underlying relationships among information elements and their evolution—this being completely true with programming languages.

- Figures and charts are better than lists. Graphics *give perspective* and *show trends*.
- Graphics enable one to compare several elements at a time in a multidimensional space by a *radar chart*.[5]

In the bottom line, figures, charts, information elements, labels, and other means of visual programming have a direct impact on perception and conception, as we will see in Chap. 3. Legacy programming technologies have hit a limit, hence the need for new programming approaches that take us further.

Programming in the large provides an overstructure. Under this main view can be built successive layers of detail served by software. If we have clear ideas about what we wish to achieve in terms of functionality—and if we properly express them through the methodology that this chapter explains—there will be no problem in supporting the required computing processes and information elements.

We need a conceptual framework in order to represent knowledge in a manner which is well organized, comprehensive, but also adaptable. Table 2.2 presents a conceptual framework aimed at supporting new software in terms familiar to end users, through a visual programming language and user-friendly interface functions.

- The challenge is to exploit the kind of reasoning characteristic of end users and their decision process.
- End users typically have a better understanding of the problem domain which they address than any programmer—even the most brilliant.

Software-literate users can therefore help themselves through *prototyping*, which interfaces between programming in the large and programming in the small. Figure 2.6 explains what is involved in prototyping through the eight major steps of this approach.

- Notice that Fig. 2.6 includes several feedbacks, which assist in adjusting and focusing.

TABLE 2.2   A Conceptual Framework for Visual Programming

Classical system analysis and programming	Interactive visual programming
1. Formal application specifications must be created and maintained.	1. Users do not need to define in the abstract what they require. They create a visual version of the application (prototype).
2. Application development usually requires months and years.	2. Application development takes hours, days, or at most a couple of weeks.
3. Professional data processing knowledge is a prerequisite.	3. Users can create their own applications, including sophisticated ones. Professional programming staff act as consultants.
4. With procedural languages, programmers must specify *how* a task should be executed.	4. Users specify *what* has to be done by means of a nonprocedural language. The generator creates the application.
5. Both system analysis and programming are formally documented through manual methods.	5. Visual programming tools are self-documenting through interactive computer support and development databases.
6. Maintenance work is a tedious, time-consuming task. It absorbs the largest share of data processing staff.	6. Classical maintenance work practically disappears. The new approach is to redefine the specifications through visual programming.

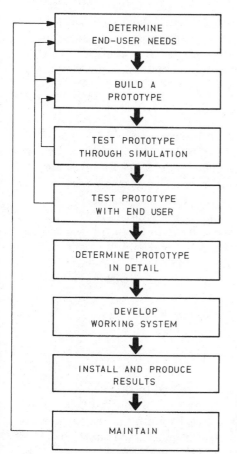

Figure 2.6 A step-by-step approach to prototyping and its feedbacks.

- Any job which is well done benefits from feedback, which leads to correction and quality improvement.

Feedbacks should be executed on line, both in connection with programming in the large and programming in the small. Programming in the small looks at the details of the software module—first through macrooperations or icons, then through machine-generated code. In a way, the applets of the Java language, which we discuss in Chap. 6, are programming-in-the-small artifacts.

With programming in the large, visual programming addresses the system context, for instance, where several media will be obtained, stored, and manipulated—or information delivered. As we have seen in Secs. 2.2 to 2.4, it also regards essential functions of the system such as database design, distribution, and on-line access.

The use of visual approaches in connection with programming in the small has to do with software development, by means of graphical solutions and by example. It also includes menu forms and routing structures (that is, the nesting of menus) as well as functional control, such as invoking functions at run time and message passing.

Both programming in the large and programming in the small need tools for representation, ascertaining that users get what they need. Both can be effectively supported through object-oriented approaches at programming and database management levels.[6] And both can greatly benefit from the languages now available on the World Wide Web, such as VRML and Java.

2.6   Synergic Coupling of New Software Technologies

What we are essentially talking about, within the perspectives set by programming in the large and the visual programming tools at our disposal, is the synergic coupling of key applications technologies, for instance, multimedia, data management, database mining, and visualization. This synergy has become a necessity because of the highly interactive environment of business today.

Visual approaches are an essential element in the effort to break out of the programming limitations of the past. As we will see in Chap. 14 in connection with the use of virtual reality as an advanced programming paradigm, we need to simultaneously address three areas which by themselves cover the whole range of a new conceptual approach to communications, computers, and software:

1. On-line data acquisition

2. Analysis and simulation

3. Interactive visualization

The synergy of software technologies we examined in this chapter helps in controlling the worries about buying, learning, and using multiple distinct products which are usually heterogeneous. Programming in the large assists in the seamless integration of different tools, but most importantly it helps to break the *programming bottleneck* from which practically all computer users currently suffer.

In a meeting in Tokyo with Dai-Ichi Kangyo Bank, Japan's second-largest bank, the chief information officer was saying that in his institution the software bottleneck amounts to 70,000 worker-years of programming work.

- No centralized software development, no matter how well managed, can meet this colossal requirement in programming.

- It is therefore no wonder that Dai-Ichi is looking to end-user programming as a way to break the bottleneck.

There is no better justification for using the agile tools now available on the Internet than the reference made in these two bulleted items. They document in a dramatic manner the extent to which the clout of centralized, mainframe-minded solutions is fading.

Let's, however, not forget the need for integration between the old and the new. The call for synergic coupling of legacy and new software arises from computational and data management requirements, but able solutions should target seamless integration of hundreds of powerful numerical analysis and logic processing functions.

Software solutions are usually based on algorithms and heuristics; what is different today is that they are addressing a broad and expanding spectrum of applications. In both an engineering environment and finance these include

- Nonlinear and chaotic systems

- The analysis of intraday time series

- Approximations for interpolation and extrapolation

- Difference and differential equations

- Multivariant transforms and other domains

Superior performance is necessary both computationally and graphically. The tools must be able to address large, multidimensional data sets, allowing their users to be more productive in less time and leaving more time for investigation and analysis.

No matter what the mainframers may say, it is simply not possible to address the expanding horizon of sophisticated implementations through old tools. Many of the better software development means which have become available during the last decade are graphics-oriented (one example is fuzzy engineering).

A similar statement can be made about fractals, strange attractors, and some of the applications of complexity theory. Optimization requirements are well supported by genetic algorithms, which are nonlinear and permit the study of dynamic system behavior. A major benefit lies in greater productivity.

- A successful visual programming language delivers at least an order of magnitude faster than alternative solutions.

- Compared to naive languages like Cobol, this ratio can reach 60:1 to 100:1 for the simpler routines and/or heavily database-oriented applications.

At the programming-in-the-large level, visual approaches help in synergic coupling because their generators employ a syntax which is typically nonprocedural. They automate the repetitive detail work, removing it from the programmer's burden. They also have components which act as control elements with system commands helping to integrate instructions written, for instance, in C++.

One of the main advantages for end users is that programming in the large is oriented to distributed database management—ideally, in an object manner. Also, in terms of basics, the tool can be learned in about 2 days, and its mechanics can be well understood by the end users—not just by systems specialists.

Visual programming approaches help in relieving some of the constraints or weaknesses present with shells, such as those available in the 1980s for knowledge engineering applications. The weak point with these shells, Art and Kee included, has been their human-machine interface.[7] They were not written for managerial use:

- Scientists want to solve a thousand things at once. That's how they understand the world.

- Managers like to do one thing a thousand times. That's how they make money.

Programming in the large through visual media provides a toolkit solution which answers this managerial requirement. In a well-written applications environment, there will be many program modules reusable in each application but also reusable through recombination in a given tool. There will also be seamless utility functions including windows, screen management, forms handling, graphical representation of artifacts, database access, and data communications specifications.

Given that competition increasingly requires the fast development of new software, the tools to be chosen must be high-level and must support rapid prototyping and the interactive visualization of applications. Libraries of user-oriented functions help to leverage the expert's work, eliminating the need to reinvent software. But tools alone don't solve problems. To survive, organizations need a new policy.

2.7   A Visual Programming Strategy and the Resulting Applications

By radically rethinking and redesigning business processes, with assistance from advanced information technology, companies can produce quantum improvements in quality, speed, and costs. In a nutshell, this summarizes the sense of the meeting in London with two senior executives of Credit Swiss First Boston (CSFB).

"We have adopted visual programming because it is a very effective solution," said the managing director of Credit Swiss Financial Products. "We use spreadsheets for programming purposes, and this job is done by the end users themselves. The central systems group now mainly provides assistance in problem areas like database management."

Other financial institutions have taken a similar position, as expressed on a number of occasions in the course of this research. They have pointed out that even though the increasing use of computer-assisted software engineering tools, fourth-generation languages (4GLs), and other software development techniques eased the implementation difficulty,

- It did not alter the need for expertise in terms of specifications and representations, or for that matter in the transition to multimedia.
- Yet, with the fast growth in the volume and complexity of applications software, much more effective solutions are badly needed.

"With off-balance sheet financial products," Ross Salinger of CSFB suggested during our meeting, "there is such complexity in the books and in the trades that the trained programmer cannot help anymore the financial analyst. The latter has to be able to develop the code he needs by himself."

This requirement is compounded by the fact that global banking increasingly requires *concurrent business* perspectives, along the lines of codesign described in Sec. 2.4.* In many financial institutions, interest in the implementation of new solutions has been fueled by reengineering, which calls for

- Setting up interdisciplinary teams to tackle fairly complex tasks
- Implementing concurrent business practices to carry them out in a successful manner.

As the CSFB commented, leading business thinkers in New York and in London believe that by merging the skills and insights of several people, concurrent business practices present significant competitive advantages. In turn, they require sophisticated support in information technology.

This new strategic approach calls for a great deal of end-user participation in software development and for attributes well beyond what CASE can offer. Particularly important is the creation of a visually oriented automated software development environment. Computer-literate end users who have become good software developers are increasingly suggesting the need of

- Visual programming policies and tools, with the assistance of semiformal graphical paradigms

---

*The same, of course, is true of manufacturing merchandising.

- Ways to ensure that the chosen measures are relevant to the overall goal of end-user programming

- Means to help in software assessment, from specifications to final code as well as applications testing

In the banking industry, for example, financial engineering pushes in this direction. As CSFB underlined, particularly challenging in modern financial applications are *complexity assessment* and effort estimation, starting with the assumptions upon which the selection of end-user programming measures is based.

"Not only the end user must do his own programming job," was stated during the CSFB meeting, "but he must also know how to do an interactive computer-based financial analysis. At any time during the day, his job requires to click on a cell and see what is in it. Then analyze its contents."

For representation purposes, the utilization of graphic system models, such as those supported by programming in the large and already used in many engineering applications, provides a concise and comprehensive mapping of reality. It enables a fast and relatively inexpensive study of essential system aspects, without the need to consider excessive low-level details.

Functional models based on visual programming approaches can form a useful basis for quantitative and qualitative input filtering, extracting from databases, processing, and producing an interactive output.

- The wider incorporation of specification modeling techniques helps the transformation from requirements analysis to software representations.

- Made through programming in the large, such user-constructed systems are independent of old programming languages and are largely based on visual paradigms.

Citibank, Dai-Ichi Kangyo Bank, and other user organizations aptly stressed, because of the compilers provided by visual programming artifacts, that knowledge of classical-style coding is increasingly unimportant. What is vital is to be able to assess the ease with which the end user can act as software developer as well as how the so-developed applications software will be tested and maintained.

2.8   Challenges in an End-User-Driven Software Environment

From the use of spreadsheets to graphical tools, the whole programming-in-the-large approach is based on the able description of high-level functions outlining the grand design. But when visual programming is employed in the context of programming in the small, it addresses the operations to be performed on individual data entities.

- Elementary functions are supported through subroutines, hence reusable software which already exists in on-line libraries.

- The end user's challenge is to recombine these modules within the new implementation perspectives, addressing the problems which arise ad hoc as business develops.

Experimentation is at a premium, and therefore simulation should cover not only a given problem, or part thereof, but also the whole business environment in which the user operates. This is written in a dual sense: programming in the large and programming in the small.

In connection with programming in the large, real-time simulation is, in essence, what a trader in the financial industry does all the time. "Most people at CSFB feel they do virtual reality every day," said the managing director of Credit Swiss Financial Products.

This statement holds true all the way from emulating market conditions to the use of advanced communications technology as a means by which the barriers of time and space can be bypassed.

- Networks permit in-depth manager-to-manager and trader-to-trader conversations around the globe.

- But there are also infrastructure issues to be addressed by computer professionals, besides the applications to be programmed by end users.

In terms of the evolution of the grand design of their computers and communications software, the more advanced industrial companies and financial institutions have passed beyond the state of an amalgam of electronic bulletin boards, on-line information services, and computer conference sessions through which bankers are already connecting to conduct business. *Virtual environments* present a new dimension and a significant leap in competitiveness and define a new ballgame, which programming in the large attempts to address. Any grand design which is worth its salt should take careful notice of the fact that in most user-driven systems, at the beginning we have only a vague idea of what can be created. As Chap. 3 explains, the perception of what can be done grows through accumulated experience, an enlarged user population, and trial-and-error approaches with quick correction.

Having worked with digital computers since 1953, I know from personal experience that even in the early years of computer programming it was that way. But as routine work and the preservation of the status quo settle in, in most data processing shops this fact of life has been forgotten.

There is a quote from Oscar Wilde that fits well this situation: "The truth is rarely pure and never simple." By some accounts, throwing money at the problem helps to solve it. But there is no documentation of that thought. Quite to the contrary, what seems to happen is exactly the opposite. Throwing money at the problem makes a bad situation worse.

Therefore, it is time to return to the fundamentals. Programming in the large through visual approaches assists in such a task. The inability to comprehend this fact and account for its existence underpins the large majority of failures experienced over the years with software projects.

What is today essentially different from the experiences of the past is that the pace of change, and associated explosion in end-user requirements, has accelerated. This makes software development a fairly different issue from what it was as recently as the late 1980s.

The new perspectives make it mandatory to find ways and means for swamping costs, accelerating the timetables of deliverables and increasing the derived benefits. Benefits tend to increase as new users steadily join the implementation environment, and as the user community as a whole grasps the ramifications of communications, computers, and software systems.

The benefits also increase when functional and other improvements are dynamically executed, a process which provides leading-edge solutions. Able solutions, however, cannot be supported through old methods, for instance, the slow-moving, inflexible, and time-consuming formal analysis for specifications, with requirements freeze and manual coding; and interminable changes to bought software packages to fit old, nonperforming procedures.

Let's integrate this with some basic principles. There are some simple rules to follow in the choice of a user-oriented visual programming language. First, it must be *easy to learn* and therefore self-teaching. *Agents* can be of significant help in reaching this goal.

Second, the programming-in-the-large approach must be *easy to use.* Hence, it must not only require simple specifications statements and icons, but also provide comprehensive and consistent user interfaces.

Third, it must be *easy to remember,* employing no esoteric graphical commands and utilizing as much as possible approaches which are natural to the end user.

Fourth, never lose sight of the fact that essentially end-user programming means *prototyping* as well as the ability to test in a mode interleaving with development—but without having these two processes confused. This can be instrumental in accelerating the timetable for implementation.

The relative importance of each of these four prerequisites varies with the application. That is why prior to making choices we should list our objectives. This statement is not limited to programming in the large or visual programming. Rather it applies to all processes concerning research, development, and implementation (RD&I) of advanced technology.

References

1. See D. N. Chorafas and H. Steinmann, *Virtual Reality—Practical Applications in Business and Industry,* Prentice-Hall, Englewood Cliffs, N.J., 1995.
2. See D. N. Chorafas, *Programming Systems for Electronic Computers,* Butterworths, London, 1962.
3. D. N. Chorafas, *Understanding Agent Technology for Communication Networks*, McGraw-Hill, New York, 1997.
4. See D. N. Chorafas, *Measuring Returns on Technology Investments,* Lafferty, London and Dublin, 1993.
5. See Chorafas and Steinmann, *Virtual Reality—Practical Applications in Business and Industry.*
6. See also Chap. 12 in this book and D. N. Chorafas and H. Steinmann, *Object-Oriented Databases,* Prentice-Hall, Englewood Cliffs, N.J., 1993.
7. See also Dimitris N. Chorafas, *Knowledge Engineering,* Van Nostrand Reinhold, New York, 1990.

3

Intelligent Human Interfaces
and Pattern Recognition

3.1 Introduction

Reference to the contribution of programming in the large to perception and cognition was made in Chap. 2. Interactive visualization enables end users to depend on tools which are as close as possible to natural language for observation and expression. As the first two chapters of this book have demonstrated,

- Visualization capitalizes on the fact that not all computer information is numbers.

- This is true even when analog information has to be reduced to digital, because that's the way computers operate.

But not all tools offer the same service. Therefore, any decision concerning choices about visualization should be connected to *perception*. Perception not only is the source of all knowledge, but also is itself knowledge by excellence: It is unconditionally genuine knowledge.

A growing number of practical examples, particularly from computer-aided design, help demonstrate that some of the current visual programming tools and projects go beyond *visualization,* in terms of user applications, to include

- *Visibilization,** the making visible of very small and very big items or concepts

- *Visistraction,* the making visible those phenomena lacking a direct physical interpretation, but having to do with concepts

These high-end implementation fields fit well with the gigainstructions per second in processing power featured by high-performance computers, but also

---

*In Chap. 6 we also call this *mathematical visualization,* a frequently used term. By contrast, visistraction is a new term.

require dramatic improvements in the understanding of perception and cognition. This chapters primarily addresses these two issues.

In terms of human understanding, the processes of visistraction, visibilization, and visualization help to translate notions, figures, and procedural steps to computer instructions. They also serve the opposite purpose, expressing the results of computer processing through figures, pictures, and moving images.

Understanding the notions which underpin visistraction, visibilization, and visualization is so important because much of the business and scientific data, and their representations, are spatial in concept. They can be mapped by means of a three-dimensional representation appropriately chosen to fit their context. And they can be made more comprehensive through the ability to interactively respond to ad hoc queries.

As we will see in Part 2, one of the major assets of three-dimensional color visualization is the quick change of a display. We can interactively alter the representation while keeping the same data stream. Or, conversely, we can change the data stream while keeping the same representation. This permits interesting experimental possibilities both in engineering and in finance.

3.2 Research on Perception and Cognition

Many rules known from studies of perception can be applied to visualization. Practically any representation can be made to fit the user's preference and visual sophistication, therefore aiding in creative thinking. We can as well take advantage of traditional metaphors or develop new ones which assist in the customization of presentation characteristics and, by extension, in perception. But before we do so, we should understand how the process of perception works.

- It assists in extracting knowledge more efficiently.
- It permits the development of more agile human-machine communications.
- It is instrumental in finding insights which otherwise might go unobserved.

In essence, the concept of high-level machine programmability ranges from cognitive complexity to the effective use of resources. Figure 3.1 shows the interdependence between cognition and software characteristics. It also notes that the programmer's skill can have a significant impact on the use of hardware and software resources.

Precisely for these reasons, a growing number of research projects investigate the basic mechanisms of perception and cognition in the human senses of sight and hearing. This is done from different viewpoints: engineering, psychological, and physiological. The goals are to

- Obtain breakthroughs in the technologies of visual pattern and speech recognition.
- Develop efficient as well as friendly human-machine interfaces for everyday use.

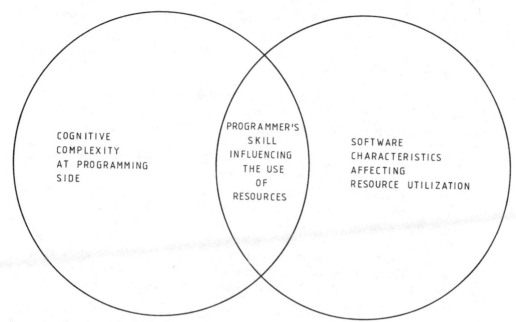

Figure 3.1 The concept of high-level programmability ranges from cognitive complexity to the use of resources.

To meet these objectives, researchers study the basic mechanisms of visual perception, conducting psychological experiments to clarify the detailed characteristics of human motion and depth perception. Subsequently, they build computer models of these functions based on experimental data.

Advanced projects are also studying human physiological indices such as evoked cortical responses. They seek to clarify the relationship between the physiological data and visual perception, while other projects focus on the character of pattern understanding, including the possible impact of psychological factors.

This effort comes none too soon. Although today's technology allows us to build machines which can recognize characters and figures, their cognitive capacity is still way below that of a human. To narrow this gap and produce more advanced technologies in pattern recognition, researchers take a closer look at human perceptual, cognitive, and memory mechanisms. The aim is to study human character and pattern recognition through psychological experiments, trying to model the human recognition process by using neural network or other approaches. We talk more about this in Part 3. This procedure is also very helpful to scene analysis and understanding.

As a step toward realizing automated scene analysis, laboratories are examining mathematical aspects of human perception of three-dimensional structure from two-dimensional images. The goal is to achieve a model-based understanding of natural scenes, comprising three-dimensional arrangements of objects. Human cognitive and behavioral processes are being studied to

- Clarify the underlying principles of information processing and communication.

- Achieve breakthroughs in developing highly advanced, easy-to-use, human-machine communication systems.

An example is the cognitive processes for visual information. Human representation and processing of visual information are effectively investigated through psychological experiments and computational analyses of pattern vision and spatial vision.

Also parallel computing principles are being examined. Neural networks in the human brain use parallel computation for information processing. The mathematical properties of connectionist models and their potential for engineering or other applications are being investigated theoretically as well as experimentally through simulation.

Similar principles apply in learning and in the motor theories of perception. An understanding of the process of learning plays a vital role in visual programming. The brain integrates all kinds of sensory information in order to gain deeper knowledge of objects in the outer world, which is targeted through programming in the large.

- A crucial issue in many research projects is the integration of sensory and visual information with motion control.

- For its part, motion control is applied to the recognition and synthesis of speech as well as of characters and patterns.

For instance, today every self-respecting telecommunications laboratory pays attention to the modeling of hearing and speech perception. Such research is directed toward the fundamentals of automatic speech recognition, syntheses, and coding techniques.

Models of human auditory processing and their applications to speech recognition and signal processing are studied through psychoacoustic and speech perception experiments. Adaptive functions of the human auditory systems, in various environments, are investigated with the aim of developing a speech preprocessor as efficient as human hearing.

Speech perception and recognition processes are studied to yield an integrated model of speech information processing in humans. Research activities include coarticulation modeling in continuous speech, representations of acoustic features in speech signals, perception of vowels and consonants, and different approaches to speech processing

The integration of speech recognition and language handling is particularly important in realizing an automatic interpreting telephone system. Means of enhancing the speech recognition rate are provided by establishing a model of the language and incorporating its word patterns. Another requirement is a method for the elimination of ambiguity which may result from speech recognition.

To correctly comprehend spoken words, it is particularly important to develop methods of inferring the meaning of sentences from the way individual words are used within a conversational context. This can be achieved through a knowledge bank that

- Includes knowledge pertaining to particular fields of interest
- Predefines the meaning implicit in terms through language semantics

To help in the process of perception and cognition, the knowledge bank must define the interconnections between words. It must also incorporate inference methods, including techniques for filtering and for predicting subsequent words. While these references come from current research projects in telecommunications, they are also most valuable in visualization studies.

3.3 Visual Programming and the Changing Dimensions of the Software Effort

As we have seen, the development of computer code has classically been a linear process. Assemblers and compilers practically copied the same step-by-step approach even as, during the last 10 years, parallel programming became an issue of considerable interest, and led to nonlinear approaches in coding schemes.

How a linear process operates is shown at the top of Fig. 3.2. Whether we come from absolute machine language or from symbolic code, we can approach our goal along the straight line in the top figure; this becomes a slow, costly, and painful process when the goal is to build fairly complex computer programs.

- This kind of limitation is always present when we work with principally linear concepts but target rather complex solutions.
- Therefore, from analysis and modeling to programming, we are increasingly interested in processes which are inherently nonlinear.

The incorporation of psychological and physiological aspects of perception injects this element of nonlinearity. This is a fact that most of the available programming languages fail to account for and that the majority of computer professionals fail to comprehend. Yet, it is vital to the cognitive process of the end user.

A good example of a multidimensional programming-in-the-large structure is provided by *Gamelan*.* This is a World Wide Web service platform which provides its users with a bewildering array of service modules ranging from a simple spreadsheet to much more sophisticated applets, for example:

- Wells Fargo Bank server
- Commission pricer[†]

---

*Created by EarthWeb, to which many other companies and private individuals contribute.
[†]robert@capmkt.com

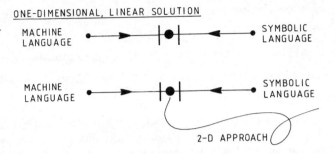

ONE-DIMENSIONAL, LINEAR SOLUTION

MACHINE
LANGUAGE

SYMBOLIC
LANGUAGE

MACHINE
LANGUAGE

SYMBOLIC
LANGUAGE

2-D APPROACH

TWO-DIMENSIONAL SOLUTION

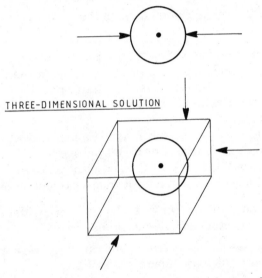

THREE-DIMENSIONAL SOLUTION

Figure 3.2 One-, two-, and three-dimensional approaches to programming and to security protection. (*Based on an original idea by Dr. H. Steinmann.*)

- Currency exchange calculator[‡]
- Commodity exchange simulator
- Derivatives calculator
- Options pricer[§]
- Mortgage calculator[¶]
- Loans pricer
- On-line portfolio computer

[‡]twendt@acm.org
[§]robert@capmkt.com
[¶]kj@broadcom.ie

- Stock tracer
- On-line tax calculator
- Java shopping cart
- Java demons

All 13 bullets are applets. Most run under Sun's HotJava browser (see Chaps. 6 and 8). Others work under Netscape. Many are n-dimensional artifacts or have the capability of becoming so. By comparison, the spreadsheet is a two-dimensional construct.

As the second diagram in Fig. 3.2 shows, persons who employ a two-dimensional approach for perception, cognition, and/or programming endow themselves with better tools than one-dimensional persons. This happens because two-dimensional concepts make available an added degree of freedom, which we can use to our advantage. The goal can be reached nonlinearly.

In computer programming, this is a much better solution which, so far, few languages have been able to exploit. One approach to converting computer code to parallel processing capitalizes on the power of nonlinearities through the use of genetic algorithms,[1] and it has obtained fairly good results. These are, however, the exceptions to the general case.

- The best example of two-dimensional programming in data processing is the use of spreadsheets.
- Graphics present another effective way, starting with the use of icons and menus and progressing toward *virtual reality* environments which are three-dimensional.

Icons are representations of familiar objects, and in their way they are the oldest human language. Its symbols are known as *hieroglyphics*. In ancient Egypt and Babylonia they were used as written means of expressing a natural language.

Pictorial writing can help in a significant way in perception. It continues to be used by the Chinese, and we also find it in traffic signs in the west. Pictures and icons are one of the better means of making personal computers more friendly, in the sense of communicating between the end user and the information which is stored and handled by the machine.

- Graphical models have become the new paradigm for thinking about systems and solutions, also for expressing meaning—hence semantics.
- They can be applied in a two-dimensional sense; or, as with virtual reality, they can be three-dimensional.

The point is that even with two-dimensional programming, which is a more sophisticated solution than the linear step-by-step approach, we are not really providing the end user with the best technology can offer. Yet, generally two-dimensional graphical models do fall under the title of *visual programming*.

- The limitations in two-dimensional approaches can be overcome through the addition of a third dimension.

- Three-dimensional solutions practically increase the degrees of freedom, which we can use to advantage.

The fourth diagram in Fig. 3.2 explains this concept. Although the two-dimensional solution is more flexible and much faster than one-dimensional step-by-step programming, this type of processing eventually builds its own boundaries, which put limits on software evolution. A third dimension changes that, making it feasible to reach the goal from different directions.

Dr. Heinrich Steinmann developed this concept in connection with security and protection in the domain of telecommunications, but it applies as well to computer programming. The defenses built along a one-dimensional frame of reference, Steinmann says, may be superb. But an intruder who thinks in two dimensions will always reach his or her goal, passing through the nonguarded gate. This gate is visible to the intruder but transparent to those who have a one-track mind. Something similar happens with programming approaches.

If the defenses are designed to withstand the security risks posed by two-dimensional thinkers in the intruder's or hacker's community, then their attacks will lead nowhere, provided the firewalls are worth their salt. But an intruder who thinks in three dimensions will be able to penetrate and reach the guarded treasures, because two-dimensional defenses are not planned to protect against three-dimensional thinking.

A three-dimensional programming environment is today effectively supported through *virtual reality* applications.[2] "A *virtual environment*," says MIT's Dr. David Zeltzer, "is a better term for computer applications in science, engineering and business." This has been further promoted by the fact that the end user's workstation has progressed in such a way that we don't need millions of dollars anymore to make realistic and interesting simulation and to develop virtual worlds through computer graphics. Technology is now providing miniature stereo displays at an affordable cost. As the faculty of the Santa Fe Institute was to underline, the whole idea of implementing virtual reality is to *significantly improve upon the presentation of information.*

More efficient presentation can have many manifestations, all of them having to do with different degrees of sophistication in visualization. But the able use of three-dimensional programming approaches requires an awareness of representational details, some of which may not be relevant to the task of manipulating and displaying graphical objects. Semantics are of significant value.

- Geometric transformation operators, such as scale and translate, have semantic meaning in graphical programming.

- Video retrieval is a more complex issue, with present methods including use of spatial pointers or text labels.

- But semantically based retrieval that relies on the contents of the video frames is much more difficult and constitutes the next frontier.

Contrary to old languages such as Cobol, visual programming and virtual reality are expanding fields, and much of their background is in three-dimensional graphics and simulation. Current work puts emphasis on *applications building*. The more advanced the solution we are after, the better able it is to cut inside the problem to emulate *real-world behavior* through technology.

The more we face these issues in an able manner, the more they permit us to extend the human senses. Therefore the key to success lies not only in building simulators that use knowledge engineering and implemention of three-dimensional graphics but also in examining in a rigorous manner how perception and cognition can be promoted.

3.4 Three-Dimensional Graphics as Tools of Perception and Cognition

In a manner similar to the telecommunications studies we examined in Sec. 3.2, colorful three-dimensional graphics can help researchers better understand complex models. Interactive visualization involves a range of techniques that enable the display, in graphical format, as well as numerical data and statistics from massive data-crunching applications.

- A three-dimensional representation process provides a picture of information elements and their internal relationships.

- The detail mapped into such picture can never be detected by the human eye looking at rows and columns of raw data.

The obvious benefit of using interactive visualization, with knowledge-enriched software, is that end users can look at a picture and immediately spot trends. This can be done with tremendous acuity.

In finance, for instance, the analyst, trader, or manager does not even have the time to mentally process the raw data under scrutiny. The market moves too rapidly. Therefore, she or he needs tools which make it feasible to immediately spot trends and exceptions. Analysts and traders must not have to think linearly about every number that comes to the screen. Because the markets are so dynamic, there is a torrent of intraday statistics whose message usually goes undetected.

Financial analysts increasingly find out that (as is the case with engineers) visualization gives them a way to investigate the potential of markets and products, by dynamically altering and tuning simulation parameters. Thus, they can interactively monitor the progress of an experiment, alter financial product characteristics, or terminate poor marketing jobs. The end result is

- Shorter development cycles
- Better market appeal of products and services

Available as a commodity by companies which specialize in computer graphics, visualization software is designed to meet the needs of two groups of users.

(See also Part 2 on Internet tools and Chap. 9 on programming tools for visualization beyond VRML.) This classification is written in an interdisciplinary sense, with better perception and cognition in the background.

One user group is made up of those interested in developing their own perceptualization and visualization environments. For these users, who are often researchers, engineering designers, and financial analysts, there are a variety of general programs as well as end-user visual programming language tool kits. These permit them to do leading-edge applications without looking at analytical processes in the traditional way.

Because such users are often working with data from many different sources, as is the case with nontraditional financial research, graphics packages must offer significant flexibility, particularly in regard to different types of data and file formats—visualizing, porting, and integrating them. What these users need is a strong model to bring in multimedia information elements of widely disparate types into one cohesive environment, not just a slick graphical user interface. When creating their displays, these power users also need speed, including rendering speed.[3]

The other group is made by casual users who look for a quick-fix approaches to perception and visualization, on a self-service basis. While these users want fairly complete visualization applications, the most important factor is friendly interfaces that enable them to see and analyze data immediately. They don't want many design details. Menu-driven visualization programs that provide standard data functions for instant viewing of color contour, line, vector, polar, and surface plots may serve them well with regard to conceptual needs.

Packages incorporating visual programming languages and graphical tool kits provide users with flexibility in how they chose to run their applications. These tools are mainly programming modules displayed as icons, with each icon controlling a particular function or subroutine. Users can customize their applications by linking together these modules, or icons, into flow graphs. Figure 3.3 shows an example.

The underlying concept, in this and similar applications, is that by linking the modules in varying sequences, end users can access thousands of imaging and visualization tasks. Different jobs can be served from this procedure, with examples being data analysis, image processing, and volume rendering.

Vendors now incorporate standardized graphical interfaces into software, replacing command-driven approaches. In this manner, anyone who is interested in visualization, and not in programming, can really get at the job by using a program that speaks his or her language.

But even though at the end-user level what a visual programming language or tool kit offers should definitely look simple, the development of more powerful tools requires a very significant amount of research in perception and conceptualization, starting with the basic notions of pattern recognition. This is the issue addressed in Sec. 3.5.

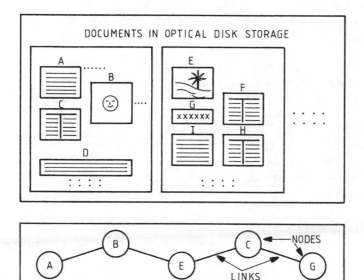

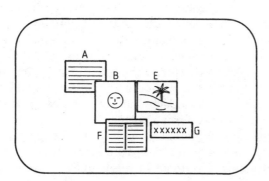

Figure 3.3 Compound electronic documents involve networked objects in a multimedia sense.

3.5 Fuzzy Engineering and the Modeling of Expert Knowledge through Patterns

The *Gestalt* school of psychology interprets perceptual phenomena as organized wholes rather than aggregates of distinct parts. A visual image or a body of knowledge, this school suggests, cannot be simply interpreted in terms of its constituents. The sum, which is the whole image, is greater than its parts—but interpretation requires rigorous knowledge.

- Looking at a bubble chamber photograph, the nonexpert sees broken, confused lines.

- By contrast, the trained eyes of a physicist record familiar subnuclear events.

The Gestalt concept is very important to visual programming because, as stated earlier, programming is a job of translation and interpretation. The process of visualization of complex patterns can be so much better understood if it is integrated with the concepts of perception and cognition along the frame of reference explained in Secs. 3.1 to 3.4.

Let's start with the fundamentals. The word *pattern* has a very broad meaning. This meaning often depends on the context in which *pattern* is used, leading to different interpretations. Such interpretations basically refer to two different levels of perception.

- A direct appearance, like an aggregate ensemble of visual impressions
- A conceptual level, which is more detailed, but also more personal to the browser

These two levels have a common background. Both are understood in the sense of a representation, which can be external, like a sketch, or internal. An example of an internal representation is the reminiscence of a phenomenon.

Basically, a pattern is a set of information. Therefore, both the external and the internal representations affect our way of thinking, leading to procedures of cognition and the learning of pattern similarities and differences.

If an industrial engineer is given the job of just-in-time inventory management, the pattern of database elements and parts that he has to deal with will most likely look like Fig. 3.4. Each one of the boxes in this flowchart is itself composed of elements which form a pattern.

To do the job in an able manner, the industrial engineer must perceive and identify the Gestalt of the production process and its component parts. The programming activity may have to do with scheduling, inventory control, or quality assurance. In the latter case the engineer may have to

- Identify the elements which caused the outgoing quality level to bend
- Detect the negative pattern that these elements formed in order to break it

The analysis of a positive or negative pattern is a programming-in-the-large job we would like to see facilitated through computers. Production processes are too complex to be studied to the level of fundamentals by the human mind unassisted. This is another example illustrating the fact that programming is a real-world activity. It is not an ossified task.

- From the user's point of view, a key characteristic is the uncertainty of the relationships among members of the data set which form the pattern.
- Either the relationships themselves or the industrial engineer's knowledge about them, or both, can demonstrate various degrees of uncertainty.

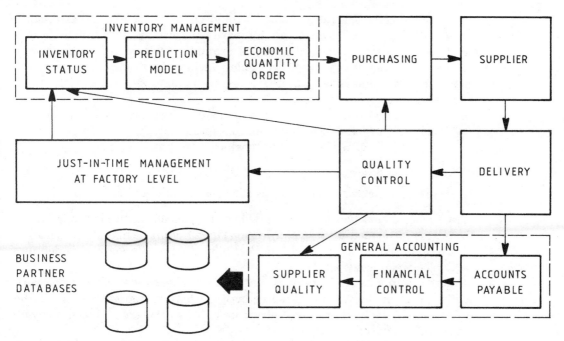

Figure 3.4 A pattern of database elements for just-in-time inventory management.

The positive aspect in this situation is that the component parts of a pattern have a certain coherence. All members of the set contain information that appears relevant to a certain phenomenon. There may, however, be ambiguous or missing relationships of hierarchy or causality among information elements, so that their membership itself may be uncertain.

Vagueness and uncertainty have a lot to do with perception, and they are part of the price to be paid for replacing crisp quantities with fuzzy quantities. The problem is that many real-life situations are fuzzy. Therefore, fuzzy engineering assists in their comprehension.[4]

To create patterns out of fuzzy information elements, we need methods of matching fuzzy sets, for instance, using possibility intervals without probabilistic assumptions. Beyond this, the fuzzy component of a problem-oriented organization and the methodology for pattern understanding may be embedded in two different activities:

- Recognition
- Retrieval

The recognition part can be subject to local matching and/or global matching, each with its primitives, which may be a function of either the user's identity or the problem's identity or of both.

In terms of retrieval, fuzzy elements could enter the search either because the query is fuzzy or because the database contents are fuzzy. In case of a search for a pattern of personal traits, for example, retrieval may be based on a fuzzy concept—not on an image facsimile—such as small nose, big eyebrows, thick hair, and round facial expression. The transition from small to big can be mediated by intelligent software.

One of the important issues related to the use of fuzzy sets to capture the imprecision of the real world concerns conceptual comparisons. These largely consist of an evaluation of the degree to which

- Two concepts described by corresponding fuzzy sets   *or*
- Two different fuzzy representations of the same concept

agree among themselves to an acceptable degree of confidence. Often this kind of analysis is termed *pattern unification* or *matching*. This is an operation defined and used in many problems. Possibility theory offers a way of defining a match between fuzzy sets.[5]

But three-dimensional graphics and fuzzy engineering don't always work together. One of the main differences between pattern representations is the lack, or partial lack, of graphical structures able to represent causal or hypothetical interactive relations.

A pattern may express the general impression of a situation which is not that strong in methodological approach or in precision of component sets. Or, alternatively, it may go deeper in associations than the usual subjective interpretations. There is therefore a problem of pattern representation strategy which both derives from cognitive processes and helps in terms of the interpretation of certain patterns.

3.6 Pattern Recognition, Clustering, and Image Understanding

Computer programs are patterns which are understood by the machine. While this statement is more applicable with three-dimensional or n-dimensional structures, visual programming sees to it that the study of pattern recognition is revealing. To improve upon our current performance, we should be ready to attack and challenge nearly every premise in sight.

Early work in pattern recognition dates back to the beginning of the 1950s, with the main effort directed to character recognition using nonstatistical methods. Statistical pattern recognition experienced a rapid growth over the two decades from 1957 to 1977, and subsequent work emphasized

- Practical applications of statistical pattern recognition
- Combined statistical and structural pattern recognition approaches

Since the beginning, it has been evident that good classification methods are needed in almost all applications, so that automatic pattern recognition can be accurate and dependable. The implementation of knowledge engineering made it feasible to combine statistical, structural, and heuristic recognition approaches.

Clustering has been often used as a tool in exploratory data analysis. Researchers organize patterns into groups or clusters in a way that patterns within a cluster are more similar to each other than are those belonging to different clusters. Cluster analysis can also be used for

- Data reduction
- Display in two-dimensional and three-dimensional space

Cluster analysis is an unsupervised classification in which previously established rules about data are not available. It is an important topic in statistical pattern recognition, which has very extensive applications in many disciplines without requiring the complex procedure of estimating the probability density.

The structure of data as represented by cluster analysis often provides useful physical insights of the measured quantity. By treating clustering as a statistical decision process, the combination of multivariate statistical analysis and statistical decision theory forms the basis for mathematical solutions to statistical pattern recognition.[6]

Pairwise comparison analysis targets a population's multivariance and can be helpful for pattern recognition both in engineering and in finance.

For image analysis, spatial clustering is a useful procedure for image segmentation. Also, as we saw in Sec. 3.5, another important development is the use of fuzzy functions in pattern understanding.

Whether crisp or fuzzy, modeling assists in reaching the goal of pattern recognition. Theoretically modeling helps in both reasoning and retrieval. However, there is a contradiction in this statement because modeling is usually general in nature while retrieval must be specific.

At the same time, however, retrieval is a way of validating the model. Models which are particularly difficult to validate fall in this class, because information retrieval is not efficient enough or is constrained for a number of reasons.

Among problem areas in visual programming where solutions are most wanted, we distinguish feature extraction, nonstationary series, matching complexity in adaptive systems, finite-sample-size effects, computational recognition, contextual analysis, statistical and syntactic models, and the automatic generation of recognition rules for complex patterns.

The reason why I am so bullish about the future role of pattern recognition in visual programming stems from the fact that this procedure and its associated tools have been successfully employed in a large number of applications including perception and cognition of characters, speech, biological signals, and biomedical images and in connection with automated visual inspections, seismic and underwater acoustic waveforms, and remote sensing.

- In some applications, syntactic pattern recognition may be more suitable.
- In others, signal and image processing is essential before recognition can be performed.

The goal of such exercises is to increase depth perception, but positive results require moving from two-dimensional representations to three-dimensional ones. To map functions for a flat surface is quite simple. By contrast, curved surfaces call for complex parametric descriptions.

- The process of *image mapping* transfers a two-dimensional image memory to the object's surface through a mapping function.

- *Reflectance mapping* simulates a surface by mapping a picture of the object's environment into it.

- *Procedural mapping* uses an algorithmic approach to generate texture values, for instance, fractals.[7]

The image which is mapped may be animated. An alternative to surface texture is solid texture. It consists of mapping from a three-dimensional texture space to the three-dimensional object. This approach involves little more than scaling and has the advantage that it is independent of the surface complexity of the object being mapped to. Because of the large storage requirements of a three-dimensional texture map, the data stream is typically generated in a procedural way.

One of the challenges is the mapping of database elements, whether images, signals, or other patterns. In Sec. 3.5 we spoke about local and global matching as well as the contributions provided by fuzzy engineering. As far as end users are concerned, their viewpoint can be expressed through a block diagram similar in Fig. 3.5.

- The end-user entity may be man or machine.

- The difference will be in the primitives.

Increasingly, research projects focus on building learning systems which respond to changes in use. This makes it necessary to observe usage patterns and to know the state of the knowledge bank. This leads to the discussion of how to project, design, and use human perception and cognition processes in spite of the growing size of distributed databases and their soft data, or fuzzy, contents.

3.7   Assisting Perception through Advanced Human Interfaces and Metaphors

Research, development, and implementation of computer-based solutions to perception and cognition are inseparable from the design and evaluation of human interfaces. For this reason, Xerox brings in anthropologists to study human aspects of new technology which it develops.

Ideally, an advanced interface will push the limits of human windows and have machines communicate as people do. This has not yet been achieved. and it does not seem to be around the corner. But there are projects using

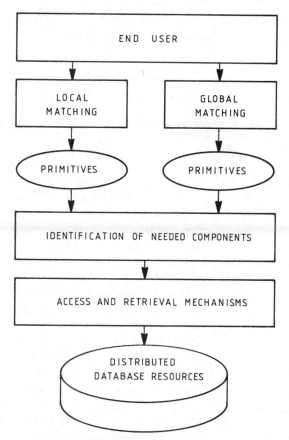

Figure 3.5 Retrieval of fuzzy information elements and patterns from distributed databases.

- Three-dimensional holograms for engineering design and architectural reasons
- Video databases which permit animation and annotations
- Digital artificial images, permitting one to integrate up to four different images
- Artifacts enabling the user to grab from different perspectives, using context understanding and autonomous agents

Fundamentally, the human window is a tutorial dialog method. It guides human-machine communication in two important ways: by structuring the dialog and by providing a fairly homogeneous conversation which is adaptable enough to the user.

The concept of human windows has both contributed to and been enhanced by artificial intelligence applications. Already in the mid-1980s, for instance, one of the best expert systems of its time—the Dupmeter Advisor—had 42 percent of its code devoted to human-machine communications.

- In most practical examples, the *dialog* plays a key role in a successful implementation.

- Experience teaches that we should have a first-class human-machine interface and a less sophisticated deep engine, not vice versa.

Specifications for user interfaces must strike a balance between encouraging use through consistency and not inhibiting innovation. An example of the search for such balance is the *desktop metaphor* for human-machine interfaces, including a system image and its components. Other, more potent, *Internet-oriented metaphors* are the subject matter of Part 3.

The desktop metaphor was created in the early 1980s for operating systems, and it was followed in the mid-1980s by icons and windows. But sometime after both achieved dominance, they started being replaced in the number 1 spot by the metaphor *agents,* as we will see in Sec. 3.8.

A basic principle underpinning the desktop metaphor has been that end users moving between terminals, or systems from different suppliers, must not go through a new learning process. They should be provided with a standard interface across different media rather than being addressed in a case-by-case, heterogeneous manner.

Within a given implementation environment, a standard human-machine interface can be expressed by an appropriate metaphor. This *metaphor* is a reference to a real-world situation that the system designer tries to invoke and explain to the machine—so that the user brings to bear the right conceptual models to the task she or he is after, when employing the system.

- Metaphors have to be embodied in the system's appearance, including graphical representation and all means of dialog.

- A desktop metaphor is tailored to the specific needs of, say, office tasks, with the understanding that merely grafting communication processes onto general office practices is inadequate.

Mobile users may require special metaphors, including navigational aids. Computer-aided design and generally computer graphics users may need high-speed access to data files linked to specific manipulation and presentation processes. Top management may require high-quality moving image communications with real-time interaction.

Although until recently the desktop metaphor was *the* metaphor, many other different metaphors are increasingly becoming a prominent part of available software. They all tend to emphasize ease of learning and ease of use. They also address basic issues in connection with their design.

In many cases, however, the word *metaphor* is used loosely to include any image that represents a given object as being something else, in order to explain it better. An example is provided by metaphorical anthropomorphisms or, more generally, by the role of metaphor in scientific cognition.

Contrary to the hieroglyphics which were in common use as a written language in Egypt for about 2500 years (3000 B.C. to 400 B.C.), computer icons and metaphors are a *pictorial* script. The contrast to hieroglyphics comes from the fact that they were a *phonetic* script.

Metaphors of computer science largely describe things made by humans that follow laws made by humans, or things that are often highly abstract and quite arbitrary. One of the risks is that once a metaphor is used for a time, it is easy to lose sight of its original meaning and treat it as though it had some other meaning.

- This problem impacts both perception and cognition.

- One way to avoid it is to enrich metaphors with paradigms.

The fact that the original meaning may be lost is not strange because services evolve and, with time, they address a wider range of users and applications. Therefore eventually there develops a more loosely defined metaphor and/or alternative interpretation(s) to the one already existing. Hence, from time to time metaphors need to be pruned.

At the semantic level, for every metaphor there must be constructed a model of the user's understanding of what the service or application is and what it has to offer. Such a conceptual model is based on the user's cognitive strengths, with the appropriate interface metaphor built to

- Leverage the user's conceptual model

- Reinforce its effects in a programming or visualization sense

Establishing conceptual models and metaphors for classes of applications and user environments can be a rewarding job. For information retrieval purposes, for example, the metaphor may assist the user in exploring a *time base,* browsing through time, locating events, helping in the recognition of a file from those displayed, and so on. We discuss these issues in Chaps. 6 and 7, in connection with the World Wide Web and VRML.

3.8   An Interactive Development of End-User Interfaces and the Role of Agents

Through a knowledge database we can derive information which is not specifically stored. This approach rests on knowledge engineering and is effective only if the language which we use facilitates search and recovery without extensive coding—which would require an inordinate amount of the end user's time.

The interactive development of user interfaces involves design refinement based on testing and the evaluation of user response. Design changes from one iteration to the next are local to the specific interface elements that caused problems. A flexible methodology does not involve wholesale replacement of interface elements, but rather a choice between interface alternatives, with comparative testing to measure which is the most usable.

- Interactive design helps in the refinement of human-machine interfaces based on lessons learned from experience.
- Solutions should be based on the premise that managers and professionals have no time to learn complex operations, such as command inputs.

The use of computers slows when human-machine interfaces are supported through lousy software, which is too difficult to understand and remember. On the other hand, asking secretaries or assistants to perform desired computer operations ends up being counterproductive.

Since managerial viewpoints vary and change, it is rather meaningless to use inflexible or fixed command procedures, or routine sequences in query execution. Ad hoc, flexible query methods which are user-friendly and easy to learn are required for all end-user application services.

Figure 3.6 shows an object-oriented solution developed by Scandinaviska Enskilda Banken along the foregoing frame of reference. The layered approach

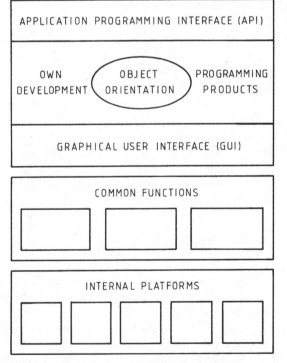

Figure 3.6 A software architecture for workstations by S. E. Banken.

which has been chosen helps to support a common structure spanning a number of different platforms while, at the same time, it permits the personalization of presentation procedures.

A good test of a user interface that is truly easy to learn is whether a person interacting with the workstation can go quickly from not knowing the system to doing her work in an efficient manner. The interface must also be consistent and comprehensible and must use a number of knowledge artifacts. This will make the solution conceptually simple, aiding in the problem's perception, and efficient, letting the end user attain a high level of productivity.

In terms of observing human strengths and limitations, the interface must be easy to remember, so that infrequent users do not have to learn everything all over again. Also, it should be error-forgiving at the user's side, and offer assurance that when they happen, errors are not catastrophic and that it is easy to recover from them.

Another characteristic of a good solution is the flexibility which it presents in the sense of future extensions and improvements. Because computer, communications, and software technologies advance to support more complex applications,

- Any current approach runs the risk of reaching practical limits, because of some badly designed interface module.

- Therefore, when new problems develop, software has to be reinvented—and quite often so do the human windows, too.

We must always account for the fact that the next generation of human windows will move beyond today's standard input metaphors and paradigms to involve virtual reality elements, such as immersive three-dimensional graphics, sound and speech, gesture recognition, and animation. They will use sophisticated artificial intelligence models and will be implemented with mobile computers, through cellular or other wireless communication media.

These new environments are likely to pose significant challenges to human-machine interfaces, particularly if we account for the fact that already the change from function-oriented to object-oriented interfaces proves to be rather difficult for designers, although it is most fundamental for end users.

- The model emerging in interface design is one based on object-oriented operating systems and frameworks (see also Chaps. 11 and 12).

- The basic object of interest in them lies in their improved ability to handle the user's ad hoc queries and multimedia requirements.

Any given electronic document can contain objects of many different types. Therefore, the system should take care of activating and handling appropriate display metaphors. *Agents,* rather than the user, must be on hand to think in terms of implementation choices, running applications, and execution of interactive presentation procedures.

Since agents know how to migrate the information elements and integrate the available functionality in the system, intelligent artifacts become the ultimate editor. At the same time, the object-oriented system should be based on an open architecture and allow flexible addition of new or upgraded functionality—as the end user desires—without any radical changes in its infrastructure.

Thanks to intelligent artifacts, next-generation interfaces will be based on some form of noncommand interaction principles. They will permit users to focus on the task rather than on the operation of the computer. The role of running operational chores will be taken over by agents without any need for user instructions other than those implicit in the job being done. While many agents will be specialized artifacts, others will be generalized and act as utilities.

References

1. See D. N. Chorafas, *Rocket Scientists in Banking,* Lafferty Publications, London and Dublin, 1995.
2. See D. N. Chorafas and H. Steinmann, *Virtual Reality—Practical Applications in Business and Industry,* Prentice-Hall, Englewood Cliffs, N.J., 1995.
3. See also Chap. 5 in this book and Chorafas and Steinmann, *Virtual Reality—Practical Applications in Business and Industry.*
4. See D. N. Chorafas, *Chaos Theory in the Financial Markets,* Probus/Irwin, Chicago, 1994.
5. See D. N. Chorafas, *New Information Technologies—A Practitioner's Guide,* Van Nostrand Reinhold, New York, 1992.
6. See D. N. Chorafas, *Statistical Processes and Reliability Engineering,* D. Van Nostrand Co., Princeton, N.J., 1960.
7. See D. N. Chorafas, *Chaos Theory in the Financial Markets*, Probus/Irwin, Chicago, 1994.

A Cultural Change Necessary to Benefit from New Technology

Whether we look at new tools as languages, horizontal software, methods, or all three together, their contribution will be limited unless we change our culture. As Part 2 explains, although our tools may be wearing out and therefore may be ineffectual, the greatest stumbling block in modern computer programming is cultural. As with every bottle, the bottleneck is at the top—and the top is our culture.

4

The Culture Underlying Visual Programming Efforts

4.1 Introduction

The language which we use forms our mind. Language exists to present whatever can be communicated. But there are things some languages transmit so poorly that we never attempt to communicate them by words if another medium is available.

- What language never does well is to inform us about complex physical shapes and movements.

- Unlike gesture and music, what we call *natural language* cannot do more than one thing at a time.

When it comes to parallelism, we can say that natural language tends to be defective. This matters little for spoken language, hence the large majority of language users are only able to serialize their thoughts. Yet, there exist exceptional people whose minds work in parallel. Wolfgang Amadeus Mozart had once said that when he composed music, he could hear the whole orchestra playing at once.

As we have seen in Part 1, with computers a "language" has primarily been a formal medium for expressing how to handle in a step-by-step fashion a given algorithm or procedure. Starting in the early 1950s with *machine language,* computer code has been oriented to serial processing and esoteric in its construction. Original computing machinery and even today mainframes, maxis, minis, and personal computers are *serial* devices. But the new-generation computers are *parallel* devices. Presently they are used as number-crunching servers. Tomorrow, with desk-area networks (DANs), they will be under every desk, as Chap. 10 explains.

Even more limiting than the serial computing aspects of current languages is the fact that they are esoteric, addressing the needs of the equipment rather than of the user. This was a relatively minor issue as long as computers were centralized in hospital looking-glass houses, and were served only by their high priests. But it has become a major handicap as computers spread and are now programmed by their users. The new principles are that

- Computer programs must be written by, and be understood by, their users—not just the professional programmers.
- The actual execution by the machine is merely a downstream process that implements the method for arriving at the solution to a problem.

This can best be achieved through graphics and an animation language. Part 1 discussed why *visual programming* constitutes an agile interface which supports expressions used in computing and database access as well as in communications. In this chapter we focus on the role of visual programming in modeling and in command instructions.

4.2   Evolution of Communications Protocols*

Any population of organisms evolves communication protocols. It looks *as if* the environment were designed to favor those living species that have the ability to generate and interpret meaningful signals which they exchange between themselves and others. This reference is vital to the programming perspective, and the best way to look at a vital issue is to consider its

- Origins
- Evolution
- Status

In terms of origins, computer programming has much to do with the evolution of science and mathematics as well as the concepts underpinning a scientific discipline. "The sciences do not try to explain, they hardly even try to interpret, they mainly make models," Dr. John von Neumann once suggested.[1] These models become feasible because we use a system of signs and rules which we call *mathematics*.

Modeling is a communications medium which becomes feasible as long as the system of signs and rules which we use is complete and is not self-contradictory. Our models—and by extension our computer programs—must bear a relational structure to the process being emulated, if not to each of its distinct steps, at least to the whole.

- Not only does the origin of scientific investigation lie in these notions, but also it helps to express the evolution of mathematics.

---

*See also, in Chap. 11, the discussion on network protocols for multimedia applications and broadband channels.

- Similar references can be made as well to the origins of computer programming because, as we saw in Part 1, programming is modeling.

Programming in the large looks at the whole, and by consequence it is *teleological*. Programming in the small is a substrate layer. It advances step by step, and it has, therefore, a *causal* nature.

Causal means that if we know the state of a system now, then we can use this knowledge to predict its state immediately afterward. Programming in the small is not precisely causal but it has a causal nature. We use our knowledge of current status to manipulate or specify what *should* happen next.

A *teleological* approach is different. The methodology underpinning it takes a whole view between two moments which are apart, for instance, from start to finish of the computer program we are planning to develop in order to meet specific objectives.

- Teleology asserts that the process under study must satisfy certain criteria.
- This is precisely what we do with programming in the large, by looking at the big picture.

In teleology, a simple event does not determine the next event; the process is treated as a whole. Both methods of teleology and causality essentially describe the same thing. The choice is a holistic view versus an algorithmic approach.

Whether teleological or causal in their fundamentals, both mathematics and natural languages are *behavioral facilitators*. We come to this conclusion by observing the impact of language on evolution. An example is *the evolution of language* itself from a simple genetically controlled signaling mechanism to *learned patterns* of communication.

Languages and protocols are important because both social interaction and industrial activity can evolve by means of signal exchange. As the communication becomes more sophisticated, a number of formalisms set in. The role played by protocols can easily be explained through this frame of reference.

- As the environment becomes more complex, it is possible to observe progressively more interesting communication protocols and support systems.
- When human-made artifacts gain learning ability, the evolution of a primitive language becomes visible, in either a natural or an artificial life population.

There are some interesting correspondences between the results obtained from experiments in artificial life[2] and what is known from the evolution of programming practices. Figure 4.1 suggests successive stages from machine language and assembler-level programming to problem representation — through the use of knowledge engineering artifacts.

The organization of Fig. 4.1 into seven successive layers is intentional, progressing toward the more complex and more demanding conditions. The upper three layers correspond to what in Chap. 2 we called *programming in the*

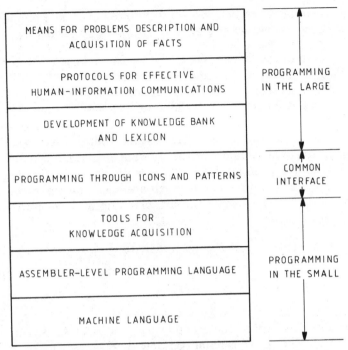

Figure 4.1 Successive layers of programming sophistication from machine language to problem representation.

large. The lower three layers consist of procedures pertinent to *programming in the small.* The middle layer is shared between these two groups as their common interface.

- Programming in the large is essentially a function of systems analysis and design, which must be done interactively through appropriate metaphors.

- Programming in the small is coding whose mechanics can be hidden from the end user if, through visual programming, she or he never goes below the interface layer.

The upper layers deal with *abstraction* of the mechanics of a business system (or scientific problem), as we discussed in connection with patterning and analogical reasoning. The lower layers are less sophisticated and address the finer programmatic characteristics of a mechanism which may be natural or artificial. The interface layer features, among other things, the evolution of *agents:*

- Intelligent artifacts (agents) represent the true automation of the middle- to lower-level programmatic characteristics of software.

- This is in contrast to classical programming which so far has been done through great cost and stress via Fortran, Cobol, or other naive languages, while sophisticated applications were not accomplished at all.

In conclusion, the evolution of human-machine protocols did not come overnight. Developments have taken the better part of 40 years. What is, however, incomprehensible is that so many people in the computer business still labor with naive computer languages and deadly, obsolete concepts. By so doing, they fail to capitalize on new developments to serve their companies and save their own professional status.

4.3 Benefits from a Visual Language

Section 4.2 has explained that, over the last 40 years, computers and communications, and their linguistic rules, constructs, and protocols, have been characterized by significant evolution. Computer artifacts can be conceived as arising as a solution to problems of common living, whether in real or in artificial life settings. This is a steady challenge to which any dynamic population addresses itself.

- Agents that work simultaneously and communicate to solve common issues can be seen as a distributed algorithm.

- One aim of several advanced projects is to find general cases in which distributed algorithms can evolve to solve nontrivial tasks.

In the opinion of many researchers, the evolution of distributed algorithms could help address several basic issues in matters such as community intelligence. Community intelligence and software literacy correlate. Both present problems which are increasingly felt and need to be solved in an able manner.

Language is the means to an acceptable solution, hence the quest for a high-level programming language which can turn the coding task inside out. Programming is a simulated process of execution or evolution, and its linguistic paradigms can be instrumental in the

- Decomposition of problems into subproblems to be solved by independent agents

- Selection of communication protocols and their screening in terms of fitness

- Development of effective methods of solving subproblems within a larger problem

In the background of linguistic evolution is the fact that higher-level tasks usually require composite subtasks, as they consist of several distinct subprocesses. Examples are parsing language, generating language, calculation and reasoning language, as well as linguistic constructs for storage and retrieval from memory.

The processes just described cannot be performed in a single pattern transformation. In fact, some cannot be handled in a serial manner at all, hence the search for parallel metaphors and their mapping into the computer.

Some projects currently conducted in leading university research centers in the United States, Europe, and Japan are embarking on the process of integrating the concepts of parallel and networked computing, with database retrieval and communications. Usually the projected solutions involve graphics.

- They stress the need to rethink and expand the approaches that object-oriented programming has made feasible.

- They also stress the importance of visual programming capabilities in human-machine communication.

It is appropriate to underline at this point that *visual* programming and *graphical* programming are not necessarily one and the same, though both in literature and in daily practice they are often confused. Visual programming does not need to be graphical.

Visual programming can be executed, for instance, through spreadsheets, although icons and two- and three-dimensional graphs are increasingly popular in human-machine communication. With both graphical and nongraphical approaches,

- A visual language can access mathematical and business functions as well as *time variables*.

- Programs can be user-written at the visual programming level and *then* enriched through generators and compiled by the machine.

Instead of focusing on the details of specific programming languages or algorithms, users address themselves more broadly to *problem understanding* and system design techniques. This can be achieved through a variety of high-level programming paradigms, including data abstraction, object orientation, rule-based expert systems, fuzzy engineering artifacts, functional icons and paragraphs, as well as other constructs familiar to the end user, which will be handled by embedded interpreters.

Under this strategy, it is essential for the end user to learn about the technology of implementing friendly languages and linguistic supports to achieve seamless programming. The end user should be prepared not to use a specific language, but to design linguistic metaphors for solving the specific problem. That's the programming-in-the-large approach which we have been discussing.

4.4   Notions which Underpin Programming Paradigms

Any valid computer programming paradigm essentially addresses issues of behavior. This is precisely what a natural language does, whether in serial writing, via icons, or otherwise, for instance, by means of speech or gestures.

Serial approaches may be enough for simple problems, but complex behavior requires bringing together several different kinds of knowledge and processing facilities, which in turn calls for a parallel pattern. There exist as well structural prerequisites because the more complex the environment, the less we can

- Evaluate what the entire system is doing

- Establish what sort of knowledge it is acquiring and/or applying

The only way to break out of serial constraints is to ensure that each sub-process has meaningful internal representations which can be interpreted by the other modules of the system, as well as by the observer, in a consistent, meaningful sense.

Therefore, a plausible approach for cognitive modeling is to construct the architecture—and associated structure—from a number of known modules capable of meaningful interactions among themselves. These modules work together on a common goal, and their joint work helps to produce a higher-level behavior. Among the crucial issues to be addressed in this approach are

- How an overall fairly complex task is divided into modules

- How these modules are organized in a networking sense

- How subnetworks are designed so that they can serve as modular building blocks

This is a process full of linguistic intricacies which become apparent in a programming perspective.

Crucial queries have to be made in order to get to know the system's behavior and the ways in which it can be influenced, for instance, how communication takes place between building blocks, how the channels are being established, and how the modular structure impacts system training.

Factual and documented answers to these queries are critical in terms of *natural language* handling. As we proceed from the simpler environment of numbers to several media, solutions are sought at different levels of reference:

1. *Symbolic through argument graphs.* These reflect belief functions about the execution of plans to achieve goals and the steps to be followed.

Analogical rules are often employed to analyze the contents of a communication. Research focuses on argument units and meta-argument units. A lexicon is constructed with lots of *abductive inferences* rather than the more classical induction and deduction.

2. *Local and distributed connectionist models,* using neural networks with a given activation value. The latter act as the threshold for classification and switching.

The brain, for instance, is distributed and localized at the same time. The pattern of activation is distributed and the main interest is in learning. This distributed level constitutes an architectural model which enables or inhibits the use of technically feasible programming possibilities.

3. *Pragmatic interpretive networks,* including feature planes, dependency graphs, phase locking, and model dynamics.

Many researchers use topographical maps and activation patterns in their work. At this level, neural network approaches also represent an interesting possibility for case-based contents understanding and as a test bed for information retrieval mechanisms which are sensitive to the relations as well as the words of a text.

Multiscale parsing at different levels of granularity, for example, applies a variety of mechanisms to extract structure from text. The output is a modification graph, similar to dependency graphs, indicating modification relations between words in the text.

4. *Pattern solutions* through models accepted or proposed for imitation; representations regarded as normative examples, templates, archtypes, copies, originals, and other fully realized forms.

A pattern can be a group of phases having several distinguishing and fundamental features in common. In linguistics, for example, a pattern is the manner in which smaller units of language are grouped into larger units.

5. *Understanding of the evolution* of communication and language, including arguments about arguments and about belief contents.

In many projects, this evolution takes place along an artificial life frame of reference.* This is a process which, in terms of the comprehension of its fine mechanics, is still in early stages and therefore far from *handcrafting*. A significant amount of knowledge engineering is used to obtain valuable results, and the expected outcome is sure to influence the way in which we program computers.

4.5   Placing Appropriate Emphasis on Visual Programming

As Sec. 4.2 has underlined, when we start with new departures, it is always wise to return to the fundamentals and take a close look at the principles which underpin important developments. When we do so, we discover that many basic principles have been forgotten along the way—and when this happens, it can lead to blind alleys.

That is what has taken place over the years with a number of computer languages such as Cobol and Fortran, whether their users want to admit it or not. Therefore, it is appropriate to return to the notions which underpin programming paradigms, as seen through the knowledge which is available today.

In their fundamentals, the concepts underpinning visual programming rest on two keywords: *visual* and *programming*. The foregoing sections have explained the notions of programming and of the metaphors involved. What has not yet been said is that it is impossible to design a perfect program on the first try. Even when designers and programmers labor hard to anticipate every potential problem, there will always be cases where users approach their work in new ways or interpret the processing elements differently from what was expected. Therefore, computer programs must be developed and refined iteratively over several versions.

- Each iteration must be subjected to user testing and other usability evaluation methods designed to uncover improvement possibilities.

---

*This reference is based on a working meeting with Prof. Michael G. Dryer, Computer Science Department, School of Engineering and Applied Science, UCLA.

- This not only eliminates future problems, but also allows us to gain insight into end-user needs that emerge from tests and daily applications.

The other keyword, *visual,* provides in essence an agile interface. Visual representation of the *spatial relationship* between objects helps in the development, testing, and improvement of information handling processes and of cross-database information retrieval procedures and effective end-user-oriented presentation. However, the employment of visual programming approaches in current software development environments is still rare, and most practices are dominated by text and numbers, in spite of significant advances in visual information technology. It is true as well that much of the gap is cultural. Few people outside specialist departments have the design or video-editing skills required to produce visual programming artifacts or even explanatory material that puts its message across most clearly.

Planning to adopt any type of visual information technology is not sufficient in terms of leading toward programming paradigms. Successful applications require a thorough understanding of the impact of visual programming as well as the integration of visual solutions with conventional data processing.

Basic to this approach is a theory of argument representation for computer comprehension of data, text, and graphs, in short of multimedia. Such theory should characterize major classes of knowledge structures, such as meaning, beliefs, storage relationships, processing relationships, argument units, and meta-argument units.

For instance, in one of the projects currently undertaken in this domain, the artifact is able to explicitly represent the beliefs of the editorial writer and his implicit opponents. This involves predictions about goals, plans, events, and states. Three types of predictions are distinguished:

- Evaluations of plans
- Causal relationships
- Beliefs about beliefs

In the background of all this effort, which is still at the research level, is the concept of dynamic creation of knowledge banks, which constitute a good way to proceed toward visual representations. Their evolution typically goes from *no knowledge* to the set of *rules* and *episodes* which permit the interpretation of a communications system, such as language, through concepts and semantics.

This brings knowledge engineering out of its earlier confines. Today, a lot of existing expert systems are basically classification-oriented. They do not really represent *intelligence* seen as the dynamic construction of the knowledge bank on the fly, which is expected to characterize visual programming projects.

Further out on the horizon is the ability to create *wisdom,* that is, understanding of the consequence of thoughts and actions. Its appreciation requires the knowledge of human personality, which in large part is embedded in the history of evolution and is largely conveyed through cultural transmission.

4.6   A Strategy of Linking to Legacy Systems

Visual programming is no mainframe business—not even one of attaching PCs to mainframes through naive protocols such as the 3270. It is a workstation-based approach typically done at the end-user level with each end user working on her or his problem. Individual applications should be implemented in such a way that they

- Can integrate new modules as they develop
- Restructure themselves for optimization reasons
- Link to mainstream applications of a legacy type

Through integrative approaches, visual programming serves a dual purpose: It opens up an effective avenue to involve end users in developing and testing their own programs. And it presents an opportunity to extend the life of old applications software, by making transparent some of its shortcomings.

One of the most pronounced shortcomings of old programs is in the domain of information retrieval from distributed, heterogeneous databases[3] and in urgently needed ad hoc interactive presentation routines. In both cases, the ability to easily describe spatial and temporal relationships through icons and graphics is at a premium. Hence, that will be the major role of visual programming in the years to come.

An example of modern information retrieval and presentation is offered by *geographic information systems* (GISs). The user interface takes the form of a map on which spacial information, such as layout, is effectively displayed. Selecting a location or an item on the map initiates retrieval of information about it.

With the retrieved information displayed in graphical form, the user interface can be effectively implemented in many other application areas, improving the efficiency of the underlying process:

- By enabling the user to view relationships between objects, important new patterns, processing aspects, and linkages can emerge.
- From programming to display, visualization increases the range of media being accessed and manipulated on line in an ad hoc way.
- For this reason, visual programming and data visualization technologies can handle a greater proportion of information on which the organization depends for its daily business.

Visual approaches are not limited to programming. They cover a wide range of human-machine interactivity, where software development is an important and integral part. They also make possible the perception and conception of patterns and semantic meaning, increasing the interface effectiveness.

Although visual programming and pattern recognition are not synonymous, they are related. This constitutes a great difference from legacy systems which have been typically insensitive to patterning requirements. Yet, many fields of activity use patterns in various ways:

- In music and literature, a pattern is the coherent structure or design of a song or of a book.

- In art, a pattern is the composition or plan of a work of graphical or other representation.

- In architecture and in engineering, a pattern is a design, style, or functional description.

In computer programming, a pattern is a thinking mechanism basic to the machine's operation. Past efforts have failed because they were insensitive to the fact that a pattern must help the end user to perceive things quickly. They were unable to recognize that a program is the interface between the human and the machine.

By contrast, today these issues lead toward an evolving concept in visual programming approaches, as we will see in the following sections through practical examples. A considerable amount of work, however, still needs to be done, since presently little is known about

- Combinations of certain classes and objects, with relationships between them, in different programming environments

- Effective linkages to be provided between legacy programs and the new software development solutions which we discuss

Finally, because of the overriding importance of pattern representation in visual programming, and the fact that patterning is also what we obtain in computer output through two dimensions, three dimensions, and virtual reality, the output of one project can be seen as the canvas on which is developed the input of another.

This is what has happened with the virtual reality solutions developed by the University of Tokyo for Tokyo Electric, by the Mitsubishi Research Institute for Chubu Electric Power, and with so many other efforts. This is also what underpins the seminal work on the understanding of linguistics through the creation and operation of artificial environments, as we have seen in the preceding sections.

4.7 Concept of a Visual Development Environment

With visual programming, what you see is what you get. The user defines a screen and associates it with an expression, without having to worry about file handling and structure. This is done through a high-level interface while processing is executed by generators.

With this approach, the small piecework involved in computer programming is standardized into a larger chunk or unit of visual programming presentation. The developing pattern identified becomes the building blocks for

- System design
- Program construction

The integration of patterns into visual programming solutions results in end-user interfaces becoming much more comprehensive and manipulative. This leads to new programming styles, and it is no surprise that the best of the new software development approaches are graphical.

As a discipline which appeals to both systems specialists and end users, visual programming must have tools. The artifacts upon which rests the new generation of software solutions include

- *Intentional* and *extentional* knowledge,[4] which cannot be mapped into the classical procedural steps but requires knowledge engineering

- *Object orientation,* with symbols used to represent knowledge in terms of *entities* and *relationships* that establish meaningful links to processes

These processes govern the creation, transformation, and other behavior of objects. *Objects* are identifiable, callable entities involving both multimedia information and commands in one package.[5]

Objects are very helpful in an effective information technology implementation, for they provide the basis for machine and application independence as well as semantic meaning. New programming solutions capitalize on the growing popularity of object databases which are typically distributed and networked. This, most evidently, increases the parallel need for graphical development tools.

Based on a concept presented by Media Systems of Karlruhe, Germany, Fig. 4.2 presents one solution toward creating a development environment. It rests on a distributed object-oriented database and uses a number of tools ranging from space control ball with 6 degrees of freedom to virtual holography.

- From three-dimensional graphics to holograms, emphasis is on patterning as well as on the agile on-line interpretation of patterns.

- Many patterns will be ad hoc, made by the user; others will be standard shapes, applied repeatedly.

For instance, in manufacturing, a standard pattern is the shape or style of a manufactured form, which may be a finished product or one of its components. Once developed, standard patterns of components may be stored in the object database and recalled at will.

Within a graphical implementation environment, objects and their relationships can be effectively represented by means of encapsulated artifacts, ranging from icons to real-life component parts, such as those used in computer-aided engineering, shown in Fig. 4.3:

- An object can have various *attributes.*

- *Values* are associated with them, documented by means of a property list.

What is particular about Fig. 4.3 is that it represents a classification effort of basic parts (not subassemblies) of a machine manufacturing company. The designers who developed this matrix worked on the principle that the more sophisticated the patterns and the way in which they are manipulated, the

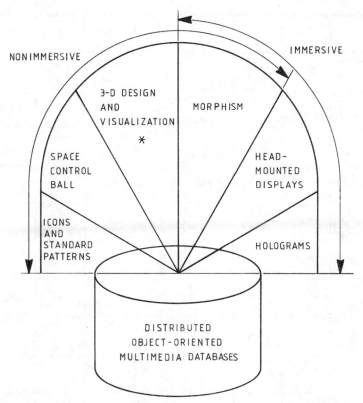

Figure 4.2 Immersive and nonimmersive tools for human-machine communications.

more assistance they provide—but also the more graphics processing power is needed. But given the steady drop in hardware costs, this is a profitable exchange.

In terms of interactive design principles, patterns of lowest-level elements and relationships between them form a building block for more effective representation in a visual programming sense:

- To find a pattern among some lowest-level elements, the analyst must look at the relationships, including whole-part, association, and messaging.

- Such relationships tie the lowest-level building blocks together and lead to the concept of *frameworks,* a relatively recent term in programming (discussed in greater detail in Part 4, Chap. 12).

Frameworks form a skeleton of classes, objects,* and relationships grouped together to build a specific application. Most application frameworks are primarily human interaction media providing a more systematic approach to

———————————

*Technically, an object is an instantiation of a class.

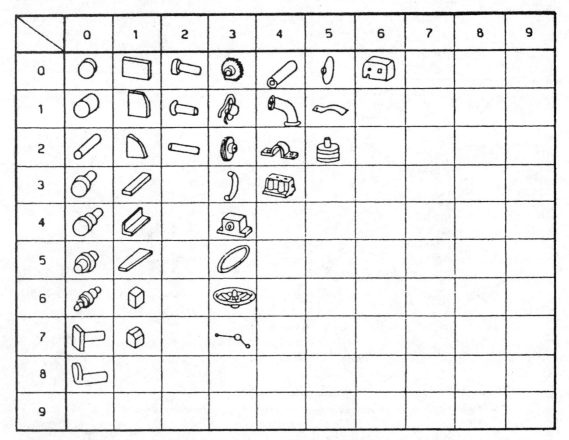

Figure 4.3   Classification matrix for mechanical elements from a project with the Osram lamp company.

building window interfaces. This will be properly documented by means of the following applications examples.

4.8   Visual Programming by Electric Power Utilities

A significant amount of the attention that has been paid to the project undertaken by the University of Tokyo for Tokyo Electric Power focused on end-user programming. This is just as valid for the production system as it is for the distribution network—and in both cases it gave good results.

According to the University of Tokyo, which helped to develop many innovations in VR connected to this project, the use of virtual reality has been particularly rewarding in regard to the development of real-time software in such domains as scheduling processes. Typically:

- As widely practiced in industry today, a PERT representation of scheduling premises is still mapped into two dimensions.

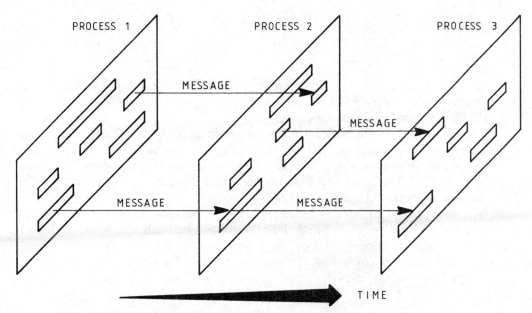

PROCESS 1   PROCESS 2   PROCESS 3

MESSAGE

MESSAGE

MESSAGE   MESSAGE

TIME

Figure 4.4 Program visualization of three processes interconnected through the arrow of time.

- But the third dimension, *time,* is very important, as it helps us to appreciate at a glance how the schedule evolves.

At Tokyo University, this principle of improved representation through visual programming has been extended to *algorithmic visualization*. It permits one to appreciate in three dimensions a family of processes interconnected through the arrow of time by means of message passing. An example is given in Fig. 4.4. (At Tokyo University, this particular attention involves 20 modules, rather than the 3 in Fig. 4.4.)

It is precisely in this connection that Prof. Michitaka Hirose distinguishes between

- Programming *in the large*
- Programming *in the small*

As already discussed in Chap. 2 and in Sec. 4.2, programming in the large is macroscopic. The visual presentation in Fig. 4.4 provides an example of the consistency of messages and protocols for effective communication. In this particular case, they are process-to-process rather than human-information communication, as Fig. 4.1 originally suggested.

By contrast, what we have called programming in the small is detailed. In an expert system, for example, programming in the small consists of statements such as

IF   <...>
THEN   <...>
ELSE   <...>

At the current state of the art, visual programming is done best at the macroscopic level or, more precisely, at the common interface level shown in Fig. 4.1. But it can also be higher than that.

For instance, a challenging financial situation such as the evaluation of a portfolio of bonds can best be defuzzified through the use of fuzzy engineering graphics.[6] Once this is done, the graphical presentation is converted by a compiler to IF, THEN, and ELSE statements, and from there, also automatically, into an assembler language such as C.

Electric power utilities are also exploiting in an able manner another major aspect of visual programming: the interactive manipulation in three dimensions of the visualized topology. At Tokyo Electric, for example, a main focus concerns process control of the production and distribution facilities—the method being used for

- New software development
- Software maintenance reasons

In the virtual reality project the Mitsubishi Research Institute did for Chubu Electric Power, primary emphasis was placed on the development of a reliability analysis approach for transmission systems. This covers a spectrum of applications from primary substations on high-voltage trunk lines to distribution substations and interconnecting links. Through graphics, the user can input the network data of power systems from primary substations to distribution substations. Also she or he can experiment with the structure of buses and connection of transformers in substations.

- The simulator evaluates reliability at each distribution substation by estimating outage and recovery for all fault modes which can occur.
- It also defines the capacity of facilities, the probability of fault of each facility, the value of load of each trunk, and so on.

Visualization effectively brings attention to the points where switching elements are turned off in the network. This turning off, for example, might have been graphically done as input data. Considered in the calculation of the recovery process of each fault mode are considered the constraints of operation of power systems, such constraints being built into the simulator.

All this has been achieved in the realm of visual programming, including the definition of reliability from the viewpoint of the customers and the development of patterns of outage and recovery. Obtained results led to the structure of a reliability criteria matrix.

Figure 4.5a shows the topology to which one of the reliability studies has been addressed, identifying a reliability level in each area. Figure 4.5b shows the display of network structure, with associated objects representing the

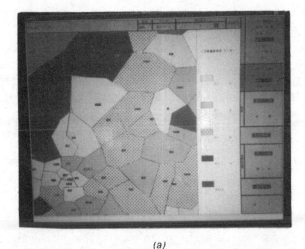

(a)

(b)

Figure 4.5 (*a*) A map of reliability level at each area and (*b*) corresponding grid of network structure.

structure of substations. Also graphically elaborated are assumptions regarding annual and more detailed load duration, the respective curves being studied under different probabilities of faults and interruptions.

Visual programming with graphical experimentation and presentation has included comparisons between the calculated value and the actual value of average outage time. The study addressed both the company's power system as a whole and its components which have been interconnected among themselves in tree- and mesh-structures.

4.9 Visual Programming and Virtual Skiing

This application of virtual reality was done by Nippon Electric, and to a significant degree it resembles the examples of the electric power utilities. In all cases, the virtual reality presentation serves as the canvas to which has been added value through visual programming.

The Information Technology Research Laboratories of NEC developed virtual skiing as a virtual reality system using physiological data. Through virtual reality the user enjoys skiing on a virtual slope. She controls her route and executes turns by shifting her weight on ski plates on the virtual slope.

- The system measures physiological data and reacts to both the user's physical movements and her mental state.

- As the slope changes, the altering degrees of difficulty reflect the skier's tension level.

- The bodily sensation is a direct feedback from slope simulation, keeping the skier's curiosity and motivation in high gear.

In connection with the virtual slope which is perceived by the skier through a head-mounted display, the system is measuring quantity of blood flow in the tip of the finger. Under *tension* the quantity of blood *decreases*; blood goes to the muscles to prepare for a fight. Under *relaxed* conditions, the blood at finger tips *increases*.

Such findings are quite important. Not only do they reveal how physiological and psychological responses can be exploited and visualized, but also they suggest that this visualization can be further processed in terms of visual programming.

The skier in the simulated landscape wears boots which assist in weight-balance measurements. With right and left coordinates, the slope simulator leads into bodily emulation as the skier is able, through left and right foot and the two ski sticks, *to program her descent* unassisted.

Figure 4.6a shows the virtual ski slope landscape, as perceived by the user. The scene of a virtual skiing ground is created by computer graphics, then displayed on the headset worn by the skier. If the skier's tension indicates a low level, the system changes the ski course to a more difficult one; if the tension is at a high level, the system changes the ski course to an easier one. A slope simulation machine is used which synchronizes the user-standing plates with the virtual slope's undulation.

Figure 4.6b demonstrates the actual setup in NEC's laboratory with the skier at center stage. As stated, the system reacts to the user's stress level and allows the latter to maintain motivation. The skier's weight transfer is measured for computing her sliding direction and speed and fingertip blood flow data, as inputs for estimating the skier's physical and mental tension level.

This solution is enriched with *acoustic sensation*. The bodily movement, the landscape change, and the sound of skiing provide a realistic environment and with it the feel of traveling over hills and valleys. Once again, the skier is able to program her own course.

This is an immersive virtual reality application. The head-mounted display of the virtual ski system has the following configuration:

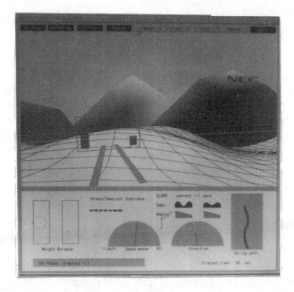

(a)

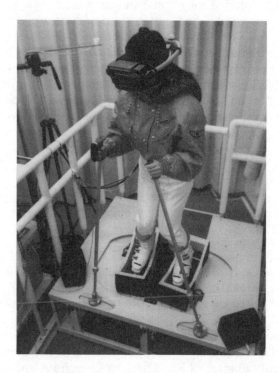

(b)

Figure 4.6 Real-time simulation of ski slopes through virtual reality.

- Two screens on which a slope scene is displayed
- Position sensor which measures the user's head position and direction of the user's face
- Earphones for acoustic displays (sound of skiing)

Another major component is the slope simulation machine. It consists of two steel plates where the user stands and an engine which tilts the two plates horizontally, vertically, and sideways. It simulates the ups and downs of the ground.

The third major module is the physiological data sensors for *blood flow* and *weight balance*. The output is an oscilloscope chart which includes

- Pulse wave
- Tension level
- Feedback

The infrastructure is provided by computer software for the analysis of data, control of the slope simulation machine, and generation of computer graphics slopes.

The system is most suitable for experimentation and, in terms of training, for beginners and for people at the early or intermediate stage of ski practice. The human-machine interaction is effected through images, and it is intensive, as the user views the virtual ski slope displayed on the screens inside the helmet. The ski plates move in synchronization with the view of the ski slope.

Figure 4.7 shows the human-machine interaction in the form of a diagram. The skier programs her own movement through the virtual slope undulations. As she adjusts the weight position on the plates, reacting to a virtual slope, the weight balance on the plates is measured.

- Data is analyzed whether the user's weight is on the front or the rear, the right side or the left side in the plate.
- The system estimates the user's speed and direction on the slope in addition to the user's mental state as a sensor establishes the stress level by monitoring blood flow in a finger.

The system uses estimated states as feedback information and generates the next slope. Intelligent software provides a self-adjusting environment: The greater the stress recorded, the easier the course becomes, for instance, a gentle slope with a few small bumps. The greater the relaxation recorded, the harder the course becomes.

For beginners, the system displays the weight balance on right and left legs on screens. Hence, the beginner is able to see how his or her movements influence the actual weight balance, which is hard to learn from verbal expressions. The user can learn how to put weight on two ski plates to turn to the left or right on the slope.

The computer stores slope, weight balance, and stress information. A *scenario*

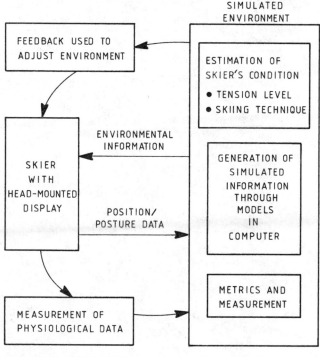

Figure 4.7 An application of virtual reality and visual programming in skiing.

can be replayed afterward. Throughout, the user can analyze her or his previous skiing and get advice from an instructor, while practicing accident-free skiing.

One use of this system is for rehabilitation of physically handicapped persons. There are many other applications, one of the most promising being its ability to serve as a test bed for visual programming activities. This is the difference between new and old software. Legacy programs are a deadweight; new ones through visual programming are a stepping-stone to greater sophistication.

References

1. E. Brody and T. Vamos, eds., *The Neumann Compendium,* World Scientific, River Edge, NJ, 1995.
2. See D. N. Chorafas, *Chaos Theory in the Financial Markets,* Probus/Irwin, Chicago, 1994.
3. See also D. N. Chorafas and H. Steinmann, *Solutions for Networked Databases,* Academic Press, San Diego, CA, 1993.
4. See also D. N. Chorafas, *Intelligent Multimedia Databases,* Prentice-Hall, Englewood Cliffs, NJ, 1994.
5. See also D. N. Chorafas and H. Steinmann, *Object-Oriented Databases,* Prentice-Hall, Englewood Cliffs, NJ, 1993; as well as Chap. 11 in this book.
6. See also D. N. Chorafas, *Chaos Theory in the Financial Markets.*

Visual Programming and Program Visualization

5.1 Introduction

In the introduction to visualization, it was said that software developments in the 1990s greatly depend on the graphical arts. Then the concept of visual programming was introduced. This and similar developments are today at a level resembling that of practical artificial intelligence applications some 15 years ago.

- Then, as now, few people had an idea of what the new development was and could do, or how to proceed.

- Therefore, only a handful of companies were able to put the skills they were acquiring to productive use.

Through real-life experiences, Chap. 4 has demonstrated how far visual programming approaches can go. And the answer is *far,* helping to revamp the whole concept of programming and immersing the end user in the picture, as shown through the example of virtual reality in skiing.

As this present chapter will document, the new perspectives which are opened in programming through current advances in virtual reality go much further than the cases we have seen so far permit us to appreciate. Visualization is significantly improving software developments, reliability, and reusability, but distinction should be made between

- *Visual programming* (VP), which revamps the programming process by visualizing it   and

- *Program visualization* (PV), where, having written a program, we visualize it for testing and maintenance reasons.

Some of the developments which took place were planned. Others came by chance. A number of VP tools came into existence as supportive to programming approaches which developed over the last dozen years, such as fourth-generation languages. Others were totally new departures.

As more powerful programming tools than those which already existed got into the job stream, it was found that they could be effectively used to create a new applications environment. Evolutionary developments take time to mature, but when they do, they set the stage for new departures.

5.2   Patterns and Visual Programming Presentation

The concept of patterning is not alien to the reader. Nor is it a secret that there is much common ground between the process of patterning and computer programs.[1] A valid paradigm is that the two are different sides of the same coin.

An object-oriented pattern, for example, is an abstraction of a doublet, triplet, or other small grouping of classes that is likely to be helpful in software development. An icon is a familiar object, a metaphor which helps the end user as a memory aid and in doing his or her programming. The rest is the work of compilers.

Many patterns regarding computing paths are found by observation and trial and error. By building prototypes and observing their application as well as the relationships established between them, we can find patterns and trace how well the execution fits the plan.

As the example of the use of visual programming for electric power generation and distribution has demonstrated, the area of visually approaching sophisticated applications is much broader than some people tend to suggest. This is not a limited scientific domain. In its fundamentals,

- Visualization is a practical reality.

- It has a widening spectrum of uses.

- It can provide a bridge between graphics and semantics, hence meaning.

General-purpose tools are, however, needed to permit significant improvements in the software development and maintenance processes. We have already spoken of the three main areas to which modern programming approaches must address themselves in an integrative way:

- *On-line data acquisition,* where real-time applications are at a premium, and with them data filtering and error correction

- *Analysis and simulation* using modern tools such as chaos theory, nonlinearities, fuzzy engineering, neural networks, genetic algorithms, and Monte Carlo method

- *Interactive visual output,* with three-dimensional color graphics and virtual reality implementation

Visual, user-friendly supports are necessary because writing more efficient software is a challenging task in itself—and the same is true of writing software more efficiently. These are a never-ending mission, not a matter of something done once to get rid of the job.

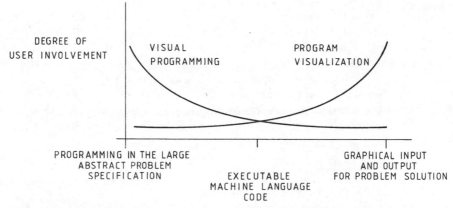

Figure 5.1 Application viewpoints with virtual reality, visual programming, and program visualization.

To a large extent, the roles of visual programming and program visualization are complementary, but at the same time VP and PV must serve domains which are their own. In Fig. 5.1 (based on the original idea by Dr. T. L. Casavant), at the right side, program visualization requires no abstraction or idealization to represent the visual elements which constitute the software modules. But at the left side, concepts being visualized have less-obvious representations, while at the same time the usefulness of the representations increases—hence the need for abstraction. In software development we progress from the left side to the right side. At the left side of Fig. 5.1, the view is more idealized and less dependent on an architecture. Hence, the VP tool is most appropriate for programming in the large, as discussed in Chap. 4.

By contrast, at the right side of that same figure, what is particularly emphasized is the more powerful input and output features. Since Chap. 1 we have underlined that I/O renewal is the most practical reason for having and using agents as well as virtual reality solutions, with program visualization being a good example.

In the left-to-right transition, the primary goal of visual programming is the specification and creation of software in a way which is much more efficient and user-friendly than has been possible through classical approaches. For its part, program visualization is important for reasons which have to do with quality improvements—from the creation and use of *development databases* to debugging, testing, documentation, and on-line maintenance.

It has already been explained why particular attention should be paid to a development database. The heterogeneity and complexity of both software and hardware elements require sophisticated tools for programming the computers of the 1990s, including monitoring and troubleshooting. A development database is essentially a necessary software memory facility into which are mapped all programming efforts—and most particularly visual programming efforts.

5.3 Providing Feedback Useful to the User

Rather than the monolithic language of the Fortran, Cobol, and PL/1 type which dominated the 1960s and (because of inertia) the subsequent two or three decades, we have today a range of programming tools that represent different software technologies and have different goals.

Since the new generation of programming tools and methodologies is to a significant extent focused on the applications domain, it helps to classify them in connection with the work to be done. In the general case, the work for which visual programming seems best suited includes

1. Programming in the large

2. Mapping of business systems

3. Visual description of engineering applications

4. Abstraction of specifications

5. Immersive approaches to computer programming

6. Partitioning and integration of modules

7. Composition for interactive software reuse

8. Prediction of correctness (dynamic testing)

9. On-line program maintenance

10. Optimization of systems performance

Visual programming and program visualization make feasible the simulated execution of software under development, the real-time comparison of routines in a library for selection purposes, as well as more-rigorous performance measurements. Because they provide a comprehensive window in human-machine communications, both act as instrumental approaches toward the goal of significantly improving the quality of software.

If we have a methodology able to assist software enhancement after initial creation and mapping, then we can use it effectively in other domains as well, e.g., software project management. But to be done in a proper manner, VP and PV require powerful visualization tools, including

1. Visual languages with pure picture semantics, assisting in drawing a program through pictures and graphs

2. Multimedia approaches permitting the handling of pictures, graphics, text, data, and voice—in short, compound electronic documents

3. Automatic compilation from picture programs to object code, either directly or through IF, THEN, ELSE statements

Visual programming and program visualization lead toward virtual reality programming systems, which is a longer-term goal. But there are also intermediate objectives which need to be met.

Fundamentally visual programming has two aspects, both of them important and novel in a technological sense, hence awaiting to be exploited in an able manner:

- Matching icons to program modules
- Helping analyze the modules of a program

The Microelectronics and Computer Development Corporation (MCC) of Austin, TX, is the first organization on record to have used visual programming to analyze the modules of a program and their interaction. In that project, emphasis was placed not only on development but also on software maintenance.

The MCC work, however, concerned serial programs, not software written for massively parallel processors, where more recent visual programming projects focus. There are evidently communalities between the two domains, both being conditioned by the fact that *the most useful feedback* for a user

- Is the one which comes from her or his own application
- Can be easily comprehended when presented in a visual manner

However, beyond these two requirements, parallel programming poses other challenges which must be answered in an able way, for instance, efficient *sharing* of resources among the programs running on the machine and multimedia *synchronization.*

To a significant extent, synchronization is necessary in all networked systems. It is based on the accuracy of the communications mechanism which we implement, in reflection of the fact that the latter is quite often a function of partitioning and mapping. Both processes can be tuned by means of run-time simulation, which VP makes feasible. How rapidly we can build a simulator is a direct function of how fast we can make a prototype helped by a visualization tool—and how well we can receive, interpret, and act upon the feedback.

Work along these lines is usually based on *worst-case* scenarios and associated design. Here again, visualization can be instrumental in helping to develop run-time programs which respond to worst-case analysis. Therefore, it can be profitably used for software testing as well as optimization.

5.4 Programming Visually, from Designer to End User

One of the better ways of looking at visual programming is to create software kernels for domain-specific applications. Incorporating domain-specific approaches into a problem-solving environment is generally possible and desirable, as it relieves the user of the necessity to program special routines.

At the same time, within an application domain usually certain well-identified computational and data-handling issues repeatedly appear in solutions to a wide variety of problems. For instance, this is the case with a powerful body of knowledge about emulation techniques, although the different details can be quite involved and are often dependent on the architecture. To solve a problem within the domain of his or her professional interests, the user must determine which routines are applicable and how to employ them. Visual programming does not eliminate this requirement, but simplifies it by substituting long programming statements with icons. Therefore VP must be

■ Supported by knowledge-enriched software
■ Able to free the user of many aspects embedded in the classical approaches to coding

When we talk about simplifying programming chores through VP, we should not forget that four full decades after computers entered business and industry, we are still using massive amounts of people to do programming work. Such work should have been automated long ago, and today VP is a unique opportunity to get out of this bad practice.

Not only must software development be simplified, but also users must be enabled to predict the consequences of the choices they are making. For instance, algorithms can be analyzed in terms of a well-understood model of computation that has demonstrated efficient implementation on existing machines—using means able to visualize the process being executed.

Attention should be paid to the fact that, even at a level of abstraction, choices in computational threads can affect performance in largely unpredictable ways. There are still many unknowns connected to processing:

■ This is particularly true of decisions concerning the match between data access patterns and the decomposition of data structures.
■ For optimization reasons, maps should be developed and presented across memory devices with nonuniform access times residing on the same or different platforms.

The development and analysis of execution patterns, for example, are very important in the case of parallel programming environments. My research has demonstrated that few programming shops today have the culture for appreciating the impact of this reference, as most still think in terms of serial programming.

Visualization and parallel processing are related in many ways. The former permits spatial relationships to be naturally assimilated, which is very important to any software effort and more particularly to that directed to parallel machines. Spatial relationships help to distinguish serial and parallel programming from each other.

■ Serial programs are only temporal.
■ Parallel programs are both spatial and temporal.

. Interest in visual programming in connection with parallel processing derives from deficiencies found in classical approaches. Understanding dynamic program behavior in a temporal dimension overloads the human ability to assimilate information and develop the appropriate patterns. This is as true of software designers as it is of end users.

- Graphical computer interfaces provide a good opportunity to capitalize on the match between parallel program behavior and its rendering.
- This is very important because at present the known processes of analyzing parallel software do not lead to appropriate analytical modeling.

Program visualization permits us to create prototype applications as well as analyze crucial features, making directly measurable demands on the underlying hardware and basic software architecture. As such, it goes beyond the now classical concepts of program development, illustrating to the programmer

- Correctness of program mapping
- A more effective partitioning of information

In programming, this makes feasible better control flow strategies. It also permits software development through visual programming to capitalize on the continuity which exists between the efforts by the designer and the comprehension by users. An example of such software continuity between the *problem* and the *solution* domains is shown in Fig. 5.2.

How much software support is realistic in a complex scientific problem or business situation? The answer is *a lot*. The critical software challenge is to enable new applications to

- Be developed directly by the end user
- Remain flexible to fit her or his changing requirements
- Be portable to any computer at the source code level.

It is not enough that new applications are easier to write than software designed 5 or more years ago. User friendliness and high performance in pro-

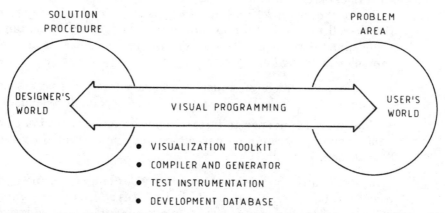

Figure 5.2   From designer to user there is a significant amount of software continuity.

gramming will never come in one big step. They are a steady business, based on continuing improvements.

Just as steady should be the search for efficient ways to overcome the heterogeneity of computer hardware and basic software, by making the existing differences seamless. This can be successfully approached through *metacomputing,* by using knowledge engineering and object orientation in software solutions all the way from the development and use of processes to data structures and data streams.

5.5   Programming in the Large and Metaprogramming

The aim of visual programming is both to ensure a friendly, high-productivity interface and to provide a powerful development environment for end users, which allows them to get involved in building applications. Another goal of the new software tools is to permit recompilation to every major platform, without rewriting code. This, of course, is a noble but difficult task.

- Most new tools abstract numerous low-level native calls into a single high-level call, making it easier and faster to write programs and interfaces.

- But rather than emulate native commands in machine code, visual programming approaches interact directly with the graphical user interface (GUI).

- This approach makes it feasible for portable applications to have the same look and feel as applications written in a nonportable native environment—without carrying much overhead.

This example stresses the *programming-in-the-small* level, discussed in Chap. 4. It is as well a good example of the implementation of *metaprogramming* concepts, the meta (higher-up) level being that of portable code.

Metaprogramming, however, has a still larger and more important domain of application at the *programming-in-the-large* level, which is the one particularly directed to the end user. In this connection, it becomes practically synonymous with visual programming.

One of the methodologies currently used with visual programming divides the overall user specification into independent modules containing distinct, well-defined entities. It also provides the relationships among these modules through a mapping language.

- The mapping language supports arbitrary levels of abstraction, ensuring a full range of details, but also an efficient viewpoint development.

- This approach is open to further innovation, for there is no standard way of viewing programming paradigms and the current processes are in full evolution.

A valid means of providing the necessary flexibility in business which has just been described is the use of *metatools,* i.e., tools which construct and manipulate other tools. This is a concept crucial to *metaprogramming* and is based on generalizing classes of tasks into their fundamental parameters, for instance,

- User view
- Designer view
- Toolkit view

The goal of a user view is to emphasize the qualities and features that a user would want in a visual programming solution, independently of how the designer and the tool interact. By contrast, the designer view focuses on the kinds of features possible in a metatool, exploring the extent to which metalevel facilities meet the needs of the user.

The VP scenario just described can have significant consequences which are not immediately apparent. In the sense of programming in the large, VP permits the development of very specific language versions

- Tailored to each specific professional class of end users and their terminology, thus tremendously easing end-user programming
- But, at the same time, providing for these different versions a common trunk and, therefore, a fundamental compatibility

The important issues in the user's view are the efficiency and ease of the tools, the features, and the functions being supported, as well as the amount of control the user has over the tools' operation.

The user does not care how a tool is implemented, or how complicated and difficult it was to build in the first place. However, the software designer's goal is to provide the full benefit of sophisticated displays to the user, while reducing the associated overhead. By combining these two aspects, a metaprogramming environment can be constructed that

- Provides useful, professionally oriented features for each class of end users
- Also allows designers to experiment with programming paradigms and gain new insight

Concerning the tool view which interfaces between the user and the computing engine, this is precisely the role to be placed at metatool level. Projecting visual programming facilities in a metatool sense and ensuring program portability between platforms are two complementary requirements which can effectively handle

- Episodes
- Rules
- Representation mapping

A behavior component acts as a buffer between raw data and the output to the user, providing for the manipulation of episodic information. In regard to rules, mathematical functions can be applied to convert individual raw event instances and organize event information. This underpins the need for a knowledge-enriched assistance in connection with a visual programming environment.

5.6   Assistance from Visualization in Programming in the Small

Graphics help in providing high-level interpretations of the behavior of program variables. This is done, for instance, by depicting the internal complexities of software by means of visual analogies. Subentities in the graphics module correspond to lower-level building blocks which make up the higher-level graphical entities.

- In some of the visual programming tools currently available, lower-level building blocks are a set of C functions that enable one to rapidly build real-time routines.
- The mission may be graphics simulation, communications management, database access, development of new expert systems, or linking to legacy data processing.

Foundation Manager is an icon-oriented programming system made in the United States. It is a graphical tool for analyzing low- and high-level local-area network (LAN) behavior. It permits network administrators to perform statistical analysis on the network's activities as well as an evaluation of protocols

- Acquiring, transmitting, and filtering data
- Displaying a graphical map of the network
- Simulating and monitoring subnetworks
- Setting alarms that ring based on operating conditions

The software runs on a personal computer, and it permits all LAN traffic to be monitored. For distributed LANs with connecting bridges, remote monitoring approaches can be configured to communicate with the Foundation Manager.[2]

A primary strength of this solution is its use of graphical components to collect data and analyze network activity, drawing a meaningful graphical internetwork display. To monitor LAN operations, the visual program constructs paths of icons, a path is a linked row of icons, and packets move through paths from left to right. Foundation Manager provides four types of icons: input, output, view, and process. Three different types of *input icons* are supported:

- Acquire
- Playback
- Remote

Acquire icons are used to obtain frames from the network, while playback icons access frames previously stored in a file. Remote icons receive packets from a remote monitoring and control component. Three different types of *output icons* are provided.

- *Dynamic data exchange* (DDE) allows communications with DDE-compliant programs.

- File icons are used to store frames in the database for subsequent use.

- Transmit icons send frames to another workstation node on the network.

View icons help to display information describing network activity. Such a display lets the user view individual frames in a variety of different formats. A map icon presents a graphical view of the network, indicating frames passing between network nodes. The statistics icon helps to describe network activity. The title icon permits the user to name a path.

Process icons are employed to perform processing on frames. An alarm issues a warning when specified critical conditions occur. The filter icon accepts or rejects frames as specified by established criteria. Sentinel determines if frames meet a specific criterion and sets a trigger. The latter can be used to control a switch icon or to activate pause control on a playback icon.

One of the interesting aspects of the Foundation Manager, as with other visual programming tools, is that in addition to being a good network monitor it serves as a fine teaching tool. It can assist LAN administrators in supervising a number of distributed network nodes; it also helps software developers to create more-sophisticated networking applications.

5.7 Evolving Landscape of Visual Programming Applications

The new generation of computer-aided design (CAD) solutions, particularly in connection with concurrent engineering, make feasible interactive, three-dimensional graphical applications for which it is easy to create prototypes through VP. They also provide the functionality required to build complex algorithms. Typically,

- A good visual programming tool is hardware-independent.

- Source code written for one machine compiles on another.

- Programs can be developed on a workstation and then run on a high-performance visualization system.

Programming in the small does not need to be inflexible. Support for cross-platform development gives the applications developer significant leeway in facing future needs, therefore in incorporating new or different modules and in porting them between platforms.

Another critical need is to enable the developer to upgrade a given program for new requirements (such as parallel processing, database mining, and network communications) and to extend the application's effectiveness beyond the traditional configuration of an applications environment.

- These performance characteristics can be effectively attained through the use of knowledge engineering and object orientation.

- A visual programming tool should contain functions for simulation, analysis, and agile management of interfaces.

Functions having a mnemonic syntax can be helpful, with applications ranging from a high-level universe to the handling of low-level drivers. IF, THEN, ELSE statements will be instrumental in a toolkit—and the contribution by object-oriented database management systems can be significant.

In simple applications, for instance, objects are added to the universe and given behaviors through task assignment. Predicates can be attached to these objects, or to viewpoints, assisting end-user programming and helping the real-time manager in its control functions.

The simulator incorporated in a visual programming construct can feature predefined event handlers with an easy-to-use control structure. A knowledge-enriched software system

- Ensures that on-line device input is properly processed, according to ad hoc or situational criteria
- Executes the application defined by the developer, taking advantage of environmental factors as they come
- Makes sure that object tasks are performed in both a local and a global sense

With visual programming solutions, objects can be added and removed from a universe container, enabling significant flexibility in applications handling.[3] Given the increasing importance of visualization, the system should include a built-in renderer able to take full advantage of graphical facilities on the host platform.

Although this may appear self-evident, there are other developments which may influence programming in the small, of which it is wise to take notice. For instance, at the University of Tokyo a sophisticated virtual reality (VR) environment is being developed without the use of head-mounted displays or data gloves which could have a significant impact on programming.

Since current VR helmets have rather poor resolution, they cannot be used for applications which require high-definition display such as CAD. Therefore, the Japanese researchers substituted the head mount with a conventional stereo monitor which generates stereo images by using liquid-crystal shutters and has a resolution comparable to that used in CAD systems. Unlike the conventional stereo monitors, however, by controlling the image rendering using a three-dimensional *head tracker,* it is possible to create an effect similar to a holographic three-dimensional image. That is the reason why this system has been called *virtual holography* or *virtual clay.*

Although virtual holography cannot create very large virtual three-dimensional spaces, it can generate a very sophisticated three-dimensional space with high resolution. It also leaves open the possibility of extending the implementation perspective into interactive programming, in a way similar to the virtual skiing example of Chap. 4.

In several situations, *force feedback* is very important. For instance, even though in drawing characters the movement of the finger is restricted over the

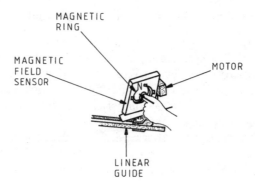

MAGNETIC
RING

MAGNETIC
FIELD
SENSOR

MOTOR

LINEAR
GUIDE

Figure 5.3 The mechanism of force feedback head in virtual holography.

surface, it is possible to draw beautiful characters very quickly. A good example of an application is the assembly of virtual objects. The existence of force feedback is needed for quick execution of a simple assembly operation such as inserting a cube into a corresponding square hall. By feeling force, one can reach the goal far more easily and intuitively.

Three-dimensional graphics can be improved by both high resolution and a force display. An example is a mechanical arm used to generate virtual force sensation. As shown in Fig. 5.3, four magnetic sensors located on the force feedback head tracker measure the location of the finger wearing the magnetic ring. Physical constraints to the finger's movement are integrated in the virtual workspace. By using virtual clay, the programmer can look around the modules yet to be written and can even touch them.

5.8   Handling Spatial and Temporal Relationships

Visual programming and program visualization are good ways to show spatial and temporal relationships. The possibility of real-time visual feedback has a direct impact on the ability to improve the software development process, as well as software reliability and maintainability.

Efficient software development requires a great deal of communications between the user, or users, and the machine. Nonuniform or poorly defined communication and synchronization interfaces make the creation of correctly functioning software a difficult task. That is why worthwhile projects in visual programming are associated with the initial specification and the creation of a communications process. Three-dimensional graphics offer significant help in the proper representation of spatial programming characteristics.

Precisely because of the power of this approach, ask these basic questions when you are considering the development of visual programming solutions:

- Where should we set the limits?

- Should we aim at a completely visual language which requires pure picture semantics?

- Or should we lower the sights and stress on dataflow and control dependencies?

The consequences of visual programming choices should be studied at both the *macroscopic* and the *microscopic* levels. While some fourth-generation languages could be used to specify functional semantics, it is not a good idea to mix linguistic constructs or revert to lower-sophistication approaches.

Programming in the large is particularly helpful at the macroscopic level, which gives perspective by describing the kind, form, functions, constraints, and boundaries rather than the details. An example of the output of this phase is *Majordomo,** a program which automates the management of Internet mailing lists.

By contrast, the microscopic approach focuses on details, and it is served through programming in the small. Microscopically, commands are sent to Majordomo via electronic mail to handle all aspects of list maintenance. The details of how this is done are not in the domain of programming in the large, but it is very important on the microscopic level—a job accomplished by looking inside text strings.

An effective visual programming solution typically supports analysis and synthesis of execution procedures, enhances communication among software modules and team members, and acts as a basis for managerial coordination of software development. Also it will facilitate the evolution and maintenance of the software product.

There are prerequisites for the able handling of spatial and temporal relationships which have been inefficiently addressed by old programming paradigms. Three types of prerequisites have been observed:

- End-use properties regarding practical issues such as comprehensiveness and user-friendly features
- Managerial issues concerned with the quality, costs, and timetable of the end product, including project planning and control
- Technical properties which deal with the method's notations and procedures as well as the automation of the programming effort

Like any software system, visual programming should be viewed from the interrelated perspective of structure, function, and behavior. Structure concerns the decomposition of the module under development into a set of interacting components as well as the allocation of function and data to the component parts.

Function addresses the transformations on data (and/or rules) without particular concern for where or when these transformations occur. Behavior regards the system's response to external events as well as the propagation of control through its structure.

---

*http://www.math.psu.edu/barr/majordomo-faq-html

The properties of software structure, function, and behavior should be mapped onto the development process in a life-cycle sense. In visual programming, these development phases should be fully interactive and should interleave with one another:

- Visual requirements analysis and specifications
- Temporal and spatial relationships to be built
- Architectural approaches and detailed design
- Compilation, testing, and maintenance

These are important evolutionary concepts regarding the way software is projected and implemented. A key role in this process is played by prototyping.

We have already spoken of the significant role prototyping can play. As a programming paradigm it permits us to construct a version of the system that can be experimented with, and provides the test bed on which to clarify the operational characteristics. It can also be used to extract information about user requirements and the distributed nature of data useful to the design.

Prototyping can also be employed in verification, helping in an interactive end-user-actuated manner to determine the degree to which a computer program fulfills requirements. Results can show whether the model performs correctly with respect to functional and behavioral needs, as well as the flexibility of the artifact to accommodate change.

Performance analysis tools can be more effectively incorporated in a *visualization environment* than in the third- and fourth-generation languages used today. Visual inspection helps both the computer specialist and the end user. It permits them to monitor hardware and basic software options to gather performance data and to profile the software package in terms of functionality and execution requirements.

In the general case, overall performance will depend on the host hardware and basic software. Currently available microprocessors possess the necessary power to handle the cycles needed for visual programming, but because the VP routines tend to monopolize the processor, visual programming is made for workstations, not mainframes.

5.9 Visual Programming and Real-Time Implementation

Visual programming will probably be used increasingly in connection with real-time implementation, with concurrent processing and communications affected by parallel event streams external to the program. Hence, these must be handled efficiently. Of concern are:

- The models of concurrency being implemented
- The granularity of concurrent components
- The communications methods being employed by concurrent components

The goal of a performance orientation and evaluation is to ensure timely response to externally generated events, guaranteeing proper processing and maximizing system throughput without unduly affecting overall reliability.

Full account has to be taken of the fact that real-time systems must interactively respond to external events within timing constraints. Hence, visual programming solutions must be enriched by dynamic simulators able to explore such properties.

A similar statement can be made about the ease of integration and the associated effort required to seamlessly work with heterogeneous modules. This requirement concerns the end-user, managerial, and technical aspects of a method, which we examined in Sec. 5.8.

In a way fairly similar to that characterizing all other software development solutions, testing should be a major part of the visual programming effort. The difference is that the results of interactive testing can be immediately visible, and this helps to create confidence in the software under development.

- As with many mathematical and procedural functions implemented by software, visual programming is characterized by the fact that its output may not be continuous functions but may feature an arbitrary number of discontinuities.

- The lack of continuity constraints on these functions and the way they are describing a given module make it difficult to find compact descriptions of test results in the classical way.

- At the same time, the lack of such constraints gives software its flexibility, while it also accounts for the complexity of testing procedures, which can be facilitated through visualization.

Real-time software development and testing increase the sensitivity to some types of errors and therefore ease some testing difficulties. Even if visual programming as such may not avoid errors which typically occur in software development, it helps to bring them rapidly into perspective.

This statement is particularly valid in connection with color graphics capabilities. As we will see in Chap. 11, there are now available object-oriented graphical architectures designed to give complete control of most aspects of a visual program in a clean and extensible manner. For instance, new graphics systems

- Allow the user to open multiple graph windows simultaneously
- Permit the user to place axes of reference anywhere in the window
- Provide precise control of how the output appears

Both the end user and the software designer can interactively control practically all attributes of a plot, such as axis direction, grid color, and the like. They can define the attributes at development time, change them interactively after they appear on the screen, and conduct a number of tests in real time as the program develops.

Designers of reliable hardware are classically concerned with manufacturing errors and wearout cases. But they can perform their analysis on the assumption that failures are not strongly correlated and that simultaneous hardware failures are unlikely.

By contrast with software, few errors are introduced in the compiling (manufacturing) phase. When they do happen at that level, they usually tend to be systematic, not random—hence easier to track.

- Software does not *wear out* in the classical sense of the term.

- The errors with which software reliability experts must be concerned are of the design and implementation type.

- These errors are not immediately apparent, and they cannot be considered statistically independent.

Whether we talk of third-, fourth-, or fifth-generation language programming— or of visual programming—it is impossible to test software completely. It is also difficult to test one's own design in an unbiased way. Therefore, a growing number of software development projects involve independent *verification and validation.* Visual programming can contribute a lot to this, as the present and preceding sections have explained.

A valid approach is to have all testing done by an independent tester. There is evidence that when an independent verification system is in place and tests are done in such a way as to yield statistically valid results, not only does the applications software get certified but also programs are written far more carefully in the first place.

Finally, an integral part of a good visual programming methodology is that all documentation must be computer-supported, very clearly done, and well organized. It must allow components to be inspected so the reviewer can verify they are consistent with the documentation residing in the development database. On-line development databases can be inspected interactively.

References

1. See also D. N. Chorafas, *Programming Systems for Electronic Computers,* Butterworth, London, 1962.
2. *Computing,* November 1993.
3. See also D. N. Chorafas and H. Steinmann, *Object-Oriented Databases,* Prentice-Hall, Englewood Cliffs, NJ, 1993.

Impact of Internet on Visual Programming Metaphors

When a modern history of computer programming is written, it will rate Internet and the Intranets as a milestone in the metaphysics of human-machine communication, which is, after all, the essence of programming. It is therefore proper to take the World Wide Web, HTML, VRML, and Java as examples of the component parts of this milestone. The other goal of Part 3 is to explain how we go from where we stand now to the place we want to be.

6

World Wide Web and HTML in a Context of Real-Space Implementation

6.1 Introduction

When end users work interactively on networks, the perception of events and conception of their meaning are executed in real time. This can be so much more effective when they are equipped with appropriate tools and most particularly a graphics programming language, which is easy to learn and employ in professional as well as personal activities.

In this chapter we look at examples of programming artifacts which have these characteristics. In the background of this discussion is *Internet,* introduced in Chap. 1. The foreground consists of the *World Wide Web* (WWW) implementation environment, *Hypertext Transfer Protocol* (HTTP), and *Hypertext Markup Language* (HTML). We will study the *Virtual Reality Modeling Language* (VRML) in Chap. 7 and the opportunities and pitfalls present with *Java* in Chap. 8.

The target of this discussion is to give an example of the assistance Internet can provide in increasing perception, a subject to which Chap. 3 was dedicated. If user programming is done interactively on a network, can it significantly increase the productivity of a labor-intensive function in an appreciable way? This is the topic which Sec. 6.2 addresses.

Internet's contribution to communications and computer technology may well go beyond network access, because it is helping to revamp the software industry. Already Internet's TCP/IP communications standard made it possible for millions of computers using different operating systems and applications programs to talk with one another—whether they are on a local area network or widely positioned apart.

Just as important is the value differentiation of Internet from other networks through the World Wide Web—its graphics-oriented subnetwork and the

Hypertext Markup Language. HTML and subsequently the Virtual Reality Modeling Language have given all computers connected to Internet a lingua franca for displaying information in graphics pages.

Another significant contribution is the ease of network access, particularly for browsing heterogeneous databases. Since 1993, when WWW and the Mosaic program for viewing its pages emerged from research laboratories, the Web has become the storehouse of many different forms of information from on-line magazines and digitized film archives or radio programs to business statistics, computer graphics, and other applications. By and large, these developments have come from universities and public research laboratories. Global solutions are at the roots of repositioning software development. New directions are becoming clear. The Web and its associated tools will prove to have a much wider market than Internet. Therefore, they constitute the most interesting implementation references.

6.2 How a Greater Perception Significantly Boosts the Popularity of the Web

In Chap. 3 we said that perception is not only the source of all knowledge, but is knowledge in its own merits. As long as we need to instruct the machines which we make regarding the execution of their duties, we need to express this knowledge clearly and efficiently. The whole concept of greater programmer productivity rests on this simple idea.

Whether it runs on Internet, on any other network, on a monolithic mainframe, or on the tiniest computer, any computer program is a *model*. More precisely, it is a dynamic model of a process, product, system, or environment that we map into the machine. The World Wide Web is an environment implemented in software. It is a model of the real world.

Behind the development and use of this or any other model stands our perception of the situation or process that we wish to represent. Thinking by analogy underpins the mapping of a real-world situation into a computer. Examples are a real-time simulator, a spreadsheet, and a relational database.

The software program which we build is essentially a *coupling* of data and commands. Advanced appliances see to it that this is primarily done in an object-oriented manner.[1] In any practical implementation, this relationship has two aspects:

- One is relatively *static*.
- The other is relatively *dynamic*.

The dynamic part typically models the behavior of the process, product, or system within its environment. (See also the discussion in Sec. 6.9 on dynamic modeling.) For this reason, developing the dynamics of a program is a challenging job, and every effort should be made not only to develop but also to sustain dynamic modeling characteristics. This is what Tim Bernes-Lee has achieved with the Web.

A comprehensive coverage assists in greater perception, and greater perception can be instrumental in the representation mission. Statistics available from the National Science Foundation (NSF) demonstrate that the World Wide Web became the dominant Internet resource, as measured by both packet count and volume. As of January 1966, it is surpassing

- Gopher
- WAIS
- Telnet
- File Transfer Protocol (FTP)

There are also some characteristics of the new landscape which differ from practices in other networks. Few Web documents are archived. Internet users show a market preference for *surfing*, or general browsing. Web browsers have become the principal tools also in connection to non-Web documents.

For the time being, at least, multimedia browsing seems to be a lower priority than graphics home pages enriched by metaindexing and search capability. Other statistics are also most interesting to keep in mind. A breakdown by topology, gender, and background shows that among the total population of Internet users

- 81 percent are North American.
- 82 percent are male.
- 36 percent have university degrees.
- The median yearly income of Internet users is between $50,000 and $60,000.

These statistics are important because they profile the Internet end-user population. Given that Web users are quite versatile in programming self-service, we could formulate the hypothesis that the foregoing four bulleted items also tell about the pattern which may characterize professionals who choose to do their own computer programming today, rather than depend on what a centralized data processing shop may produce 2 years from now.

Service providers are ready to help Internet users with visual programming. Palo Alto–based W3 and Philadelphia-based Group Cortex, for instance, have released tools that enable World Wide Web site administrators to collect sophisticated information in real time. Based on data being collected, Hypertext Markup Language pages, and other Web applications tailored to the end user are made available interactively on the fly.

Possible applications range from delivering images to highly targeted corporate memory facility services, to visual programming solutions. But there are no standards, and each product approaches the problem of narrowcasting of information to users in different ways.

- W3's Personal Web Site toolkit (PWS) runs off common Web-log file tracking registration as well as off tools developed in-house.

- Group Cortex' SiteTrack makes maximum use of Netscape's Server Application Programming Interface to track users through a site with or without registration.[2]

Web sites such as HotWired also support on-the-fly customization. Internet experts predict that these are the first of many similar tracking and site enhancement products to be brought to market. New developments are expected to radically change the way end users, as well as professional programmers, look at how they dish out HTML pages and other content.

6.3 Targeting a Quantum Jump in Programming Productivity

Asked about the single most important reason which made WalMart the number 1 retail chain in the world in the short space of 20 years, its founder, the late Sam Walton, answered: "We were always ready to turn on a dime."[3] This is what the programming profession needs today more than anything else.

Turning on a dime is important because different people look at the Internet, and the Web, from totally different viewpoints. Bill Gates considers it to be a global virtual arcade getting ready for electronic commerce. What others particularly appreciate is its news groups and their role as virtual meeting places. Still others lower their sights to the level of electronic mail. My personal hope is that

- Internet, WWW, and the tools which they are supporting will be instrumental in radically changing the programming culture.

- In the whole world of computers, communications, and software, this cultural change is the salient problem of technology. (See also the discussion of the need for a cultural change in programming in Chap. 1.)

Figure 6.1 helps explain the transition necessary to put such a change in programming policies and attitudes into effect. The first row outlines the objectives: End users will be happy to pay in low-cost microprocessor cycles, *if* they can get something in return. The second and third rows compare visual programming to the conventional languages of the old school.

Some of the potential contributions of visual programming to software were discussed during the Pasadena Workshop of 1992. NASA, its organizer, invited experts from the research community with the goal of identifying software needs and associated challenges. As expected, the majority of the participants were concerned with the software question. The consensus was that

- Software is indeed the grandest challenge, and major resources should be allocated to significantly improve current conditions.

- Whether in communications or in computing, no real breakthroughs can be made until the software bottleneck is broken.

The Pasadena workshop highlighted a better direction for research, develop-

OBJECTIVES	– RAPID PROTOTYPING – SAVING TIME, WORKFORCE – PAYING IN CYCLES

NEW LANGUAGE	– DESIGNED FOR LOGICAL PROCESSES
	– GIVING SUPPORT FOR
	   ∗ USER INTERFACES
	   ∗ DATABASE ACCESS
	   ∗ DEVELOPMENT AND DEBUGGING

CONVENTIONAL LANGUAGE	– USE WITH WORKSTATIONS – USE WITH MAINFRAMES, AND – PAYING IN TIME, WORKFORCE

Figure 6.1 Layers of reference in modern approaches to programming.

ment, and implementation of information technology. It underlined the need for *software solutions which are very dear to the user*. It also brought in evidence that Ada, Fortran 90, and C++ do *not* answer the software challenges of this decade and beyond.

But this is still far from becoming a general consensus. Yet, from Cobol and Fortran to C, the majority of widely used programming languages were not designed for parallel computers. Neither do they have a truly object orientation, nor are they made for visual programming.

Experience shows that patchwork solutions don't meet fast-evolving requirements. Therefore, the effects of a facelift here and a facelift there do not last for very long. One aspect of the software problem, the Pasadena Workshop suggested, is advancements in visual programming technology.

- Achieving ever-greater levels of peak performance is not the only challenge which faces the information technology profession.

- The most significant job is to make this higher level of program performance easily accessible to, and understandable by, the end user.

The cultural bottleneck lies in both items. I expect that by programming the network rather than the computer, we could change the current programming images. *Flexibility and adaptation should be at a premium.* The five topmost characteristics of good visual programming are that

- It is easily accessible by end users.

- It contributes to significant productivity.

- It is flexible and dynamic.

- Operation is very fast.
- It supports an open architecture.

Because there should be software-hardware codesign, these five characteristics of good visual programming tools are written in both a software and a hardware sense. Notice that these concepts are the exact opposite of the rotten strategy which has been followed so far by some computer vendors, who have always tried to lock user organizations into a proprietary architecture and its obsolete programming languages, turning what used to be a systems solution into a cash cow for several decades.*

The other reason why for over 30 years programmer productivity has been dismal lies in the fact that the user organizations themselves have not been that aggressive in getting better performance from the efforts of their people. Yet, significant increases in productivity are not only most welcome but also necessary—and they are doable.

An example from World War II helps document this thesis. When Henry J. Kaiser and his "boys" committed themselves to building the Liberty ships, not only did they go against current (and the then-established) shipbuilding practices, but also they radically changed the way in which ships were built.

- At the time, the best U.S. shipyards produced a cargo ship of 10,000 to 15,000 tons in 210 calendar days.
- The prefabrication and open-space assembly methods Kaiser introduced, from his background in building huge dams, first cut the time in half, to 105 calendar days.
- Then Henry Kaiser created stiff competition between his Richmont, CA, and Portland, OR, shipyards and radically shrank that timetable.

When Kaiser said that a couple of weeks per ship would be enough, many experts shook their heads and said it could not be done. Yet, the Portland shipyard—managed by Edgar F. Kaiser, the founder's son—took only 10 days from keel laying to launch. In a few more days, the cargo was out on the ocean bearing weapons and other supplies to the U.S. soldiers at the front.

Established in September 23, 1942, this record is a stimulant to any profession, and there is a big lesson in it for programming and programmers. Internet users should never forget this example.

At the company's Richmond shipyard, Clay P. Bedford cut this astonishingly short time in half. At 3:27 p.m. on November 12, 1942, Hull 440 was launched in just 4 days, 15 hours, and 26 minutes after the keel was laid.[4] Speed and high quality did not characterize the construction of only freighters. Henry Kaiser's Vancouver yard was credited with building its aircraft carriers in one-third the time a regular U.S. Navy yard would require to construct a similar vessel.

---

*Dr. Carlo de Benedetti said in a CNN interview during the 1996 Davos meeting that IBM has a gross profit margin of 55 to 65 percent on its mainframes.

While many people look at Internet as a communications highway, I am more intrigued by its other aspect—the major contribution that a global perception of the application being developed can make in programming. Hence the decision to dedicate Part 3 to this issue. I think that we can match Henry Kaiser's record with the Liberty ships in software productivity.

Just as important is to ensure that an open architectural standard will prevail. The hope is that the market today is wiser than in the past, and will not go for arm twisting by this or that vendor, no matter its fame. But what is an open architectural solution, and how far it can be brought?

The classical example of an open architecture in software is Unix. Because of its wide market acceptance, Microsoft's Windows plays a similar role in masking hardware design details. But the sense in which I am using the notion of open architectural policies and practices is much wider. My paradigm is the World Wide Web.

6.4   Understanding and Appreciating the Contribution of the World Wide Web

Developed at the European Laboratory for Particle Physics (CERN) in the early 1990s, the World Wide Web brings together Internet's disparate networked resources. It makes them accessible by using a point-and-click interface at the end user's site. However, some of the most rigorous requirements for a transaction environment are not present on the Web. The Web protocols are

- *Hypertext Transfer Protocol* (HTTP), which addresses client/server handshaking and communications

- *Hypertext Markup Language* (HTML), the protocol for document formatting

The salient point in connection with HTTP is access compliance, both to terminals and to other Internet environments being accessed through the Web, for instance, WAIS, Gopher, FTP, and E-mail.

One of the functions targeted by HTTP is the breadth of communications setups supported by the terminals. This brings into perspective issues related to connectivity. Indirect connectivity may be served through X.25 through dial-up access to Internet information providers. Ethernet and Token Ring are often used for direct connectivity.

An important feature of the protocol is proxy client support, which enables the terminal to behave as if it were an intermediate server. Thus, with appropriate permissions it can gain access through firewalls erased for security purposes.

Generally speaking, access compliance is an issue meriting significant attention, and much more needs to be provided than is today available. Proxy client support is important because currently the weakest link in the Web is in this domain:

- Rigorous security measures are vital.

- But also authorized clients must pass through firewalls.

In this duality lies the key to how the system operates. Basically, the Web works by linking information together using hypertext, building hyperlinks into documents that can be transported, and assisting the user in mapping one piece of information into another. This interlinked structure of information elements can be stored anywhere on the Internet and anywhere in the world.

A user could travel from database to database around the globe while reading a few Web pages. She does so in a seamless manner, without realizing that she changes information structures. Because browser software (such as Mosaic, Netscape's Navigator, Microsoft's Explorer, MacWeb, HotJava, Spyglass, and other routines) used to access the Web allows graphics, sound, and video to be displayed, WWW has become by far the most popular Internet resource.

One of the major contributions made to the art of computing by the World Wide Web is that it introduced a standard syntax for referring to and accessing Internet hosts. The basic normalization is done through

- The uniform resource locator (URL)
- The uniform resource name (URN)

But at the same time, Web designers left the standards they developed open for further enhancement. The URL supplies a standard nomenclature for addressing Internet services by means of Web browsers. It is not, however, known whether it can hold its own without further enhancements, as further advanced applications develop.

The importance of the World Wide Web is not limited to the fact that it has brought a new paradigm to on-line interactivity, or that it is steadily enriched with third-party contributions. Careful readers will pay attention to future implications in groupware solutions much more powerful than Lotus Notes and other alternatives which are closed architectures.

- The feasibility of in-house Web structures comes increasingly under examination, and it helps to ensure that the market for Web technology is much bigger than that for Internet.
- This leads to *intranets* which can be more efficient business architectures than any other brand, greatly capitalizing on third-party contributions. (See Sec. 6.8.)

When these facts sift down to the information systems community, there will be a rush to invest, in one way or another, in leading companies in the Web. The market will experience also plenty of fallout from Internet to the intranets.

In Internet sites, World Wide Web servers currently hold information estimated to be more than 7 million pages. To this should be added the downloadable files on some 15,000 Gopher and FTP servers as well as the content of thousands of news groups.

Database mining is necessary to exploit the networked information resources. Some are impressive in terms of the facilities they offer. For instance, 3Com has

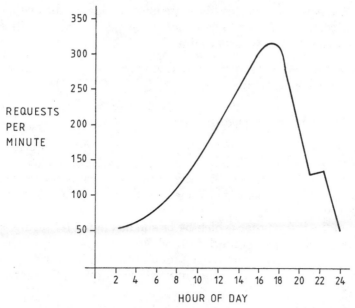

Figure 6.2 Intraday statistics on request per minute for text on the World Wide Web.

a database of 140 possible acquisition candidates and tracks everything that happens in those companies, down to personnel changes.

The relatively large quantity of information available on Internet continues to grow as a function of time. Indeed, this is part of the problem of information overload currently experienced on the Internet. Another problem is the questionable value of much of the available information as well as the possibility that a browsing trail may lead to a deadend.

- Even the best search engines available today are far from perfect, but their capabilities are evolving.

- As with all computer applications, success in finding what one wants still depends on the skill with which the user constructs, queries, and selects keywords.

Figure 6.2 shows a leptokyrtotic distribution of requests per minute for text on the Internet.* These are U.S. statistics. Other graphs address images. Interestingly enough, the image curve has about the same distribution, although it is slightly below the text curve shown in this figure.

To effectively use networked resources, and therefore the World Wide Web, the user needs a browser. The browser presents the user with a screen on

---

*A leptokyrtotic distribution is not exactly bell-shaped (normal), but neither is it necessarily skew. It has a peak which tends to be sharp and usually features fat tails, as in Fig. 6.2.

which Web pages are displayed. Netscape's Navigator, for instance, will automatically connect the user to its own *home page,* which is the first page of any Web site and acts as a table of contents.

- From there the user can scroll up and down, as the page can be bigger than the screen displaying it.

- Flexibility is maintained by the fact the user can employ embedded hyperlinks to jump to other pages.

Hyperlinks can be words that are highlighted in a different color, a picture, or a signal on the screen. Clicking on the link causes a new page to be displayed. This may be another page within the same document or a page at a completely different site. It does not really matter where it is, as the browser finds it automatically.

To keep the information which he or she has found for future reference, the user can either save it on hard disk, where Netscape will be able to view it as a file, or print it. Saving the chosen information on the workstation does away with the need to reconnect to the Internet, but it can lead to garbage collection problems.

6.5   Hypertext Markup Language and the Programmer

Users create an Internet Web page using the Hypertext Markup Language (HTML). This is Internet's publishing code. The Hypertext Markup Language permits the end user to select a link from a two-dimensional graphical representation of a scene or object which constitutes the reference.

Etymologically, a markup language is a set of codes designed to identify the generic parts of database objects. In this way, such objects can be displayed interactively on various types of computers. For example, the Hypertext Markup Language uses

<h1>	to indicate the start of a primary heading
<p>	to identify a paragraph
<i>	for the start of a word or phrase to be set in italic

HTML defines what Web documents can look like and how Internet resources can present themselves. HTML pages are usually presented in edit form. A good exercise would be to convert them in graphical form, in this way demonstrating the power of visual programming. However, Web clients differ considerably when it comes to the finer points of HTML compliance. Organizationally, the HTML kernel specification could be cast into levels:

- Basic structural specifications

- Extensions for rudimentary image handling and simple text enhancement

- Technical specifications for forms

- Extensions for tables, mathematical formulas, and multimedia support

HTML Version 1 addressed the first two bulleted items. Versions 2 and 3 address, respectively, the functionality implied by the third and fourth bulleted items. There are also other extensions for document body handling proposed by Netscape developers. They include standards for image alignment and resizing as well as control of the type size.

Other enhancements will surely come in connection to security standards, as an effort is now made to develop norms of secure HTTP transmission and HTML pages. This will involve

- Authentication

- A reasonable level of secrecy

- Message auditing

A requirement for the latter is the creation of a message audit trail from sender to end receiver, through digital signatures. Audit logs can be automatically created during navigation and displayed from the main menu. They can constitute hot lists, served by agents and cross-indexed according to a number of search or audit criteria.

With on-line access becoming an easy-to-use commodity, the barriers that have kept information from flowing between different brands of computers and software have begun to crumble. A growing number of users employ the World Wide Web not only to communicate information but also to share the same programs—in spite of having different, incompatible platforms.

Advantage can be taken of the fact that WWW pages are encoded in HTML, and these documents steadily update themselves with new data or links. This is typically accomplished with the help of underlying commands or scripts.

- Such documents are multimedia and can even change based on their own commands.

- The rub, however, is that HTML pages are fixed. The user cannot alter them once they have been delivered.

A good example of how HTML is helpful comes from newspaper publishing. In theory, it should be possible to publish a newspaper without any manual effort at all, since with a database publishing system all text, graphics, pictures, and navigation tools are held separately as objects in a database.

When a reader requests a particular story, a modeling program in the database can use one of several templates, to build the customized newspaper on the fly. This is delivered interactively exclusively to that user. The challenge is speed of response and flexibility. The overcoming of obstacles has led to some imaginative projects, which we study in Chap. 15, such as MIT's News in the Future and the Internet edition of the Sunday *Times* of London.

It is precisely because of environments like the Web and tools like HTML that the Internet promises to overhaul the software business, creating a whole new set of players and plays. New programming solutions that ride on the Web's open standards, such as Java (see Chap. 8) and VRML, promise to make it easier for diverse machines from various manufacturers to communicate.

The contributions are polyvalent. For instance, Microsoft is providing on the Web HTML extensions that will add multimedia capabilities for users of its Internet Explorer browser. The tactic of releasing innovative but proprietary HTML extensions has been used as well by Netscape Communications which, in early 1995, incorporated into its Navigator browser the ability to

- Display backgrounds
- Produce tables
- Wrap text around pictures

A different view is that browser vendors have began to respond to user requirements, and associated complaints when such requirements are not met. As a result, significant improvements have been included in HTML Version 3.0.

In conclusion, Internet and its World Wide Web created an infrastructure for delivering information to computers virtually anywhere. Something similar is now happening to software, which seems to be entering a time of evolution, shedding its past policies and images. If this effort succeeds in changing the embedded, slow-moving culture of programming, it would be the equivalent of turning a supertanker on a dime.

6.6   Why the Web's Implementation Horizon Continues to Expand

In all likelihood, the new software order will reflect the character of open networked solutions. If the current Internet policies are upheld, barriers to entry promise to be minimal. High technology enables the deconstruction of the old economic model which prevailed in the software industry. Protocols such as HTTP and languages such as HTML, VRML, and Java are instrumental in this evolution.

Using network access extensions as their spearhead, many vendors are now trying to capitalize on the rapid growth of Internet, whose revenues totaled an estimated $1 billion in 1995 and are expected to grow to between $10 and $20 billion by the end of this decade. Beyond new products are cooperative deals with cross-licensing technology aimed to deliver scripting and programming features.

Among the predominant strategies is to develop a *community* on the Internet, analogous to a television channel, providing users with subscriptions to select information resources by third parties. Enhancements to HTML and to browsers brought with them significant stock market activity connected to start-ups. Even though most of these companies are quoted on NASDAQ, The American Stock Exchange has developed an *Internet index*.

Alliances will most likely play a vital role in new software developments. As of December 1995, Microsoft, Spyglass, and Sun Microsystems established a collaboration. Intuit and Netscape Communications have agreed to integrate their software offerings, in a move to render the World Wide Web safe for banking and commerce. Visa and Mastercard made a similar deal.

Intuit will incorporate its Quicken financial software with Netscape Navigator, the user-oriented software and Web browser. The two companies hope to lure large banks and other financial institutions into Web commerce which, if done, will help spread the World Wide Web into the mass consumer market through home banking.

Security is, of course, everybody's concern; and Intuit will offer free access to what it considers to be its secure site on the Internet, the Quicken Financial Network. Once connected, this network will provide access to Intuit's databases, technical support, and financial partners such as

- American Express
- Bank of Boston
- Chase Manhattan Bank
- Home Savings of America
- Smith Barney
- Union Bank
- Wells Fargo Bank

But as we have seen in Secs. 6.4 and 6.5, nobody has yet provided a fail-safe solution for security. If there were a breach or account information were stolen, this would be a severe setback for banking services. It is therefore wise to proceed very prudently with Internet banking.

One of the major problems in enhancing security is that a lot of people, including systems experts, don't understand the distinction between *private* and *open networks*. Even private networks are raided, as it happened in the 1994/1995 timeframe with Citibank's network, which was infiltrated by Russian hackers from St. Petersburg.

- Whether private or public, networks today transfer so much money and other financially valuable information that their existence makes them an extraordinarily tempting target for criminals.

- In spite of this, organizations and people trying to protect their data, from transmission to storage, use less caution than with paper money and checks.

In Amsterdam, there are hackers for hire, ready to break into any network and any database. Because tampering with valuable information is not going to disappear, in the coming years some of the most sought-after intelligent software packages will address security issues.

Another reason why the Internet user community cannot shy away from increasingly more challenging problems in the security domain is that, as access to the network expands and the applications get more sophisticated, infiltrators get smarter. At the same time, software and hardware heterogeneity becomes a limiting factor. Still another challenge at the roots of network operations is the way software is created, distributed, and used. Programs such as spreadsheets or word processing packages are written for a particular type of hardware and basic software. Even if they have been developed for the same operating system, programs from different software makers will not work easily together because data must be arranged in a particular way for each commodity offering.

For instance, frequently a spreadsheet package cannot deal with text from the word processing package, and vice versa. As a solution, some vendors offer *suites,* a collection of programs sold as discounted bundles surrounded by new code to make it appear that the different routines actually mesh with one another.

This may work in a closed proprietary environment, but not in the open landscape Internet sponsors. Different suites don't match, and this requires even more interface software, which has been recently called *bloatware.* The result is a spoilage of both development effort and computer power.

Until and unless these applications-related problems are solved, Internet use will be more or less limited to relatively simple database accesses and basic communications routines. There are many issues to be addressed as real-time network connectivity and the managing of databases move forward by pushing the available technology and creating de facto standards.

The thrust toward open specifications comes at an opportune moment because as Internet and other networks expand, many users are running out of patience over being forced to test their pages against multiple browsers. Even some Web sites feel obliged to serve different pages to different browsers, which takes extra server processing power and storage capacity while it handicaps the implementation of real-space concepts.

6.7   Real-Space Applications Using Networked Resources

Information technology at large and the World Wide Web as a specific global implementation eliminate geographic distance. *Real space* is wide-area real-time execution but with a difference. Through intelligent networks, database mining, and high-performance computers, it is feasible to concentrate logically—not physically—in any one point

- Globally selected information elements and patterns
- Information elements which respond in a dynamic, ad hoc manner to end-user selection
- Multimedia bit streams whose concentration is not permanent but ephemeral

Real space is a new concept. Until recently only the most technologically advanced financial institutions and industrial corporations had the skills and financial resources necessary to practice it. But with Internet, and most particularly with the Web, this has changed tremendously.

Any Web user today can effectively work in real space. Clearly, this issue can have vital implications for the competitiveness of persons and of companies. Working in real time through an open architecture permits real-space mining of widely distributed databases.

- The advanced technology underpinning the first world's economies depends to a large extent on radically new departures not only in communications but also in database mining.[5]

- While in the majority of cases in the corporate world the needed solutions are not so well understood, Internet and the Web see to it that clear-eyed individuals are often ahead of corporations.

As explained in Part 1 in no uncertain terms, next-generation applications will have little in common with today's data processing-oriented handling of information. At the heart of this statement is the very significant change which took place in *time* and in *space*.

It is no exaggeration to say that our views of the nature of time and space have changed over the years, with time becoming the fourth dimension. Up to the beginning of this century, people believed in an absolute time.

- Each event could be labeled in time in a unique way.

- All time measurements agreed on the time interval between two episodes.

This is no longer the case. The change started with Albert Einstein's theory of relativity, which killed the idea that there was a unique absolute time. With this, time became a more personal concept, redimensioned relative to the observer who measured it.[6]

A similar notional change happened with directions in space. It used to be that a person had one home, and a company had a market near its office, factory, and laboratory. Today consumers have many homes and jet around the world. Companies have become multinational, operating in different time zones. Both are being *globalized*.[7]

What is happening in the world of business had a precedent in physics. When scientists tried to unify gravity with quantum mechanics, they had to introduce the idea of *imaginary time,* which is indistinguishable from directions in space. In their way:

- Scientific laws do not distinguish between past and future, which makes prognosis a memory facility.

- Neither do scientific laws discriminate between episodes taking place in different places—although business laws do make such distinction.

But scientific laws started having a cultural impact on organizations. "The increase in disorder or entropy with time is one example of what is called an *arrow of time,*" says Dr. Stephen W. Hawking,[8] "something that distinguishes the past from the future, giving a direction of time."

Internet and the Web come at an opportune moment because, in the business world as well as everyday living, globalization obliges us to be aware of the direction of time. As a result, competitiveness implies the ability to bring into one point events which happen in different places, compressing topological space into one integrated reference point:

■ Television reporting does so, both in connection with political and social episodes and in regard to financial or scientific events.

■ The information superhighway adds a multimedia dimension to this same process. It also makes feasible the interactive exploitation of databases in real space.

Real space is, however, a concept in full evolution. It develops as we gain experience in implementing it.[9] Propelled by applications, it grows in sophistication. The classical real time is no longer enough. Global organizations have to operate at any time, in any market, for any product.

The virtual dome example, which we study in Chap. 14, explains the practical sense underpinning this idea.

6.8   Intranet: Mapping the Real-Space Environment into the Communications and Computers Systems

Networks are hooking together entire corporations, permitting companies to merge selected operations on-line; connecting in real time to business partners, customers, and suppliers; and even linking people with their home appliances and cars. Part of these communications and computing services is provided in real time through public networks, but in business an increasingly important role is being played by private enterprisewide systems—the *Intranets*.

From a business perspective, an Intranet is a private Internet. As such, it constitutes a most important factor contributing to a company's competitiveness. Its services go beyond groupware, and the World Wide Web may be the best paradigm in this regard. If *Internet* focuses on

■ Long-haul interbusiness communications

■ Communications between business and consumers

■ Communications among the consumers themselves

then the recently coined term *Intranet* stands for the private enterprisewide information solution. Evidently, it entails a great deal of communication. It also features hardware and software components which may well be heterogeneous, but they should be operating as an aggregate in a seamless manner. That's why the Web is the best metaphor.

What corporate users expect from their Intranet is explained in Fig. 6.3. While most of the so-called enterprise information systems are largely patchworks of computers working in batch, not only on-line, Intranet identifies a company's *real-time and real-space network* which links its sales offices and factories—or the bank's branch offices and headquarters—both at home and

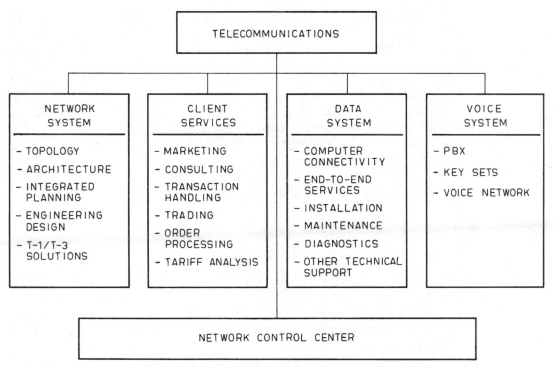

Figure 6.3 Functional overview of network services supported by a major bank.

abroad. Therefore, intranet is a rich area of growth during the coming years. It impacts business partners and makes feasible virtual corporations. Therefore, wise managements will be paying a lot of attention to Intranet solutions.

This needs to happen for reasons of both competitiveness and survival in a market more demanding than ever. Continuing competitiveness suggests the need to identify in real time, and to map in real space, all crucial parameters governing market behavior. As an example, the four parameters with the greatest impact on currency exchange are

- The cost of supplying liquidity

- The probability that a transaction takes place inside the bid-ask spread

- The autocorrelation of the exchange flow

- An asymmetric information factor, the heat wave

Written at a level of average sophistication, most models today follow the easier way of expressing transaction price changes as a linear function of contemporaneous and past order flows. They also provide for adjustments to the standard deviation for serial covariance of the errors induced by discrete price structures, doing so through least-squares techniques.

However, not only is the behavior of financial markets most often nonlinear, but also not all the parameters in a model can be identified with confidence. Typically, by using a time series of observations of transaction price changes and trade initiation, these parameters are estimated by maximum likelihood or a similar nonlinear procedure.[10]

The drawback is that this requires strong assumptions about the distribution generated by the processes in question. One approach used to avoid this shortcoming is an estimation strategy based on the generalized method of moments (GMM), which jointly addresses the system of equations governing the transaction and quoted price processes.

Currency exchange is a good example of the real-space paradigm and the necessary mapping procedures for bids and asks, because it is a global trade. Every day $2.4 trillion changes hands, which is more than 35 percent of the gross national product (GNP) of the United States. Both risk and opportunity exist in these statistics.

Realistic modeling is, of course, the keyword, and it must be admitted that in several applications today we are faced with not only the need for real-space information elements but also *algorithmic insufficiency*. For increasingly more sophisticated applications we constantly need new algorithms:

- If one consults the textbooks, what exists is a handful of approaches that are always the same.

- But both operating environments and the nature of the applications with which we deal vary.

Hence we have to find new algorithms. The problem for many user organizations is that they typically do not have the skills to do the job. Neither do they have the culture. Able solutions require new departures as well as the ability to choose parameters, map them into the system, and record (or estimate) their values. We also need to adjust in real space a criterion function based on moment conditions implied by the model, as well as to produce comprehensive visualization results in real time.

6.9 Gaining Advantage from Dynamic Modeling and Animation

Classically, models are made by first creating two-dimensional geometry on a work plane and then extruding or stamping this profile through a three-dimensional space. Such work planes can be generated fairly easily, and interaction is possible between two-dimensional and three-dimensional geometry.

- Work planes and profiles are copied, translated, and rotated as the application requires.

- But with new tools (see the discussion of VRML in Chap. 7) better profiles can be created by projecting data and entity locations from three-dimensional space.

As implementation requirements grow, the now-classical approach of first going through two dimensions shows its limitations. By contrast, the newer, *dynamic modeling* solutions deal with parametric, solid modeling which is based on constraint management. This should be the chosen approach from now on.

The discussion is most relevant to applications in the World Wide Web—whether on Internet or the Intranets—because WWW provides the environment on which it can be implemented. Dynamic modeling eliminates issues such as model design history and over/under limits. By means of this solution, users can concentrate on designing while surface data is created from numerous sources. On the Web and its databases, surface data can coexist with solid data which is generated through the model. Object orientation offers distinct advantages in this connection, both at the level of the three-dimensional programming language and in regard to the distributed object databases.

Figure 6.4 suggests in a nutshell a methodology for programming in a network setting and prototyping in an object environment. (See also Fig. 2.6.) The described procedure targets a range of services, from the establishment of specifications to prototyping proper, two levels of testing, and the development of the target artifact.

New three-dimensional programming languages, such as VRML, see to it that when beginning a design, users are presented with one or more initial viewports, each with its own set of visualization tools and commands. Menus help in controlling dynamic zoom, rotate, pan, and viewpoint visualization and in showing or hiding control aspects. The user can activate different models to see one or more elements in each viewport. This increases interaction through the ability to work on any part at any time. Interactive design should be easily accessible regardless of relationships or viewpoints which it involves. Parts can be saved into an assembly file type of naming scheme, either individually or in relationship to others. This scheme can be interactively modified through a work session.

Advanced commodity software currently allows for both dimension-driven and individual feature modification. In this way, users do not have to worry about the order in which the model's different components were initially created. Programs are available to offer dynamic part rotation in shaded, wireframe, or hidden-line removed modes. Dynamic part rotation provides high-level assistance.

On either the Internet or the intranets, Web-type environments can be instrumental in supporting design verification tools. These permit programmers and designers to explore all aspects of the model being created, doing so inside and outside through a variety of dynamic visualization schemes. One key advantage of this approach is that the resulting virtual mockups eliminate the need for full-scale physical prototypes.

- Three-dimensional scanning and interference checking functions enable models to be viewed from any perspective.

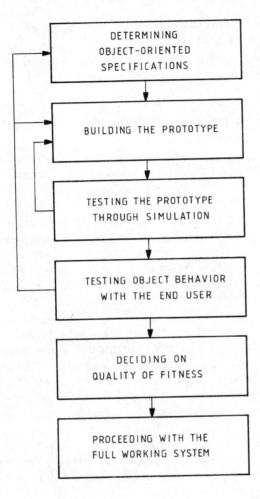

Figure 6.4 Programming in a network setting and creating a prototype of an object environment.

- Models can be projected as shaded solids for realistic visualization, while components and subassemblies are added or removed for viewing hidden areas.

Along the same frame of reference, models can be sectioned with a dynamic three-dimensional scanning plane, following any trajectory to check for areas of conflict. Interference between components can also be highlighted by audio cues. The evolution of VRML, which is covered in Chap. 7, should be seen from this perspective. Dynamic modeling ensures that space allocation studies can be performed to add components to an existing artifact. A two-dimensional cross-section view can be displayed simultaneously, as required by the project. Multiple parts should be supported without an extra assembly module.

For constraint management purposes, the user can establish relationships between different features. Such features are named and then selected to be grouped together. If a part is cut into two elements, the software automatically names the new body as a new part. At any time,

- The relationship between two features may be deleted, or redefined and reassigned.

- Elements can be named for different part creation purposes, or for manipulation and selection.

The difference between what static CAD can provide and what Internet or Intranet resources can ensure is that with the latter groupware can be executed dynamically, in real space. That is how automobile manufacturers, among others, now hook up their design laboratories which are located on two different continents.

What changes with Internet, the Web, and VRML is that, up to a point, users can do away with expensive private networks. They can also dispose of the parochial languages which dominated computer-aided design for over 20 years. As we will see in Chap. 7, VRML sees to it that the design of solids is achieved by complete primitive generation and modification.

Furthermore, as the sophistication of applications increases, the need for animation capabilities, to be controlled in real time, also grows. Animation, for instance, will allow engineers to evaluate how moving parts of an assembly interact, while precision measurement tools can be used to check distances and angles. Concurrently with animation can be employed

- Dynamic three-dimensional scanning
- Interference checking
- Two-dimensional cross-section functions

Such a procedure permits designers to evaluate their models by using realistic rendering (see Chap. 7) and applying precise measuring capabilities in a real-space sense. They can also visualize complex mounting and dismounting operations.

Dynamic modeling and animation also have significant sales consequences. They provide a realistic real-time tool that can be used by the sales staff and taken directly to the customer. The objective of extending the implementation perspective is to allow the customer to better visualize the design. This also helps to ultimately shorten the transaction process. Let's keep this in mind when we talk of VRML.

References

1. See also D. N. Chorafas and H. Steinmann, *Object-Oriented Databases,* Prentice-Hall, Englewood Cliffs, NJ, 1993.
2. *CommunicationsWeek International,* September 1995.
3. Sam Walton, *Made in America — My Story,* Bantam, New York, 1993.
4. Albert P. Heiner, *Henry Kaiser, Western Colossus,* Halo Books, San Francisco, 1991.

5. D. N. Chorafas and H. Steinmann, *Database Mining,* Lafferty, London, 1994.
6. Dimitris N. Chorafas, *How to Understand and Use Mathematics for Derivatives,* vol. 1: *Understanding the Behavior of Markets,* Euromoney, London, 1995.
7. See also D. N. Chorafas, *High Performance Networks, Personal Communications and Mobile Computing,* Macmillan, London, 1996.
8. S. Hawking, *A Brief Theory of Time,* Bantam, New York, 1988.
9. See D. N. Chorafas, *Rocket Scientists in Banking,* Lafferty, London, 1996.
10. Dimitris N. Chorafas, *How to Understand and Use Mathematics for Derivatives,* vol. 1: *Understanding the Behavior of Markets* and vol. 2: *Advanced Modelling Methods,* Euromoney, London, 1996.

7

The Virtual Reality
Modeling Language

7.1 Introduction

The Web's Virtual Reality Modeling Language (VRML) provides a good way to encode three-dimensional graphics, so that Internet can effectively handle them. End users can display these encoded elements on a computer monitor, manipulating them through a pointing device. Let's also keep in mind what Chap. 4 has underlined: Because of the Intranets, the market for World Wide Web technology is much bigger than that for Internet alone.

The experience with widely networked visual programming solutions is just starting, and there are several competitors. Among languages addressing this goal, VRML seems to be the best positioned, and it is attracting the greatest public attention. But it is not the only one. Others include the Multitasking Extensible Messaging Environment (MEME), Manchester Sane Description Language (MSDL), and Labyrinth. (See also Sec. 7.8.)

The fact that a common language is needed to control three-dimensional graphical objects and scenes has been known for years to CAD users and other people working with interactive graphics. In the sense of wider networking, the more general aspects of this need have been brought into focus at a meeting organized by Tim Berners-Lee in the spring of 1994, during the first annual WWW Conference in Geneva, Switzerland.

Up to that time, several companies and laboratories had been working independently on providing a graphics capability. But heterogeneity called the tune, and these experiences were instrumental in the process of getting together a draft specification.

The designer of VRML is Mark Pesce. Version 1.0 of its specifications was released in the fall of 1994. It is based on the Open Inventor ASCII file format developed by Silicon Graphics, which has been adapted by SGI's Gavin Bell to operate in a networked environment.

VRML incorporates concepts and means to reduce the data transfer. Java, which we study in Chap. 8, has similar features. The VRML solution tends to be more application-specific, therefore requiring more time for specifications, which in some cases may be a nuisance but in others is an advantage.

In either case, a common standard for networking sees to it that other interactive users with incompatible systems can handle the artifact on their screens, zoom to get a better look at the details, or take different views of it. In this manner, VRML ensures a new level of interactivity on the Web and provides good quality three-dimensional graphics and user-controlled animation.

7.2   Comparing HTML, VRML, and Their Objectives

The Virtual Reality Modeling Language was designed to assist in the task of describing multiparticipant interactive simulations involving three-dimensional graphics. These are real-time constructs, essentially virtual worlds networked by means of Internet and hyperlinked with the World Wide Web.

Following the 1994 Geneva session, the institution of a WWW-VRML mailing list permitted a number of participants to collaborate on the first version of VRML. This list expanded rapidly, reaching over 1000 members and leading to a draft version of the specifications which was ready for the fall 1994 WWW conference. Basically,

- HTML is a method of describing two-dimensional text and images.

- VRML is a method of describing three-dimensional objects.

While HTML gives the user the ability to describe a document's properties, VRML permits the description of the important elements of a three-dimensional scene—polygons, rendered objects, surface textures, lighting, and other spatial properties or effects. When a VRML file is called, the user sees first a scene that can look very realistic, depending on the quality of the rendering. (For a discussion of rendering see Sec. 7.5.)

For instance, a design engineer may take a three-dimensional CAD model of an internal-combustion engine and, by encoding it in VRML, create a file that other designers can display on their computers without the need for the original CAD program that created the model. This is very important because from PHIGS to GKS and IGES—all designed to be *the* solution to CAD file transfers—there exist a host of incompatible graphics standards.[1]

HTML is an important language in the Web context, but in terms of sophisticated applications the wave is away from two-dimensional and toward three-dimensional and virtual reality perspectives.[2] This is true both in engineering design and in the more general landscape of Internet users, including games and financial applications.

An example will help to explain this transition. Until fairly recently, to analyze a chip design with millions of transistors, available CAD tools modeled the transistors only in two dimensions. Depth was ignored because the main action takes place at the surface of thin films on the silicon. But as technology advanced, this is no longer satisfactory. The width of the transistors approached the thickness of the surface films, and the electron activity at the sides of a transistor has to be modeled, too. To do so, advantage must be taken of three-dimensional CAD tools, which include sophisticated, high-level features. For example, in addition to a comprehensive set of two-dimensional and three-dimensional drawing and editing tools, commodity software now handles solid object modeling, photorealistic rendering, three-dimensional walk-throughs, key frame animation, complete color control, and extensive lighting control.

These concern professional three-dimensional graphics tools. Not all apply to VRML at its current release—but some do. Many aspects of virtual world display, database mining, and networks can be specified by using VRML. Therefore, the Virtual Reality Modeling Language is intended to become the standard language for interactive simulation inside the Web, and its impact will increase in direct proportion to the drive toward multimedia and animation.

Images are a vital link in understanding the realities represented by multimedia information, or simply by numerical data. By looking at images end users are gaining new insight, which permits them to manipulate analytical functions with ease.

As already explained, the origins of VRML date to the spring of 1994. At the first annual World Wide Web conference, a birds-of-a-feather session was organized to discuss virtual reality interfaces to WWW. Some of the participants described their projects as intended to build three-dimensional graphical visualization tools, and all agreed on the need to have

- A common language for specifying three-dimensional scene description
- Well-defined and universal Web hyperlinks working with this language

The dominant idea has been that of creating a metaphor of the Hypertext Markup Language for virtual reality. With this the term *Virtual Reality Markup Language* was adopted, but the word *Markup* later was changed to *Modeling*.

- HTML can connect sound and other objects.
- VRML can connect hypertext in space, and it does so with a click.

In Fig. 1.5, we see the progression from the bottom up, from Internet hardware and software to World Wide Web, Hypertext Markup Language, and Virtual Reality Modeling Language. Notice that between HTML and VRML there has been a layer of browsers and other support services. We talk about MPEG, JPEG, MIDI, and MIME in Sec. 7.3.

One thing distinguishing VRML from other three-dimensional design tools is that it addresses itself to a wide population of end users. As far as professional engineering designers are concerned, VRML does not necessarily need to be the ultimate in the line of progression. For instance, as a higher layer than VRML can be taken one of the established three-dimensional CAD languages, such as

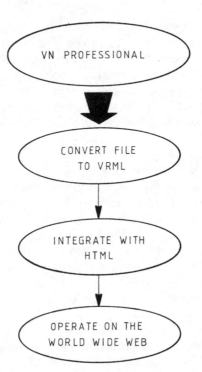

Figure 7.1 A level of sophistication in graphics above VRML.

VN Professional. (An applications example with PV Wave software is given in Fig. 9.2.) The concept is shown in Fig. 7.1. This approach

- Will create the ability to graduate to a more sophisticated tool
- Will help service providers to offer the full range of functions described earlier in this section
- Will do away with the need to generate incompatible versions of VRML, because of unilaterally developing add-ons

The conceptual sequence is then that VN Professional converts to VRML which uses the facilities of the service layer and of HTML. As we saw in Chap. 4, not only is HTML supported in the Web environment which runs on the Internet, but also it may be a basic feature of an Intranet.

This chain of increasing professional functionality can deliver useful services because HTML addresses the structure of the documents but permits different views. It supports user references, but also for display purposes it is necessary to have *viewers*. The concept of VRML is to help define the type of a viewer:

- Film
- Sound
- Graphics
- Icons

- Data
- Text

In conclusion, from spring to fall of one year, 1994, a new and powerful visual programming language was created. This speed of delivery is another important characteristic of the Internet culture. Unburdened by the bureaucracy, compromises, and delays characterizing the large standards institutes, mainframe vendors,* and mainframe user organizations, Internet moves fast and establishes norms having a global impact.

7.3 MPEG, JPEG, MIDI, and MIME

The most important norms which existed already and on which the development of VRML has been based are MPEG, JPEC, MIME, and MIDI. In this section we briefly review what they stand for.

- MPEG, the Moving Pictures Expert Group, has two standards, MPEG1 and MPEG2.
- JPEG is the Joint Photographic Expert Group.
- MIDI is the Music Instrument Data Interface.
- MIME stands for Multipurpose Internet Mail Extension.

MPEG is the norm for movies, and it promotes two standards. MPEG1 defines a bit stream of compressed video and audio optimized to fit into a bandwidth of 1.5 Mbits/s. It is a norm which can be easily applied in a compression and decompression sense.

The second standard, MPEG2, is used for digital satellite TV. It is relatively easy to decompress, but it is quite difficult to meet its requirements for compression. MPEG2 operates at 3 to 10 Mbits/s.

- While MPEG handles movies, JPEG addresses itself to still pictures.
- The MIME interface complements the underlying norms necessary for multimedia presentation.

Well established in industry, the MPEG1 and MPEG2 chips decompress video data for smooth and sharp replay of digital video and audio signals. Both chips, and particularly MPEG2, are at the crux of technology that can access multimedia on Internet.

The two MPEGs and MIME are so important because experts are convinced that with new visual programming languages in place, such as VRML, major new programming efforts will develop relating to multimedia. Through Internet,

---

*Rechristened as *systems integrators,* whatever that means.

users will be able to upload and download complex audio and video programs, by employing multimedia PCs with MPEG chips. (The MPEGs sell for about $35 each.)

Demand for the two MPEGs was about 10 million units in 1995, but it is expected to hit 60 million units in 1997 and 220 million by 1999. Note that MPEGs are used not only for multimedia on Internet but also in connection with the new generation of video compact disc (CD) players.

To keep up these norms, the MPEG group meets under the auspices of ISO to work on standards for digital sequences of images as well as audio compression. Emphasis is placed on compressed bit streams implicitly defining decompression. MPEG, however, leaves the specific compression algorithms up to the individual manufacturers.

JPEG provides the norms for images, more specifically the special compression and conversion formats for pictures. These norms specify the density of compression; for instance, edit out 20 percent of the format. The Joint Photographic Expert Group also meets under the auspices of ISO.

- The JPEG standard has been designed for compressing either full-color or gray-scale images of natural scenes.

- Its users say that it works well on photographs, but it is not that good with lettering and line drawings.

Furthermore, users comment that with JPEG the decompressed image is not quite the same as the one the user started with. The other side of the argument, however, is that JPEG achieves much greater compression than is possible with lossless methods because it is designed to exploit limitations of the human eye.

There is always a trade-off in technological choices, and JPEG is designed to compress images handled by humans—not for a computer-intense analysis of images. At the same time, the norm is flexible because

- The degree of loss can be varied by adjusting compression parameters.

- The image handler can trade off file size against output image quality.

- Decoders are able to optimize decoding speed and image quality.

As explained, JPEG addresses still-image compression. Another committee, *JBIG*, works on binary image compression, such as faxes. Still another effort, known as *MHEG*, sets multimedia data standards.

Notice that MPEG and JPEG meetings usually are held at the same place and time. But they do differ in the participants to their sessions, having few or no common individual members. Their aims, delivery requirements, and charters are also different.

For their part, musical instrument manufacturers have agreed on a digital serial interface. MIDI makes it possible to simplify the connection of instruments by using a reasonably high transmission rate. This ensures that there are no major delays in transmitting large amounts of musical bit streams, especially in real time.

- Machines equipped with MIDI use an RS 232 interface at 31.25 kbits/s, while normally RS 232 works at 19.2 kbits/s.

- Higher transmission rates are possible, but the problem is that the bit error rate (BER) also increases.

MIME, the Multipurpose Internet Mail Extension, is a necessary extension for conventional Internet mail programs. Many Internet products today are supporting it. It is designed to decode and execute simple programs sent via E-mail.

As an ASCII-based document processor, MIME specifies norms for the Internet community, particularly for text messages. It does not address multimedia which, as we have seen, are taken care of by the other norms.

Critics say that even for text, MIME is inadequate when the applications of users require character sets richer than the 7-bit ASCII, for instance, Chinese or Japanese language text. Neither can it be used for voice mail. This is, indeed, a limitation. But because MIME has been designed as an extensible protocol, it will probably evolute as a function of user requirements and time.

7.4 Platform Independence in the Design of VRML

The fact that a given language, in this case VRML, is independent of platforms and vendors is important not only because it supports an open architecture, but also because this strategy enlarges its applications perspectives. A special challenge with visual programming is the ability to extract knowledge in real time from masses of data leading to models, simulations, and experiments. This strategy poses a number of challenges:

- How can we communicate our ideas and insights to others through a multimedia presentation which is comprehensive?

- How do we comprehend the complex relationships of multiple variables and their origin(s) from different sources?

- How can we interactively analyze the fundamental relationships represented by the information elements we manipulate?

Object-oriented solutions are an evident candidate in providing a valid answer to these questions. The same is true of knowledge engineering, particularly of *agents* residing in the nodes of the artifact. Figure 7.2 presents an integrative view of the facilities we would like to incorporate into our tools.

The support structure described in this figure is important because, as a platform-independent graphics programming language, it must at the same time address

1. A higher level of design perspectives

2. Lower-level issues, such as formatting and portability among platforms

3. Heterogeneous operating systems on which the language should run

Today VRML is supported over four operating systems: Unix, Windows 95,

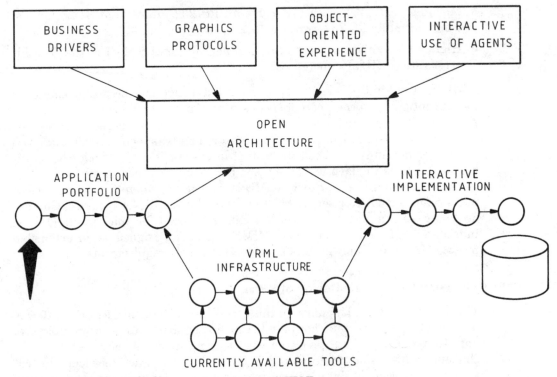

Figure 7.2   A framework for platform independence with VRML.

Windows NT, and System 7 of Macintosh. Other additions may be made in the future. However, because the graphics language is so new, it is still too early to say what the market will demand, as well as which of the supported operating systems and database management systems may provide the best background facilities and which of the OS and DBMS vendors would benefit by massive applications development support by third parties and end users. My guess is that top of the line will be Windows 95 followed by Unix, while object-oriented DBMS will hold the upper ground in terms of competition in the graphics domain. The market will decide. (See also in Chap. 10 why network appliances are not considered valid candidates for the implementation of VRML.)

In terms of lower-level issues, after a considerable amount of deliberation, the Open Inventor ASCII file format (by Silicon Graphics) was selected. It supports complete description of three-dimensional scenes with polygonally rendered objects, lighting, and realistic effects. The developers as well decided that

- VRML will not be an extension of HTML, because the latter is for text, not for graphics.

- The new graphics language has to have the ability to work over high- and low-bandwidth connections.

- Both platform independence and extensibility should continue to characterize VRML design.

Currently VRML has a file format designed for delivery and use of three-dimensional objects and scenes over the Internet. As an example of the facilities which it provides, a new scene can be loaded if specified by the name field.

Another key design factor is that VRML requires a much more finely tuned network optimization than any other language preceding it—including HTML. The graphical characteristics of VRML will see to it that, in contrast to HTML, its scenes are

- Composed of many more *in-line* objects (See Sec. 7.5)
- Supported on-line by a greater number of networked servers

A wise choice has been to depend on subsequent releases of VRML rather than going at once for a high level of sophistication. During the language's definition, it was decided that, with the exception of hyperlink features, Version 1.0 of VRML will not support interactive behaviors.

Since its first version, VRML made feasible the creation of virtual worlds, but Version 1.0 has a limited behavior perspective. The worlds which are created contain objects which have hyperlinks to other worlds, HTML documents, or multimedia types—an extension to electronic mail which follows the MIME norms.

When a viewer selects an object to create a hyperlink within a WWW browser, a VRML world is launched. For instance, in connection with E-mail this may contain pictures, animated sequences, virtual reality artifacts, or different attached documents other than text files.

- This facility makes VRML viewers an important companion to standard Web browsers, for navigating and visualizing the Web landscapes.
- Successive versions will most likely allow for richer behaviors, including the handling of motion and real-time multiuser services.

Basically, the processes of manipulating graphical objects and VRML scene descriptions have many similarities. For example, the concept of a class of objects is an analog to the VRML group structure. The VRML separator applies a transformation to an object which does not affect its predecessor objects, because it acts independently from the rest of the hierarchy.

As a graphics language, VRML describes objects in terms of polygons created by connecting data points. This and other embedded features facilitate the conversion of more-classical object handling procedures to VRML descriptions.

VRML uses a cartesian, right-handed three-dimensional coordinate system. By default, objects can be projected into two dimensions in the direction of the positive Z axis, with the positive X axis to the right and the Y axis up. However, a modeling transformation can alter this default projection. Figure 7.3 shows an example. The upper half has two solids: a sphere and a cone. They are expressed

3-D VIEW

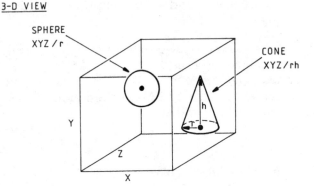

2-D VIEW

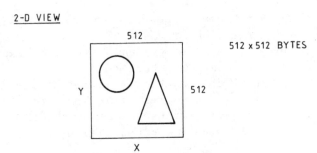

Figure 7.3 A three-dimensional view of the world and, by default, a two-dimensional view.

in an *XYZ* coordinate system. The lower part is a two-dimensional presentation by default presented, for example, in 512×512 byte format.

Simple situations can be effectively handled through existing conventions. The standard unit for angles is radians. The standard unit for distances and lengths is meters. The file with a description of this scene is VRML. To open this file, the user needs an VRML view able to do the calculation of the picture.

- Interactivity is necessary when another person is in the picture.

- With the early version of VRML, the issue of *interactive behaviors* was sidetracked because designing a language able to answer this requirement is a tough job.

Still, it is no less true that a sophisticated artifact needs to express behavior of objects communicating on a network. Although such languages do exist, they are to a large extent parochial. Also keep in mind that the goal of VRML has not been that of describing polygon objects, but rather one of serving visual programming purposes—and effectively supporting the implementation of a viewer environment.

7.5 Nodes, Anchors, and the Rendering Perspectives

VRML defines a class of objects able to serve three-dimensional graphics. These are the *nodes,* whose characteristics help define what kind of object the node itself is, which parameters distinguish this node from other similar nodes, and what kind of child nodes (filials or pertaining objects) this node has. We will talk more about the role played by the nodes of languages in Sec. 7.7.

An important node is the *WWW Anchor,* which loads a new scene into a VRML browser, when one of its filials is chosen. The WWW Anchor behaves as a separator, handling the traversal state before traversing its children and then surfacing.

- How a user chooses a filial of the WWW Anchor is up to the browser.
- The description field of the WWW Anchor allows for a prompt to be displayed.

Basically, the WWW Anchor is a group node performing a transformation of the scene's current state to preserve it while its filials are traversed. Its mechanism permits one to attach a name to the entire group. An important element, as well, is the *WWW in-line node* which makes it feasible to store VRML scene graphs as a series of separate files in one or more locations.

The WWW in-line node reads its filials from anywhere in the Web. Reading the filials can be delayed until WWW in-line is displayed. The artifact's box may be nonempty, which means it has at least one dimension greater than zero. Or it may be an empty box.

Instancing of a node, aliasing or multiple referencing, means using the same instance of that node multiple times. VRML's USE word indicates that the most recently defined instance could or should be reused. However, nodes cannot be shared between files.

The extensibility of VRML is supported through self-describing nodes. Those nodes which are not part of standard VRML must write out descriptions of their fields. This is done right after the opening of the mode:

- It consists of the definition of *fields* as keywords.
- This is followed by a list of *types* and names of fields used by the node.

There are many other issues that a visual programming language should address as it becomes more sophisticated. One is how to avoid redundant effort by creating *macros* from existing visual programs. The user should be enabled to select tools and objects to place in the macro as well as facilitated in choosing the macro option.

User-written real-time loadable modules must be manipulated as objects. These modules should be characterized by portability and other advantages without the disadvantage of heavy overhead. Also the module builder should present simple user-friendly interfaces.

Functions must be provided to load objects that enable the setting and retrieval of named variables and handle errors and generally control execution. It is important to support good user visibility besides providing effective language commands.

Useful lessons can be learned from existing graphics tools for three-dimensional presentation and applications in virtual reality.[3] For instance, during the last few years, simple *shading,* which dominated CAD solutions, is being enhanced with

- Texture mapping to produce surface patterns
- Radiosity to model diffuse lighting
- Reflection mapping to take care of shiny surfaces

If shading is one of the keywords in three-dimensional graphics and virtual reality at large, another one is *rendering.* Renderers are crucial components of modern visualization systems, as well as of all cases involving both visual and acoustical presentations.

- Rendering concepts are integrated into systems to generate high-quality visual walk-throughs in virtual worlds.
- Particular efforts toward real-time *radiosity* are made in connection with visual simulation.

But *visual rendering* is computing-intensive, therefore requiring high-performance graphics workstations. In simple terms, *volume rendering* is a direct technique for visualizing space primitives. This is accomplished without the need for intermediate conversion of volumetric objects to *surface rendering.*

Surface rendering is an indirect approach used to visualize volume primitives by first converting them to a perspective surface representation and then rendering them to the screen through more-conventional techniques. With both volume and surface rendering, the underlying process is that of converting geometry to images. This is not far from the definition of visualization.

Sophisticated rendering systems are typically assisted by an object database which can be interpreted in real time through visual and acoustic renderers. Done in conjunction with visual images, *acoustical rendering* requires the synchronization of output as well as physical simulation of room acoustics.

- Integration of acoustical and visual rendering is done through the definition of appropriate object attributes and the real-time synchronous display and replay of visual and acoustical effects.
- The visual and acoustic renderers are, in many respects, very similar, but the propagation speeds of light and sound cause algorithmic differences.

Experts who are concerned with the steady enhancement of scenes of graphical objects see two ways to render through software. One is by means of *ray tracing,* an approach based on physics, throwing a ray in object space.

The other is to improve upon rendering by means of *radiosity*. The metrics rest on the computation of the exchange of energy by all objects in the scene—breaking the scene into patches consisting of edges (links), vertices (nodes), and color in vertices.

Radiosity can be assisted through software or hardware. The better approach is to custom-make the software in order to exploit to the fullest degree facilities supported by the hardware and those mapped into system design. There are, however, no uniform rules on how an application should be optimized.

No one language answers in the most perfect manner all the issues discussed in this chapter—at least not from its first version. Care should therefore be taken to provide for upward compatibility so that visual programs already written don't have to be rewritten when upgrades take place. Elder versions should act as a subset of newer versions.

7.6 Basic Characteristics of the Facilities Supported by VRML

Graphics, particularly three-dimensional graphics, will characterize most advanced computer applications by the end of this decade. So it is no surprise that software developers working on the Internet thought of the need to enrich the World Wide Web with a three-dimensional programming language. The evolving environment of virtual reality applications also pushed in this direction.

Some of VRML's basic characteristics naturally come from the fact that concepts leading to the development of three-dimensional programming languages have been around for nearly 20 years, since the beginning of computer-aided design. But in the sense of implementing them on a fast-growing public network, the effort of supplying the Web with a three-dimensional language, which we have seen, is recent.

In the short span of two years, the Virtual Reality Modeling Language became the most promising of a number of three-dimensional modeling efforts addressing a networked computing environment. Much of its importance derives from the fact that it provides a compact grammar which permits Web users to navigate and interact with realistic virtual spaces and places. As a text-based language, VRML describes how to construct three-dimensional images on the fly. In the sense of a three-dimensional design tool, Release 1.0 is limited—but it is fairly user-friendly. Many people believe that its growing popularization will lead to an explosion of graphics applications on the Web. It will be enriched with still-better human interfaces, will operate in a real-space manner (see Chap. 6), and will be rendered interactively, at the end user's request.

VRML browsers transport users to a growing variety of solution spaces with images and scenes constructed on the fly in a customized way. Cognizant people predict that currently available tools and approaches would be enhanced with the development of sophisticated gateways served by agents and permitting different scenes to be created following the retrieval of pertinent Web pages.

There is every reason to believe that this is doable in a networking sense. The effects will be comparable to the Web's Common Gateway Interface (CGI), but they will address multimedia solutions going beyond currently supported facilities. In present-day environments,

- The exchange of information between a Web browser and a helper application is handled by MIME.

- MIME definitions select and launch the right VRML viewer application, extending the current two-dimensional Web services to three-dimensional space.

This transformation is known from the implementation of computer-assisted engineering projects, starting with the first experiences when CAD software made it feasible to create and handle three-dimensional representations of objects. The solution space which is created supports

- Multiple points of view on engineering designs

- Virtual light sources and shacks

- Light and texture filters and other visual effects

I don't look at VRML as a substitute for CAD software, and therefore I judge some efforts leading to this approach as misguided. It will not serve VRML to try to be all things to all people. Rather it is better to look at VRML as a substrate of a professional CAD language. To help explain this concept, Fig. 7.1 showed an example with Visual Numerics Professional, but it can be any other top-of-the-line three-dimensional CAD shell.

- The three-dimensional CAD software creates the tool at a more sophisticated level than common VRML.

- The service provider generates the files and ensures the distributed database access.

A VRML level-of-detail (LOD) command allows a viewing program to choose among a set of uses of a given object, based on the user's distance from that object. A top-of-the-line CAD tool can add characteristics which are presently lacking from the first release of VRML.

An evolutionary path suggests the wisdom of this approach. It is quite normal that the first effort regarding VRML concerned a specification designed to normalize three-dimensional modeling work done at different companies, into a single unified programming language. This strategy

- Assisted in leaving behind the confusion which exists in incompatible CAD files

- Continues to help many organizations concentrating on means of moving away from the two-dimensional flatland.

As we saw earlier, among the options evaluated in the process of VRML's initial design was the Open Inventor File (OIF) format, which is based on ASCII—a necessary requirement in keeping a link to HTML. It has, however, been necessary to add to it networking properties which developed the original file format into the current VRML infrastructure.

The Open Inventor File is an object-oriented three-dimensional tool kit, supporting complete rendering. However, in its original form it was both hardware- and software-specific. Other object-oriented choices have been made in connection to VRML. They are discussed in Sec. 7.7 along with concepts which help define the syntax of the language.

7.7   Infrastructure and Syntax of VRML

Object-oriented solutions started with *Simula* in 1968. The concept is nearly 30 years old, but the effective implementation of object technology, on a larger scale, and popularization are relatively recent. Object-oriented software is discussed in Chap. 11.

VRML is an object-oriented language but with a difference. While in other programming languages the objects are organized in a random manner, the files in VRML reside in a *scene graph*. This is a hierarchical structure dictating the sequential order in which nodes are to be parsed.

- As we saw in Sec. 7.6, the *nodes* of VRML are objects which can contain any type of multimedia information.

- Using a node, the programmer can represent a series of points located, for instance, at a subset of defined coordinates.

As discussed in Sec. 7.5, nodes can have child nodes. Being objects, nodes may be reused through instancing. Links and separators are artifacts which enhance the ability of one node to affect another node's state.

In VRML parlance, nodes can be actual shapes or commands that affect the way shapes are drawn. Nodes have names. Version 1.0 of VRML defines 36 nodes as well as the mechanisms by which other nodes may be brought into perspective.

A node can have none, one, or more fields. Fields are variables with parameters that describe size, color, rotation, or other characteristics. These characteristics can encompass a number of variables. The nodes of VRML can be divided into three classes:

- Shape
- Property
- Group

A vital part of VRML's infrastructure is the Object-Oriented Graphics Language (OOGL) for the World Wide Web. This is a nonproprietary format with an easy-to-extend browser. Another fundamental element is the declarative nonprocedural language known as *Cyberspace Description Format* (CDF).

- Both VRML and CDF are essentially descriptions of a three-dimensional world. They are not algorithms centering on step-by-step procedures.

- Both VRML and CDF tend to be platform-independent, requiring relatively small bandwidth and having an object orientation.

- Finally, both are characterized by expandability and feature a concise syntax, which constitutes one of their advantages.

VRML's file format for the interchange of virtual worlds is AFF (which stands for A File Format). It consists of tags with specific properties able to compose a three-dimensional virtual world. This is the virtual world targeted by the Virtual Reality Modeling Language.

The syntax of VRML includes the rules for placing and ordering terms. It addresses values as well as punctuation and guides the programmer in writing language statements and in the three-dimensional graphics description which she or he develops.

VRML's coordinate system uses radians, making it easy to describe angles of rotation and orientation. The graphical language expresses its worlds in terms of *xyz* axes in the cartesian coordinate system.

- The rotation operator specifies the axis and amount of rotation in radiants.

- The scale operator controls subsequent shapes along the three axes and is expressed as a vector.

- Translation is used to describe a transformation of an object occurring parallel to the coordinate system.

The elements and commands of VRML can be combined in a number of ways to create objects, landscapes, or general scenes. The language also defines two camera nodes known as *orthographic camera* and *perspective camera*.

The orthographic or parallel projection translates a three-dimensional object or scene into a two-dimensional plane without any perspective division. (See also the example given in Fig. 7.3.) By contrast, in a perspective projection objects are sized up, which is a handy facility from the end user's viewpoint. For instance, in a three-dimensional scene translated onto a two-dimensional plane, they diminish as they travel away from the camera.

Another important VRML definition concerns the three light nodes: directional light, spotlight, and point light. The directional light node gives the end user control over the objects which he or she manipulates. Spotlight is a source located at a fixed three-dimensional coordinate with illuminating rays.

The flexibility of VRML is demonstrated by the fact that extensions to the language are possible, supported by self-describing nodes. The risk, however, is that the graphics language can become quite complex, moving away from the population which was supposed to serve since its beginning—the typical

Internet user. That's why in Fig. 7.1 I have suggested a superstructure of existing CAD languages which can satisfy the needs of professional users.

In conclusion, a major challenge related to the wider application of VRML in the Internet community comes from the fact that it addresses the total population of on-line users, from scientific applications to the casual consumer. An example of the former is the effort at the National Center for Supercomputing Applications (NCSA) to use VRML to model objects in cosmology. Other scientific efforts are in the fields of genetics, molecular biology, and particle physics. Medical practitioners, chemists, and biologists are employing VRML in connection with experimentation and simulation and to understand the behavior of systems as well as to improve the visualization of results. While VRML is a good graphics language, that sort of wide-ranging expectations can end in overkill.

7.8 Beyond VRML: MEME and VRML+

As we have seen in the preceding sections, in its current Version 1.0 VRML is a combination of three-dimensional graphics and active modeling. It is a meaningful step toward network-based three-dimensional design and the delivery of virtual reality applications to the typical Internet user. The language supports agile visualization tools which make feasible

- End-user interactivity
- The description of object behavior
- Patterning operations
- Real-time object animation

But not all problems connected to interactive three-dimensional graphics have been solved. A further piece of critical software is an interactive development package. There is currently available a tool pointing in this direction known as Multitasking Extensible Messaging Environment (MEME), by Immersive Systems.

- MEME should not be confused with MIME, which is a multipurpose Internet E-mail extension.
- MEME's goal is to permit programmers to create virtual worlds and act within them.

In its current status, MEME includes a modeling language which is a competitor to VRML. The same is true of *Labyrinth,* whose specifications found their way into the VRML set of specifications. A similar statement can be made about the Manchester Scene Description Language (MSDL) developed by the University of Manchester.

Individually and together, each one of these contributions has targeted both general and special aspects of three-dimensional design and modeling, all the way to the on-line rendering of emulated goods and services. An example of how far-reaching this statement can be is provided by Project Virtuosi, by Nottingham Trent University and British Telecom.[4]

Only imagination limits the use of VRML for fairly advanced applications able to combine three-dimensional graphics with virtual reality settings. A good example is virtual meeting spaces, giving a much broader perspective to the more classical approaches to teleconferencing of the past.

Virtual conferences are a fundamental implementation in connection to virtual offices and virtual companies. They should be exploited by organizations using VRML to create virtual meeting places. Some telecommunications companies start employing VRML to define a system of virtual phone booths, extending these efforts toward virtual multimedia environments of networked clients and resources.

- An example of facilities presented by VRML at the level of the casual Internet user is three-dimensional interfaces that permit one to browse the contents of Web servers.

- The current release of VRML, however, lacks animation as well as tools to handle different types of behavior which some users may wish to add to their tool kit.

Since a scene graph is downloaded to the end user's computer in its entirety, there is no awareness on the part of the server that a user is present in a scene. Nor is there an embedded ability to make a virtual reality out of being in a scene. This is another example on the need for a higher layer than VRML, to avoid overloading this language with so much complexity.

Similarly lacking from the current VRML release is the concept of object behavior. With Version 1.0 a scene behaves as a single object. It can be rotated, zoomed, or redrawn as a whole rather than in terms of individual nodes and parts. Work is, however, underway to make feasible much more sophisticated end-user actions with three-dimensional scenes. This project is known as VRML+.

At least according to current plans, the functionality being embedded into VRML+ will permit the representation of users through customized entities. These are known as *digital actors*.

- Digital actors exist within a scene, their movements being communicated to other people and actors viewing the same scene.

- For many applications, this value-added facility will be an important element in interactivity necessary in virtual spaces.

While a great deal of performance is achieved under current modeling conditions, it is good to remember that with Version 1.0 VRML is still in its beginning. Even if most people today limit their visualization applications to three-dimensional spaces, users tend to extend their interest to walk-throughs in a virtual space, an example being architectural walk-throughs.

7.9 ActiveVRML; Combining VRML and Java

By using a VRML browser it is possible to fly through the World Wide Web environment, picking up information as one goes. Proceeding along this principle, Microsoft's *ActiveVRML* will allow users of personal computers to create three-dimensional multimedia effects rather easily on the Internet.

- ActiveVRML combines three-dimensional animation with two-dimensional cartoon-style graphics and synchronized sound effects.

- This creates considerable potential in the advertising, education, and entertainment markets as well as in other applications.

Technical support for the system will be built into the future versions of the Microsoft Web browser, Internet Explorer. No doubt, other vendors will develop similar facilities. However, keep in mind that always in information technology, "my solution is better than yours" means that it is also incompatible with what already exists.

One interesting aspect of the future evolution of VRML is an integration of sorts with Java. (See Chap. 8.) Java is being used as a VRML language because it permits developers to build audio graphics. Silicon Graphics employs Java as an enabling means to create VRML tools, but its use requires powerful workstations at the user site which can handle the applet in an ad hoc dynamic manner rather than as standard pages.

- VRML could be used in conjunction with Java to benefit from facilities embedded in both languages.

- For instance, Java will create the virtual machine which interfaces to VRML or acts as its substrate.

Not only software and hardware vendors but also some tier-1 banks are now looking at Java-VRML-Internet as the way to deliver applications in a rapid way, without going through floppy disks and the messy old routines. Being ready for business ahead of others has always been a powerful competitive advantage.

The concept underpinning this strategy is simple, but it can be far-reaching. Figure 7.4 explains the background notion behind the statements being made. At the base, providing the connecting link, is Internet with the World Wide Web and HTML. User organizations have different options in building an overstructure:

- VRML-Internet

- Java-Internet

- Java-VRML-Internet

The choice of partnerships among linguistic constructs should not be random, nor should it be made lightly. The best strategy is one which rests on

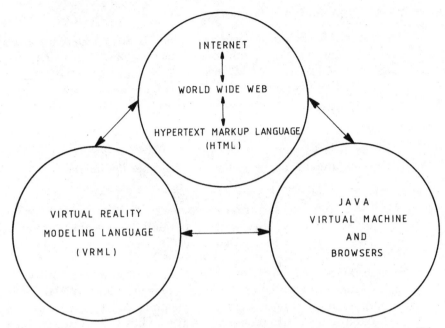

Figure 7.4 The Internet-Java-VRML connection can provide the user with competitive advantage.

competitive reasons. What will give to our company, or to our project, the market edge today? What should we do today in order to stay competitive over the next few years? How can this be done in a way which guarantees fast delivery, at maximum efficiency and lowest possible cost?

References

1. D. N. Chorafas and Stephen J. Legg, *The Engineering Database,* Butterworth, London, 1988.
2. See D. N. Chorafas and H. Steinmann, *Virtual Reality—Practical Applications in Business and Industry,* Prentice-Hall, Englewood Cliffs, NJ, 1995.
3. See Chorafas and Steinmann, ibid.
4. See H. Steinmann and D. N. Chorafas, *An Introduction to the New Wave of Communications and Networks,* Cassell, London, 1996.

8

Java—A Contrarian View

8.1 Introduction

The search for better software and more efficient languages is as old as the computer business itself. But with the exception of the mid-1950s, almost consistently linguistic solutions and software developments have been lagging behind breakthroughs in hardware. In a systems sense, this has created a significant imbalance.

Many experts today believe that, originally designed for appliances and then converted for use on the Internet, Java embodies key attributes of a new software era. They also think that these attributes will characterize the years ahead. They feel that Java will be a winner because of three technical reasons.

- It is an *object-oriented* programming tool, based on C++, which is generally accepted as *the* object language.

- It works as a *real-time interpreter,* which makes it feasible to abstract from hardware details.

- It addresses the database at *page level,* visualizing a variable page size—the *applet.*

None of these three issues is really new. And none of them alone, or even all three taken together, can make Java a smashing success. A revolution in computers and computing will come only if there are cultural changes in the user community, while technical breakthroughs are leading to dramatic uncovering of new solutions, which become universally accepted.

It is conceivable that Java will be successful, but its degree of success will not be just a function of the forementioned technical features. In the 1970s, Univac's Mapper also had new and interesting technical features, but it was a flop because computer users were not ready for a cultural change, and because of miserable and greedy marketing by its vendor.

This chapter has both good news and bad news for Java.* Most particularly, it examines the technical issues behind the new language and evaluates how far these can go in turning it into a new programming standard—and from there making it a marketing success.

Interpretation, object orientation, and page-level database access are no breakthroughs of the 1990s. They date back to the 1950s, 1960s, and 1970s— each time being hailed as the nearest thing to a new messiah in the art of computing. I have treated extensively

- *Interpretation,* in D. N. Chorafas, *Programming Systems for Electronic Computers,* Butterworth, London, 1962

- *Object orientation,* in D. N. Chorafas and H. Steinmann, *Object-Oriented Databases,* Prentice-Hall, Englewood Cliffs, NJ, 1993

- *Page-level* database access, in D. N. Chorafas, *Interactive Message Services,* McGraw-Hill, New York, 1984; and D. N. Chorafas, *Interactive Videotex— The Domesticated Computer,* Petrocelli Books, Princeton, NJ, 1981

The integration of all three concepts into a *multimedia system* has been critically examined in D. N. Chorafas, *Intelligent Multimedia Databases* (Prentice-Hall, Englewood Cliffs, NJ, 1994) and D. N. Chorafas and H. Steinmann, *Virtual Reality—Practical Applications in Business and Industry* (Prentice-Hall, Englewood Cliffs, NJ, 1995).

With this background, I have prepared the present chapter to promote discussion—and dissension—not just on Java but on any language which is sure to follow it on the Internet. It is appropriate to be critical about the characteristics of a programming artifact, given its probable generalization over myriad public and private networks which are now in operation and under development. A contrarian view brings perspective.

8.2   A Brief History of Java and the Paradigm Shift

Cast in the role of a universal computer language, Java is a long shot in the intense networking environment of Internet and the Intranets. For any practical purpose, it is still in its development stage, and the implementation of the Java virtual machine in the Netscape browser (Version 2.0) is slow to come online—but it will.

The Java history started in 1991, with the intention not of developing an Internet language but of assisting in writing control software for computer chips that run microwave ovens and other state-of-the-art household appliances. James Gosling is the programmer who originally developed *Oak*† (later renamed Java), and he reconfigured it several times over in the early 1990s,

---

*The purpose of a book, and the aim of its author, is to educate, not to impart personal preferences. However, a critical evaluation of a new tool cannot escape the expression of opinions. No analysis can be 100 percent objective.

†After the tree outside his office window.

successively targeting cable-TV set-top boxes, video-game machines, personal computer CD-ROMs, and other devices. Every time a restructuring has taken place, it looked as if Oak might finally find a marketing base—but this did not come so fast. Even its name seems to have been a problem, because other companies had already used it for their wares and, therefore, it couldn't be easily protected with a trademark.

Then Sun Microsystems decided to change not only the name of the language but also the marketing approach. *Oak* was dropped for *Java*. This is a slang term for coffee, dating to the days when the best brews came from Indonesia. Then, in a stroke of genius which emulated Netscape, Sun marketing people made the language available free of charge on the Internet.

One of the strong points of Gosling's work has been that in his artifact he embodied most of the major advances in computer theory, and in programming practice, of the past half century. Java is object-oriented, and it enables programmers to write in small, self-contained subroutines.*

Basically, the language seems to be fairly robust, while providing software developers with flexibility. Less assurance is provided by the statement made by Java's pros about security. In principle, before Java allows a line of code to be executed, it determines whether the command is legal. The problem is that

- The theory necessary to prove whether the computer program has been tampered with is still in its infancy.

- Only years of practice, not just classical testing, will tell if Java is foolproof in regard to hackers and other perils.

Virus Implementation Language (see also Sec. 8.3) is the term used by security expert William Cheswick of AT&T Bell Laboratories to describe Java's browser, HotJava.[1] While this may be a little exaggerated, it is no less true that the language lets programmers embed small pieces of software in World Wide Web documents, and this comports security risks.

Java's customized programs do not run on the Web server but rather on the computer that belongs to the end user. This makes it easier to process complex exchanges of information but also requires powerful PCs. We will look into this issue in Chap. 10, in connection with network appliances. Furthermore, it opens the way to viruses and metaviruses. The years ahead will tell how big this risk may be.

Opinions vary regarding the contributions Java can make in turning the network into an interactive computer, but they are generally favorable. "I think quite positively about the future of Java," said some systems experts in response to an earlier draft of this chapter. This has not been a universal opinion.

---

*In the early- to mid-1950s, those of us programming in machine languages religiously followed that practice. Reusable chunks were called *subroutines* and they were incorporated into assemblers as macros.

Among the strengths of Java is that it works with various makes and models of computers and software. If, in the longer run, the language proves to be *reliable* and *efficient,* then its clout may range beyond Internet's World Wide Web, becoming a tool for many applications. A plus for Java is that in 1995 it was seen as one of the hottest things in cyberspace.

■ More than 100,000 copies have been downloaded by software developers who try out the new language.

■ Thousands of applets have started to pop up on the World Wide Web, in a growing variety of applications.

Central to Java is the concept of *applets.* These are small applications and display programs linked directly to a Web page in the same way as static images and text are. Applets can be seen as flexible minipages. Each can be 1, 2, or 3 kbytes or more. The developer of the applet defines its size.

A negative about Java is the time it takes in networking. The WallStreetWeb, from Bulletproof, starts the page with a welcome. Then it says, "The WallStreetWeb Java applet is loading, this takes 60 seconds or more. Please wait...." These 60 seconds are an eon in interactive computing (more about that when we talk of network appliances in Sec. 8.6 of this chapter and in Chap. 10).

Java has its own browser, HotJava. It also works in conjunction with other browsers. This flexibility in association is a good design choice. Focusing on a Java applet, HotJava springs to life with

■ Animation

■ Sound effects

■ Dynamic displays of data

As expected, Sun Microsystems has developed a library of applets. There are as well applets, supported by HotJava, which reside at other Web sites and can be browsed. These include utilities, applets to spice up a page, for programmers only, collections of applets, Java-powered home pages, educational applets, games, and other diversions.

■ Examples of utilities are WebTap, HTML Sizer, HTML Verifier, Geographic Information Server, Prototype Shopping Environment, Option Pricer, and Commission Pricer.

■ Applets for Spice Up a Page include Magazine, Interactive Vector Graphics Display, Nervous Text, and New Improved Nervous Text.

■ Among educational applets notice A Simple Neural Network, Color Perception, Statistics, Interactive Simulation of Eddy, CMOS Gate Demonstration, Computer Graphics, and Fast Fourier Transform.

Eventually, Java will allow live data updates and direct two-way interaction, but this facility is not yet here. Another problem at present is that well-supported software libraries and applications routines that streamline a programmer's task, and make her or his work more productive, are still written for Java.

But the user community grows. A number of leading venues on the Internet, including c|net and Time Warner's Pathfinder—as well as competitor software developers such as Microsoft—now use Java applets. Some link to the wire services to display live news tickers running across the screen.

The general consensus in the communications, computer, and software industries is that Java applets will make working with the Web more interactive. They will ease the chore of downloading to the user's computer, where they process data transmitted from a Web server.

To its fans, Java is the programming language of networks. Or, to use Sun Microsystem's slogan, "The Network Is the Computer." "There is a paradigm shift every 10 to 15 years," says Marc Anderssen, a Web wizard, designer of Mosaic and cofounder of Netscape Communications. "And we're in one right now."[2]

Java is indeed a paradigm shift, but it is far from clear that it will bring an era of network appliances substituting today's personal computers with dull set-top boxes and game machines. For less than $1500 today, a user can buy a Windows or Macintosh PC that comes with loads of built-in software and hundreds of megabytes of storage and for a little more money can include a graphics processor MPEG1 or MPEG2. (We will return to this issue in Chap. 10, when we talk of desk-area networks.)

8.3 The Challenges of User-Friendliness and Security

Some of the cognizant people who have seen an early draft of this chapter commented that "it sounds like being anti-Java." This is not true. But a contrarian approach stimulates thinking. Therefore, the reader should welcome it.

In the long run, I believe, Java and similar structures will be driving the development of more flexible and interactive languages. Though it will be a while before users' software and hardware are able to reap the applets' benefits, this will prove increasingly important over the coming years as the novelty of Web surfing wears off, and users demand more than just static Web pages.

Java has attracted lots of attention because it enables programmers to create dynamic, interactive artifacts on the World Wide Web. But the language also has limitations: The more important being that it is not user-friendly, but is intended for expert programmers. The second major drawback concerns security.

To overcome the limitation of user-friendliness, a project at the Media Laboratory of MIT is creating *Cocoa*, as a Java-for-kids language. The goal is to permit everyone to generate dynamic, interactive artifacts without being an expert programmer.

Restructuring for user-friendliness is important if we view Internet as the new medium for construction of concepts and not only for communications purposes. Rapid-to-learn and easy-to-use programming languages will be necessary to develop new software tools enabling people to:

■ Share dynamic artifacts on the Internet

- Collaborate on modeling and design projects

The capabilities I am describing are not difficult to develop, but somebody must do the job of putting muscle to bare-bones Java. As it now stands, in spite of the fact that today it is a hot issue, the Java language is technically a *simple* C++ with no overloading. Its primitives present just one line of inheritance.

- This is a simplification that somehow had to come
- C++ has too many features and, therefore, is too complex

Also C and C++ have not been networking languages, while Java intends to be one. Some of the dressing which is necessary may come from other computer languages. For instance, in terms of network linguistics for remote clients, a Java+ could integrate HTML. And for more effective presentation services, it should combine Java with:

- Three-dimensional visualization and visibilization solutions, using VRML
- Knowledge engineering artifacts, using KQML.[3]

Finally, neither Java nor any other network computer language will strike gold until and unless it solves crucial security problems and, therefore, gives confidence to the user community. There are a number of people who think that Java is unsafe in its present form.

Reports of problems with Java's security have started coming out of university computer science labs. Problems on Web sites range from annoying to catastrophic, such as deleting crucial information from an end user's disk storage.[4] A growing number of researchers say that Java's defenses against *poison applets* are inadequate.

Some technology whiz kids now say that the theory behind Java is inherently risky; others believe the flaws are not in the theory but in the practice. "Java is not theoretically unsound," says Edward W. Felten of Princeton University, "but I think there is some reason for concern about whether one can build a system as big and complicated as Java without making mistakes that will compromise security. I personally run my browser with Java turned off most of the time."

8.4   Object Orientation, Database Pages, and the Use of Applets

Because the subject of what Java can and cannot offer to the Internet user community is complex, prior to examining its current and potential applications domains, we focus on its technical characteristics and what these mean for the end user.

Object programming is well suited for networking, where attached computers will function as multimedia communications devices rather than as more classical calculators and typewriters. (See also Chap. 11.) On the network, what the user needs to know most is information about an object.

Object orientation meshes well with interpretation because its origins can be found in *Simula,* the simulation language developed in 1968 at the University of Trondheim, under a grant from Univac. Interpretation is essentially a real-time simulation. We talk more about it in Sec. 8.5.

There may be problems with object orientation in an Internet environment due to the extreme diversity of files. This is true not only in regard to interconnected information providers, but as well of software suites which will be invariably used, and most likely will require bloatware to work together.

Some experts think bloatware will not be necessary because one major advantage of the Internet is that it is served by more than 100 TCP/IP protocols. But these protocols and their suite will not make miracles; nor should the transport of information elements be confused with the mining of distributed heterogeneous databases.[5]

Short of limiting Internet to personal computers with specified file formats under relational or object DBMS, the case will eventually arise where hierarchical and Codasyl files will have to be addressed interactively on-line. This will create major problems ranging from unacceptably long response time (an example is given in Sec. 8.2) to the use of significant resources at the database level and the associated costs.

IBM saw this problem coming and, during Comdex 1995, the Las Vegas event, tried to exploit it by espousing the concept of network appliances—with the added remark that the database work and much of the processing should be done at central locations by mainframes. Such "solution" means stumbling backward toward the future, and it will be surely unacceptable to the large majority of Internet users.

Quite contrary to what mainframers say, creating a new database concept with *applets* like the one implied by Java seems to be one of the opportunities for truly a distributed information system (DIS). Such opportunities do not come too often in information technology.

- The notion underpinning a DIS approach is far from novel.

- There is good reason to exploit as far as possible the capabilities provided by applets.

Let me, however, immediately add that applets will not be able to solve single-handedly the challenge of multimedia warehousing and visualization. The better way is to proceed by combining language strengths. In a January 1996 meeting in the Silicon Valley, in California, with Teknekron, I saw an interesting application of applets in which the company's own development language, TDL, meshed well with Java.

Teknekron uses a bridge between the two languages, where TDL objects are handed to Java for display. This can be instrumental in terms of faster performance, allowing transmission of only updates, not a full table of quotes where much of the information is repetitive. Such an approach is indeed efficient in terms of network utilization.

The use of pages first came to light in the late 1960s when IBM was working on the concept of *virtual memory*. Officially announced at the Bergen

Symposium of 1968, the notion of *paging* became one of the pillars of information technology in the following years:

- Paging was invented in the late 1960s to extend central storage into disks, because high-speed memory was then very expensive.

- In 1979, paging was reinvented and used with Prestel, the British interactive videotex system, following the seminal work by Dr. Sam Fedida of the British Post Office.

From storage to presentation, these references revolve on the notion of a *virtual machine* within a computer or a network. The fact that the fundamental notions date back to the 1960s and 1970s in no way diminishes the impact that Java, and its successors, may have on computing. But it is wise to recall that the underlying concepts are not new and only our goals have changed. A different way to look at this issue is to say that there are always advantages to be gained from studying what has happened in the past and trying to derive some useful lessons. If we don't learn from our successes and our failures, we will be condemned to repeat the same mistakes.

Based, then, on the three concepts of object orientation, paging, and interpretation (see Sec. 8.5), I look at Java as a computer language which caught the eye of the Internet user community, but has not yet been subjected to rigorous testing in a systems sense. The fact that it was designed for appliances and then converted for network computing is no proof of infallibility.

"Technically, everything becomes more organic," suggests Mark Pesce, who developed the Virtual Reality Modeling Language (VRML) discussed in Chap. 7. Technically, yes; but not yet politically—and when we talk of global networking, *politics is part of the system*. The giant hardware and software vendors have not yet had the last word, but they know that just as with VRML and HTML, millions of computers now have the Java virtual machines installed as part of Netscape's Web browser software and Sun's competing HotJava.

"Netscape's technology is not that scalable," said a major vendor in a recent meeting which addressed Internet, the Web, Java, and browsers. Then he added, "The company's projected server is not going to get wide user acceptance." We shall see.

In terms of technology, the Java virtual machine seems to be able to update itself automatically by calling over the network for the latest extensions, a fact which may permit new entrants to monopolize services. This poses challenges to the companies which during the past decades dominated the hardware and software industry worldwide. The easier way out for them is to adapt. But the management of change presupposes a painful conversion of cultures, which is not everybody's baby. It is easier to be negative than to be proactive.

8.5   Strengths and Weaknesses of an Interpreter

Interpretation is a process known since the 1950s, but it has been downplayed in favor of *compilation* because it absorbs computer power as a sponge does.

The low-cost but very powerful new generation of microprocessors have altered that perspective. However, it is wrong to combine interpretation with low-MIPS *network appliances,* as some vendors today contemplate.

An interpretive system resides in the machine, and it remains there through the solution of the problem. In this way, the code is never translated to the absolute machine language of the real hardware, but acts as a metalayer.

- Java's developers say that they have overcome the problem of machine and operating system (OS) heterogeneity through applying the process of interpretation.

- This may be true, but the interpretive process is very expensive in terms of processing cycles, reducing by so much the power available for end-user applications.

Precisely for this reason, in the late 1950s, when crucial decisions were made about computer programming solutions, compilers were chosen over interpreters. Figure 8.1 contrasts the two procedures; it also suggests that emulation and horizontal microcode can be alternatives to a pure interpreter, but the cost is still paid in CPU cycles.

My recollection is that the reason why in the 1950s—when crucial decisions were made in programming—compilation gained ground over interpretation was that the latter is very expensive in machine cycles. If we forget the lessons of the past, we will be condemned to repeat our mistakes.

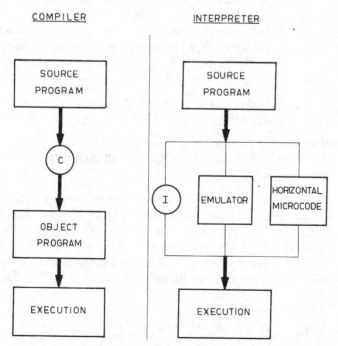

Figure 8.1 Compilation and interpretation are two different procedures.

- As its name implies, the interpreter translates, in real time, a program written for one type of computer to another heterogeneous piece of equipment. The original program might even have been written in machine language.

- By contrast, a compiler translates a higher-level language code into machine language. Compilation usually happens off-line, but this does not exclude run-time compilation.

Other things being equal, interpretation is much more elegant than compilation, because the process is flexible and it has to be executed in run time. An example from the mid-1950s is the Internal Translator, which we discuss in the following paragraphs. Another example of the preference for interpretation over compilation, from that same time frame, is the run-time interpreter of the Bendix computer.

Over the long time frame of four decades, however, the interpretation process was shunted aside because it was too expensive in CPU cycles. Its overhead added to that of the operating system, database management system, and transaction processing routines.

Technological advancements, however, may make designers less thrifty in CPU cycles. With desk-area networks (DANs), which we discuss in Sec. 8.6, this concern over cycles may change. If n microprocessors are dedicated to one user, then one, two, or more processors can be earmarked to work as interpreters.

A different way to look at this issue is that, at the current state of the art, Java's process of interpretation, because it slows down execution, has to be tested against the target market. There is a penalty to be paid in performance, which many Java enthusiasts forget.

The penalty associated with interpretation is lower as the efficiency of the interpreter increases. Based on my 47 years of experiences with computers, I believe interpretation will reduce computer power by an order of magnitude or more.*

- A Pentium chip with about 200 million instructions per second (MIPS) will perform at less than 20 MIPS.

- This is still lots of power, nearly 20 times that of an IBM 370/145 mainframe of the early 1970s, but not enough for the complex uses to which PCs are being put these days.

To my knowledge, the most efficient interpreter ever written was IBM's Print 1. It was developed in the mid-1950s, and its purpose was to make an IBM 401 scientific computer look as if it were a 501 business machine. In so doing, it reduced the 401 power by a factor of 10.

Also in the mid-1950s, another of the famous interpreters of the old age of computing was the Internal Translator (IT), written by Dr. Alan Perlis of

---

*Sun says interpretation will reduce machine power "only" by 30 percent or so—a statement which technically is senseless applet by applet but might stand on a total job stream if only a few applets are executed.

Carnegie Institute of Technology. Dr. Jim Bachus used the IT when he developed Fortran. In fact, the original name of the first scientific higher-level language on record was *Fortransit* (For-Trans-IT), which some people had nicknamed "for transit."

- The "for transit" concept is important with Java because Sun's language does not have a straight interpreter but uses intermediate code.

- This makes it more flexible in keeping its design dynamic but also creates a number of problems in terms of cycles and, eventually, implementation.

There are, for instance, integration problems. Because Java is a garbage-collecting environment, the system goes idle for a while as cycle stealing takes place on the chip of the PC. Garbage collection has also the problem of destroying memory contents unintentionally.

To overcome machine idleness problems, some vendors now work on a Java architecture which may be able to avoid this problem by means of multiple chips. This is exactly the opposite of what the advocates of network appliances say. Alternatively, this means that most vendors are building their own Java versions which, as expected, will be incompatible with one another.

A further problem that some vendors are addressing comes from the fact that Java is not that easy to employ if the programmer is the end user. The better interface, in this connection, is through applets. If the user has a battery of applets, then Java programming can be easier, but some of the system's flexibility is lost.

Because the reference unit of an applet is what its developer makes it, the developer must have some experience in computer programming. She or he needs such experience to

- Optimize the applet size
- Put its content into packets
- Normalize its behavior

This argument of optimization of applet size and behavior can be taken still further. Java is no free lunch, as some people have suggested. The value to be derived from any interactive programming system largely rests on a few key factors:

- Dynamic content for pages
- The ability to deliver them quickly
- On-line facilities to change them quickly

All three factors are very crucial in adding value for reasons of competitiveness and differentiation. This means not only developing new applications but also taking existing applications and moving them into a network. This is a job to be done in a flexible, interactive manner while always keeping in mind the cost associated with interpretation.

8.6   Network Appliances and Desk-Area Networks*

An *appliance* can be a facsimile machine, a car, a handheld device, a television set, a refrigerator, or some other gadgets. The sense of an appliance is that it is *simple* and *specialized*. It can do just one job. That's why what some vendors say about "network appliances" is a deception.

- The fact that Java was originally developed to get microprocessors inside consumer appliances to talk to one another does not mean it should be used only with appliances.

- Instead, a much more ingenious use is with desk-area networks (DANs), that is, networks at and around the end user's workplace.

As we will see in Part 4, an excellent example of a DAN is the *ViewStation* developed by the Massachusetts Institute of Technology. The MIT approach has the advantage of being more flexible. It permits one to integrate current machines and software with those already in place.

Another example is MANNA, the desk-area network by GMD-FIRST, the German government's research laboratory in Berlin. This laboratory has also designed an operating system to run effectively many microprocessors at the service of the same user, regardless of whether these chips are specialized or address the same job.

Not only is this fiat of chips very useful on its own merits, because it represents polyvalent resources dedicated to one user, but also it renders important services while operating on-line. The sophistication of what can be done through desk-area networks cannot possibly be matched by present-day workstations, let alone dumb $500 machines.

Contrary to a mainframe which uses one microprocessor for, say, 500 users, and to a PC, where each machine has one microprocessor or nearly so, a DAN has a two-digit number of microprocessors per end user. For instance, MANNA features 32 chips. Therefore, two key advantages that a DAN offers in connection to Java are that

- It eases the pressure on the cycles that a microprocessor must provide.

- It can allocate one or more microprocessor fully to Java interpreter(s) which absorb cycles as a sponge.

As we have already seen, because Java is based on the process of real-time interpretation, its programs run more slowly than those written in conventional languages. Other things being equal, it needs more powerful processors than a PC, rather than what low-cost network appliances offer. Hence, desk-area networks may be a good bet.

---

*This section is a snapshot presentation. A much more detailed discussion can be found in Chap. 10.

Also, Java is object-oriented; and, as we will see in Chap. 11, while object solutions have many advantages, they also have prerequisites. For instance, the power of objects is best exploited when they reside in main memory rather than an auxiliary storage.

One of the Java applets for engineering measurements provides a good example of what I mean.* It is connected to eddy-current-sensor simulation, and given the proper processor and main memory, it provides an attractive implementation of the image loop.

- The procedure is one class loading one image.

- Time depends on the size of the images.

The applet is fully resizable when shown with external views. The demonstration was made at CeBit '96, the Hannover, Germany, event, as part of simulation of sensors using Internet. The artifact made the applet pages look pretty; but as always, response time is a problem.

When Arthur van Hoff, of Sun Microsystems, wrote the Java interpreter, he provided an imaginative solution which, however, is power-hungry. (See also Sec. 8.10 on virtual machines.) All applications should account for this fact, rather than promoting cycle stealing, which works to the detriment of the application and the end user.

- As far as serious computer use is concerned, it is technically insane to talk of Java and network appliances at the same time.

- Vendors who think they can pull the leg of the user community by distorting technical facts will find that their customers desert them.

It is at the same time proper to suggest that the platform strategy Xerox PARC invented, and on which has been based most of the workstation and PC technology, has reached its logical conclusion. This came in the form of the card-slotted PC industry and of the Windows OS.

The next wave is the DAN implementation with its concept of a network operating system. This must be tuned to provide computing resources and database mining on a global basis. As the World Wide Web demonstrates, solutions have to be found totally independent of the hardware platform and without requiring expensive kinds of conversions.

Historically, hardware-dependent approaches and expensive transpositions have slowed progress and made system solutions so much more complex. Any product that requires the average application to be changed is a bad one. Users do not like to have to alter their software, and in some cases they may not even be able to afford to do so. We must always remember that there is a huge installed base in applications software which should not be upset.

---

*It can be retrieved on Internet: *www.javasoft.com* or *www.netscape.com*. The Eddy Current Simulator was developed at the University of Kassel, Germany.

8.7 IPv6, New Standard Protocols, Videotex, and Page Formats

Even if the component parts of what seems to be a new solution have existed for a number of years, the way in which they are combined makes a lot of difference in the market's reaction to the product. Not only should the offering be sound and able to create market enthusiasm, but also it should sustain itself in the market's mind. "If the headline is bigger, it makes the news bigger," W. R. Hearst once said.

To ensure that their marketing efforts are successful, the sponsors of JavaScript, VB Script, Cyberdog, Lotus Script, and other entities should be willing and able to learn a lesson from the Internet itself. In terms of eye-catching technical headlines, what makes the Net so powerful is its strict use of *standardized protocols*.

- Standardized protocols let all computers participate in a collaborative service.

- Normalization and standardization amplify the power of an open network solution.

In their way, Internet's de facto standards resemble the role IBM played in the 1960s and 1970s, as well as that of Microsoft from the mid-1980s until today. The keyword is *general acceptance*. But general acceptance is a chimera when there are so many incompatible scripts in a row.

Before, however, we look into programming and paging formats, let's examine the evolution of TCP/IP itself. Will general acceptance characterize the next generation of Internet protocol, IP Version 6? The reader must be aware that IPv6 is designed to run on both these networks:

- High-performance networks, such as asynchronous transfer mode (ATM)

- Low-bandwidth networks, including wireless

The opportunities presented by IPv6 will come from its ability to become a de facto standard. But this concept of standard protocols conflicts with the business interests of software and hardware vendors. As experience since the early 1950s helps document, the different versions of Unix served much more the vendors' interests than the users'. (Let's keep this idea in mind when, in Sec. 8.8, we talk of a growing number of languages and browsers on Internet.)

The question has been posed on a couple of occasions of what may be the advantage of IPv6 in connection with visual programming. The answer is support for *visualization bandwidth*. Database bandwidth and processing bandwidth are significantly increasing. So do the requirements for visualization and visibilization, because greater bandwidth helps in human-machine communication.

The original IP was a great protocol, but it is nearly 30 years old. It no longer meets current needs. IPv6 is designed to work with the asynchronous transfer mode, which is expected to dominate the late 1990s and beyond the year 2000.

The question is, Will vendors and telecommunications companies be eager to adopt a standard IPv6 version?

- TCP/IP gained general acceptance because it was sponsored by the Department of Defense (DoD).

- IPv6 seems to be a good protocol, but will DoD stand behind it? If not, who will have the might to do so in a diffuse user community?

A similar query can be made about other premises advanced by experts in connection with Internet. For instance, will software companies no longer have to create unique versions of their products for machines running different, incompatible operating systems? The theory may be good, but in practice this is hype.

Just assume for a moment that standard protocols will be a feasible proposition—from programming to database, networking, and human interfaces. This would bring the liberation of users and their software applications from hardware platforms: "Write once, run anywhere." But is it realistic?

The problem with "Write once, run anywhere" is no different from that of another swiping generalization, "One data entry, many uses," as well as the repeated claims by this or that vendor that he or she offers "a natural programming language." Theoretically, all these ideas are excellent. But practically, vendors cannot deliver what they promise. (See also in Sec. 8.8 the reference to the failed UNCOL and MIA projects.) In my years of computer experience I have heard such arguments so often that I have become immune to them.

Also to be found is a fair amount of misinformation and misorientation. In mid-1995 I looked at companies said to be cognizant on Java to understand how it evolves, how it works, and what it might or might not reach in terms of deliverables. The issues topping the list in this research have been

- How the concept of the virtual machine is being used

- How applets should be developed and used, from cradle to grave

- What's the best facility of handling some form of page-level programming

Critical to all three questions was to define, in a factual and documented manner, what can be done with an applet. For instance, the user can download a page. The applet does the viewing job for the user, but this presupposes that

- The user knows how to structure applets.

- She has the data she needs to download.

- She can download information through the network.

Subsequent research has demonstrated that some of the first users of applets were badly misinformed. Some thought that the most applets could do is to play Tic-Tac-Toe on a network. Others felt that the applet concept is still at a rather primitive stage of development. Still others stated that the size of applets is frozen. Three common misconceptions are

- Applets are 64 kbytes—no less, no more.
- Applets are oriented to the mass market.
- Their use is not recommended for professionals.

All three statements are wrong. As we have seen, applets are the size that their developers make them. And applets are sophisticated enough for professional use—even if professional requirements are an order of magnitude more rigorous than those for the mass market. At the same time it is no less true that while there is potential in Java's applets, it will take much more work than what the current release offers to make it a first-class system.

The contribution that applets can make in altering current programming concepts has not yet been approached in any meaningful manner. In my judgment, not only is a further-out system solution missing, but also

- The applet today is a passive object.
- It cannot work on itself, hence its value is rather limited.

To take a lesson from the videotex experience, the way the applet currently stands is something like a videotex page and its *filials* (*sons* in Java jargon). As videotex demonstrates, passive pages become obsolete very quickly, which indeed also happens with many of the databases hooked onto the Internet.

With few exceptions, the page format of applets seems to be too limited for moving computation beyond conventional sites and vanilla ice cream procedures. In terms of *real innovation,* I have in mind MIT's new research project "Things That Think" and its goals:

- Explore ways for moving computation beyond conventional sites
- Develop agents able to sense the movements or feelings of their owners
- Lead to changes in everyday life and the way we work

Videotex-type pages and formats, adopted by Java, are unfit to explore designs associated with thinking objects. Our goal should be smarter instrumentation—from flexible manufacturing to polyvalent services in banking—not reinventing the past. The new generation of computer artifacts will not necessarily fit into kilobit containers or other types of strait jackets, but applets can be useful in limited jobs.

8.8   The Growing Number of Languages and Browsers on the Internet

Dominant companies in computers, communications, and software know well that technology permits them to raise roadblocks while officially stating exactly the inverse—that what they are after is to develop a better product. As we will see in this section, it will be neither the first nor the last time that some vendors use the red herring strategy.

Nor should we forget that there is a difference between intended functionality and currently available services. There is as well a growing amount of heterogeneity on the horizon as companies with a long tradition of proprietary solutions are forced to enter into product competition on Internet's open landscape—so as not to be left out in the cold.

As Java spreads across the computers and communications devices, some 30 companies are said to have signed up for *JavaScript*. This is a programming artifact used by several brands of commodity software on the Internet, including Netscape, to create Java's applets.

- The current version of JavaScript is being distributed to developers over the Internet, at no cost.

- JavaScript will be included in the next release of Netscape's Web browser as well as other off-the-shelf routines.

But to the trained eye with experience in successes and failures which during the past four decades have characterized software for computers and communications, much of the euphoria about Java, HotJava, JavaScript, and other recent constructs seems exaggerated. Remember Taligent and Magic Cap in 1994? Overstatements are indivisible from the dawning of a new era, but they should not be confused with reality.

This exaggeration becomes hype when network appliances take center stage. Optimists think that programming languages such as Java may make it possible to cruise the Net without a personal computer. Others say that users will do so with a PC but without Microsoft software. Still others curse Microsoft because it did not jump on the Internet. (Recently, however, it converted its Visual Basic, a language now used by some 3 million programmers, to create Windows applications.)

At a 1996 working meeting in Silicon Valley, CA, in which I participated, Java was characterized as the next generation of Basic. All the user needs, it was said, is the interpreter running on his or her machine, since the interpreter is the key component sustaining the virtual environment. One of the participants suggested that

- The Web turned Internet into a virtual disk drive.

- Java changed the virtual disk drive into a virtual computer.

Another person said that he sees the applet as a diskless artifact. Then he quickly added that, contrary to what many people think, Java does not have access to anything in the environment. To get access, the user has to go through the object's class library.

One of the interesting aspects of this discussion is that in the opinion of several specialists present at this and other meetings, Java and applets can have other users than Internet. For instance, private and semipublic networks today are being managed by a database administrator (DBA). Tomorrow they may be run through Java.

This notion of substituting applets for the DBA is interesting, but not that clear. What is much more likely is that not just Java but every artifact running on Internet, including the World Wide Web, may well find its way into enterprise networks—the Intranets. WWW structures are not necessarily limited to the Internet landscape, even if this has been their first home.

In this sense, Microsoft should not have delayed using Internet as the information infrastructure of a global laboratory. Bill Gates seems to have rapidly appreciated the damage caused by the delay, and a transition is currently taking place.

Based on Visual Basic, *VB Script* contemplates moving programmers to the World Wide Web. And Microsoft's Object Linking and Embedding (OLE) technology is being adapted to let software objects communicate over Internet to create Java-like applets.

- Proprietary authoring tools originally designed to create multimedia content for the Microsoft Network are as well being recast for the Web.

- As the popularity of the Internet increases, it is sure that neither Java nor VB Script and Blackbird, renamed Active X, with all their merits and demerits, will be alone on the Net.

Other companies, too, which have been late in joining the Internet bandwagon are now trying to catch up. Apple Computer launched *Cyberdog*. Apple says Cyberdog will make Net surfing much easier. Some specialists suggest that this piece of software is Apple's last chance to make an impact on the Internet.

Based on the IBM-Apple OpenDoc software standard, which so far has had no particular business success, Cyberdog is an artifact competitive with Java. Apple promises to make software modules work together *as if* they were part of one and the same application. This is another kind of hype, similar to the promises made by Taligent about object frameworks, or by IBM in connection with the first incarnation of its Repository.

The original Repository was based on the idea of *decompiling*. Decompiling is a claim which surfaces time and again in computer technology—even if there is evidence that the task of decompiling is not doable in any practical, sustainable sense. One proof of what I am saying is UNCOL, a priority project by IBM in 1958 which led nowhere.[6]

Apple claims that the solutions which it will bring to the market will make it feasible to add Internet links to existing applications which were not written for WWW. This will supposedly be done without necessarily decompiling. Such a claim, too, is not destined to be successful, as documented by the failure of the Multimanufacturer Integration Architecture (MIA) by NTT, Fujitsu, Hitachi, IBM, and DEC.[7]

IBM is working on its own Web-executable language, a combination of a new programming scheme called *Bart* and *LotusScript*. LotusScript is the development software that the mainframer will ship with an upcoming release of Notes. For its part, Netscape will bundle Java into the next release of its Navigator browser, but will also promote *LiveScript,* its own language based on Java.

Statistics on current users of the Internet can tell a story about which way the chips might fall. Published information shows that 38 percent of all Internet connections were from Microsoft Windows clients, 31 percent from XWindows (therefore Unix), 20 percent from Macintoshes, and 21 percent from all other types of clients. At least 58 percent of requests originated from personal computers.[8]

In conclusion, any vendor afraid of being left behind in the Internet race comes up with a new script and hopes that developers and end users will build their own custom modules by using its language and associated supports. But given the diversity in hardware and software, cognizant people in the Internet market are not so sure of a scenario where "this" or "that" brand will dominate. Only time—and the user community—will tell.

8.9 Marketing Savvy, Open Networks, and Competitive Edges

As far as one can tell this early in Java's public life, a competitive advantage of the new language lies in the fact that programs written in Java could run on many digital devices, from computers to machine tools, automobiles, power meters, TV set-top boxes, burglar alarms, and different home appliances.

In 1993, General Magic had made more or less a similar statement in connection with its operating system—that it could be everything to everybody. Lots of companies, including AT&T and some Japanese firms, flocked to the virtual engine concept which was advanced, but nothing has happened since then. Why did the Magic Cap fail? I asked this question at the Silicon Valley, CA, meetings, and here are the answers I got:

- Its technology was not mature.
- The product was difficult to use.
- The product had a lot of rough edges.
- Sales did not focus correctly on the market.

We shall see in the coming couple of years if Java's forecasts materialize and to what extent. Today, however, the product is too generalized. It does not focus. Financial applications can profit from applets, but neither Sun nor other vendors seem geared to exploit that track.

A new product has a much greater chance of capturing the market, and of becoming a cash cow, if it is focused, efficient, flexible, and offered at reasonable cost. This is not true just of software but of any commodity. We have, however, to guard ourselves against a vicious cycle:

- Efficiency sometimes brings success.

- Success usually brings growth.
- Quite often growth results in inefficiency.

This has happened with IBM and its mainframes. This may also happen with the Internet, and in Sec. 8.8 we saw some reasons. Java, its clones, and its applets are not immune to the cycle of growth and decay which, in some cases, is fast.

If Java fails, it will be a pity, because people who have had experience with it say that it is a very compact language and gives a rather robust code. It permits one to define interfaces and provides facilities for change in clauses. Hence, it has flexibility. Some experts suggest that Java may be replacing C++ as a programming system because it works at higher level, has simpler compilers, and assembles to machine language. They also point out that Java applications tend to have half the bugs of a C++ program. But most people with Java programming experience refute the argument that it does or will replace C++. They do, however, point out that, as of today, in terms of programming groups' traffic on the Internet, it is about equal among Java, C++, and Visual Basic. While currently the market is leaning toward Java, there is a widespread opinion that 1996 and 1997 will be critical years for the success of this language. Much will depend on how fast Sun and other vendors can come up with a focused, comprehensive marketing program—and whether they deliver a real-time compiler.

Another factor which will influence success or failure is the cultural change on the users' part. A change in concepts and procedures can present interesting opportunities to revamp the bank-client relationship that should exist in software development. Another cornerstone to marketing success is proved security, an argument which is just as valid for any form of networking.

Still another factor in success is the steady delivery of third-party software. "The value of the military lies in its continuing ability to deliver," said George Marshall. Will JavaScript, VB Script, Cyberdog, LotusScript, and the other offerings be able to deliver and to continue delivering? The answer is less than sure because a sprawling network tends to be chaotic.

Some of the prevailing unknowns are the result of the heterogeneity which is bound to reign on an *open-network* environment like the Internet. As Fig. 8.2 suggests, the network is the computer, and it should be programmed interactively. Judging from original intentions, no Java program will really reach all parts of the target computer. Therefore,

- The vendor assures the users that Java will not unleash viruses to infect their systems.
- But nobody can really be sure of this, as applications continue to evolve.

The power of Internet comes exactly from its open-network features and from the associated stream of steady evolution. Internal translation can help to make Java's promises come true. The question of cycles left aside, there is significant potential in this solution of a computer within a computer. However,

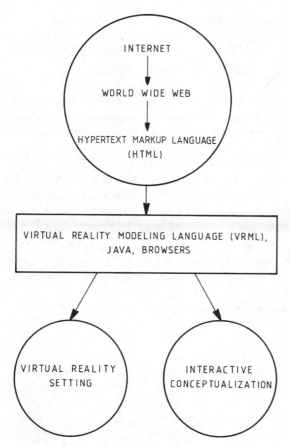

Figure 8.2 The network is the computer, and it should be programmed interactively.

- *If* security is not iron-clad and viruses or tampering starts to spread or hackers have a ball

- *Then* this may be the end not just of Java, and similar interpretive schemes, but of the concept of an unregulated Internet as well.

From mainframers and software manufacturers to state regulators, there are a lot of people waiting to punch a hole in the notion of open networking, and of an open society as such, as defined by Dr. Karl Popper. This is another aspect of the political issues involved in systems solutions, introduced in Secs. 8.2 and 8.4.

Assuming that security will not be a problem, and that microprocessor technology will provide the necessary increase in power at zero cost, interpretation presents technical advantages which must be rigorously studied. A factual and documented answer is needed to the query, How far can the chosen approach permit otherwise incompatible computers to use the same Java software?

At the current release, this is limited to the applets stored within pages on Internet's WWW. Users, the vendors say, will be able to purchase or rent software routines for specific tasks as they need them, whether these objects are intended for a one-time use only or for many uses.

The idea is that by distributing bits of fresh Java code across the Web, one could automatically and instantly bring new capabilities to millions of computers and their users. An interpreter's ability to hide incompatibilities prevailing in the community of users could rewrite the rules of the software industry, the pros suggest. We shall see.

Finally, as with any other product, a great deal of the success of Java will depend on marketing wizardry. Netscape captured 70 percent of the market for WWW browsers by giving away its software. Sun Microsystems followed the same initially profitless approach, informing Internet users that Java is for free.

This strategy is familiar to Sun, since in the early 1980s it promoted the growth of Internet itself by shipping free Internet Protocol (IP) software with every Sun computer. But in that case its profits came from the sale of its workstations, while now margins will be very slim with the network appliances it promotes.

It goes without saying that in the end the company expects its initially profitless approach to turn a profit. Anything that increases Internet traffic is bound to add to Sun's bottom line at the hardware end. But how successfully will Sun Microsystems market Java in the years to come?

Eric Schmidt, Sun's chief technical specialist, got results as Java's top marketer. His successor, however, is a former IBM employee. Quite independently of what assets Alan E. Baratz has, and no doubt he was chosen because he is knowledgeable and active, IBM is the wrong training ground for a new software product which must move very fast in the market at rock bottom cost in order to survive. Just look at Taligent. (See also Chap. 12.)

8.10 The Business Opportunity of a Virtual Machine in the 1990s

Folklore has it that once a computer is equipped with Java client software, it can run any Java application that comes across the network on a hyperlink. What's more, it can do so independently of its manufacturer and the operating system under which it runs. Like any generalization, this statement is hype rather than substance.

But there are also merits in the concept underpinning the Java approach. As contrasted to the software dinosaurs of mainframes, small Java programs may hit the PC the way E-mail does. If these small routines are flexible in size and format—and proactive rather than passive—their existence will be consistent with the fact that Java and its likes aim to turn the Internet into a parallel processor.

- The underlying concept is that of a flexible virtual machine.

- Its software will let any computer simulate an engine standardized by the interpreter.

As far as any Java-type program knows, the simulation is the genuine article: It is a computer with processor, monitor, memory, and disk drive. The virtual machine executes small modular routines by interpreting their commands, guiding the real computer to perform all the tasks needed to execute them.

Small page size has a virtue. If the virtual machine program is contained to a one- or two-digit number of kilobytes, it may eventually get used in cellular phones, camcorders, TV sets, automobiles, refrigerators, and other appliances. Lots of equipment which is today enriched with microprocessors would have enough storage to hold and run the applets that come its way.

This, however, is a generalization. Sun Microsystems, Microsoft, Oracle, Apple, IBM, and other Java sponsors must make up their mind about their market goals. Artifacts that target all market segments at the same time end up nowhere. Focus will permit one to

- Taylor Java to the targeted applications.
- Remove the rough edges which exist.
- Add functionality without an inordinate amount of cost or complexity.

The first basic decision is, For whom are these artifacts made? Are they for the professional user market, in which case they must be sophisticated, flexible, and dynamic; or for the mass market and kids games? Therefore, they can be simple but also offered at a very low price.

- *If* the target of the projected virtual engines is the professionals and not the mass market, *then* the offering should rather be designed around the concept of high-level basic software.

Applications such as concurrent engineering and 24-hour banking, or others of a work group nature, will need their own software developers who must be able to easily extend the basic networking routines offered by the vendor.

After the market goals of the virtual machine, 1990s version, have been set, a lot of technical questions must be answered. For instance, will there be an integration of Java and the Virtual Reality Modeling Language, as we saw in Chap. 7? How will the professional user be able to describe a three-dimensional scene's important elements, and how will she or he download them? How will a VRML file be called, in a networkwide sense, and manipulated through applets?

Efficient on-line network access and transport mechanisms require good compatibility and high modularity. Both are necessary to empower a wave of end users who, individually, may be great professionals in other fields but in software terms will be small developers. Let's also keep in mind that the better the solutions provided for professionals, the more they will open the gates of a global communications and computers in the coming years.

References

1. *Scientific American,* November 1995.
2. *Time,* January 22, 1996.

3. See D. N. Chorafas, *Agent Technology for Communication Networks,* McGraw-Hill, New York, 1997.
4. David L. Wilson, "Experts Differ on Security Threat Posed by Java Computer Language," *The Chronicle of Higher Education,* July 12, 1996.
5. D. N. Chorafas and H. Steinmann, *Database Mining,* Lafferty, London, 1994.
6. See D. N. Chorafas, *Programming Systems for Electronic Computers,* Butterworth, London, 1962.
7. See D. N. Chorafas and H. Steinmann, *Solutions for Heterogeneous Databases,* Academic Press, San Diego, CA, 1993.
8. Thomas T. Kwan, Robert E. McGrath, and Daniel A. Reed, "NCSA's World Wide Web Server: Design and Performance," *Computer,* IEEE, 0018-9162/95.

9

Other than Internet Programming Tools for Visualization

9.1 Introduction

The tools which are necessary for virtual reality and visual programming must not only respond to current requirements but also be able to cover a widening range of applications. Any approach limited to the visualization of current, classical programming chores will be ineffectual and incomplete.

Contrary to programming, virtual reality technology allows users on a network to meet and interact in computer-simulated environments.[1] This can nicely lead to concurrent program development. Therefore, a legitimate question is, Are the tools at our disposal able to serve in a concurrent programming sense?

Many experts who follow engineering technology today are convinced that in just a few years, cyberspace applications will be a key element in the design process. And those who think that it is a mistake to include examples of animation in the visual programming frame of reference, because "they have few, if any, characteristics of computer coding" are wrong.

Although it is still early to have a documented opinion on how great an impact immersive virtual reality (VR) will have in programming, eventually the impact will probably be major. We are not yet there, but we should not forget about this possibility.

Furthermore, immersion is just one of the alternatives—it does not monopolize the VR field. But clearly as technology develops, it will impact current coding practices.

- Visual programming and VR immersion will prove to have common elements, as it is being appreciated that both involve the user's interactivity and interaction with the graphical images.

- The added value comes from the fact that both in interactive programming and in an immersive environment, the user is not just viewing on a display screen but becomes part of it.

On-line interactivity and immersion in computer code are, however, complex and their able handling requires some of the most exciting advances in computer technology over the last few years. Though significant developments are taking place in programming tools, as this chapter will show, we are not yet at an immersive state—but we might reach it.

The reference to currently available *tools* is in the plural. The fact is that both software developers and end users now want more choices, even if more than 80 percent of the programming effort comes from 20 percent or less of the programming platforms available at any time.

9.2   Idealized Processes and Sophisticated Requirements Handling

Virtual reality provides techniques for an intuitive presentation and manipulation of *massive data* as well as of idealized descriptions of states and processes which reflect the physical and logical worlds. As we have seen through a number of practical examples, a basic demand of modern software is that execution be done in *real time,* including

- The evaluation of the computation model under development
- The provision of a visual continuity to human perception
- The subsequent execution routines in a productive, conversational manner

Any mathematical model is based on abstraction and on hypotheses. We may err on both counts. The abstraction might be too coarse, and one or more of our hypotheses might be wrong. Testing is an integral part of model development.

Testing is also an integral part of model usage—a fact that has begun to be generally appreciated. In January 1996, the Basle Committee of Banking Supervision of the G-10 countries published the Market Risk Amendment, which follows the line of the Federal Reserve and promotes marking-to-model of a bank's trading book. It also specifies *backtesting* throughout the life cycle of the model.

In connection with the second and third requirements, real time is obtained by an image refresh rate of at least 15 images per second for visual presentation and an 8-kHz sample rate for auditive presentation.

As experience is acquired with interactive mathematical and procedural models, and given that the demands posed in their regard are expanding, it is no longer sufficient to think of simulation as just a computational paradigm. We must incorporate into the solution the possibility of generating and controlling *virtual worlds,* and of improving *rendering* and *motion.*

Interactive possibilities must be provided for any graphical environment, motion and depth of field must be effectively handled, development must account for invisible surfaces casting shadows as well as live action, and reflection maps must be developed. Other rendering issues include spotlights with softness controls, antialiased vectors with highlights, different stochastic and filtering algorithms, and other high-performance requirements.

As far as motion is concerned, the development tool should permit inverse kinematics, synchronization of motion to sound track, real-time gesture motion input, and path animation. Objects will be pointing at other objects. Developers and users must be able to view and render from lights, and a flexible, dynamic view projection is a must.

Visual programming and subsequent program visualization must be able to convey multiple sensory information—not only visual but also sound or touch— to make environments truly realistic. This has to be done interactively, as underlined in every case where such references have come up.

Chrysler is developing a VR implementation on car design projects and expects that the exercise could cut a big chunk off the 3- to 5-year car design process. It will do so by permitting engineers to spot inconveniently positioned technical and end-user problems, before they surface in expensive prototypes.

Because both visual programming and virtual reality have so much to do with the ability to think and react in real time, success will depend on not only improvements in the classical sense of software development tools but also the ability to gain new insights into human behavior. As artificial systems become more *real,* they will pose thorny technical questions which, in turn, require further departures from the leisurely legacy programs of the past.

Chances are that these departures will significantly affect a number of professional fields. Tracking the performance of financial assets against the larger market is a challenge for analysts, who must follow hundreds of ever-changing numbers. Traditional financial research never did this job in a meaningful sense.

Nontraditional financial research has established that it is much more effective, in terms of interactive presentation, to convert the numbers to a three-dimensional schematic of colored icons. This permits one to effectively symbolize individual stocks or bonds, and their values, within grids representing financial markets and industry sectors. Such solutions, however, require steady, seamless access to distributed heterogeneous databases and must also draw on real-time feeds from financial wires. We talk about seamless access to databases by the end of this chapter.

The early experience with visual programming helps as well to document that, in terms of applications development, it is much more effective if the end user can easily remodel the developing construct in a way that prompts him best. In the years to come, we will hear a great deal about *program customization.*

Software customization solutions go well beyond the visual perspective. They involve fine-tuning of the sensory and psychological factors in a way similar to that which makes a VR world "real." This is a major technical challenge in itself, and it can be a major contributor to improving the user's ability to absorb information.

Satisfying all these requirements is, evidently, a taxing business. Solutions must place emphasis on the presentation of logical worlds and the interaction with their virtual features which are an essential dimension of the representation. Let's keep this in mind when, in the following sections, we speak of specific visual programming tools.

9.3 Critical Components of an Interactive Three-Dimensional Visualization through PV-Wave

The able, interactive representation of simulation results addresses the human senses. The most exploited today, and during the last 40 years, is the visual sense whether through tabular presentation or graphics. However, as several applications have demonstrated, the presentation dimension becomes more sophisticated when it is characterized by

- Multimedia, with coordination of visualization, sound, and other channels
- Dynamic visualization techniques
- Event sequences executed in real time

Exploited through virtual reality, multiple sensory and other channels lead to presentations which promote the sensation of "being there." This goes well beyond the old interactive approaches where passive computer graphics dominated. But three-dimensional computer graphics will have a great deal to offer if they address three areas of interest simultaneously—not just the output.

We spoke about this fact in Chap. 8. The concept and procedure are considered in greater detail in this chapter, in conjunction with non-Internet visual programming tools. As a memory refresher, the three areas to which reference has been made regarding the need for interactive handling are

1. On-line data acquisition
2. Analysis and simulation
3. Interactive visualization

They should be preferably executed in real time and in a parallel mode rather than serially. Also, sophisticated applications will typically take place in multiprocessing environments: While each user works on his or her personal workstation, in a share-nothing mode,* the servers will support many users.

Table 9.1 presents further details on the aforementioned classification and includes different programming tools, each with its specific contribution. In Table 9.1, 1 denotes the function which the shell serves best while 3 denotes the least developed of the three key functionalities. The rightmost column is informative and refers to visual programming facilities. A better explanation of the programming support connected with each tool is given in Table 9.2, developed

---

*Typically in a client-server setting.

TABLE 9.1   How Different Commodity Shells Answer the Visual Programming Needs

Product	On-line data acquisition	Analysis and simulation	Interactive visualization	Comments
PV-Wave	1	3	2	Assembling to a Basic-type language (not to be confused with Visual Basic)
Interactive Data Language (IDL)	1	3	2	Like PV-Wave
MatLab	3	1	2	Assembly to C
Mathematica	3	1	2	Assembly to C
Application Visualization System (AVS)	2	3	1	Object-oriented, could run on parallel processors
Power Visualization System (PVS)	2	3	1	Like AVS

in collaboration with Dr. B. Pedrazzini of Eurodis Technology, Regensdorf, Switzerland.

Designed by Precision Visuals and currently sold by Visual Numerics, *PV-Wave* has been strong in analyzing the data flow. Visualization is second of its competitive advantages. A similar statement is valid in regard to *IDL,* which has the same origin as PV-Wave (at the University of Colorado) and so far has been implemented in connection with research and development projects.

The block diagram in Fig. 9.1 shows the work flow in PV-Wave applications. It starts with data access both from databases and from data feeds from information providers.

■ The original release was sequential and involved four steps prior to presentation.

■ The new release permits one to bypass the transformation step; also, if necessary, the data analysis.

In contrast to PV-Wave and IDL, both *MatLab* and *Mathematica* are strong in the analysis and simulation domain (graded as number 1), with visualization the second competitive advantage. This is reasonable if we consider that their wider implementation has been for some time in the domain of vector and matrix analysis operations. In fact, the name *MatLab* is an acronym of *Matrix Laboratory.**

All four shells considered so far offer interactive numerical computations with graphical capabilities. As such, they have applications in many areas of science, engineering, and business, from physics, applied mathematics, control theory, and machine design to finance.

---

*Connected to the development of Linpack and Eispack, Fortran packages of matrix computations.

TABLE 9.2 Vendors, Product Characteristics, and Programming Support

Product	Vendor	On-line data acquisition	Analysis and simulation	Interactive visualization	Programming
PV-Wave	Visual Numerics, Boulder, CO	Data access for different formats	Basic math, statistics, signal processing, and image function	Two- and three-dimensional and user-defined visualization	PV-Wave language (also C or Fortran)
			Optional: additional gridding, math and statistics functions		Optional: graphical user interface design kit
IDL	Research Systems, Boulder, CO	Data access for different formats	Basic math and statistics functions	Two- and three-dimensional and user-defined visualization	IDL (C or Fortran)
MatLab	The MathWorks, Natick, MA	C-like interface	Matrix/vector-oriented tool boxes for different application areas	Two- and three-dimensional	MatLab language
Mathematica	Wolfram Research, Champaign, IL	C	Matrix/vector-oriented	Two- and three-dimensional	Mathematica language
AVS	Advanced Visual Inc., Waltham, MA	Typical three-dimensional data format support	Optional: libraries for special application areas	Three-dimensional volume display with real-time rotation	Visual programming environment (C or Fortran)
PVS*	IBM	Fast data access (up 100 Mbits/s)	Analysis procedures written for multi-processors	Three-dimensional volume display with real-time animation	Visual programming environment (C or Fortran)
VoxelView	Vital Images, Fairfield, IA		Optional animation and mathematics packages	Three-dimensional Voxel display	Visual programming environment
apE III	Tara Visual, Columbus, OH			Two- and three-dimensional visualization	Visual programming environment
Voxel Visualization	State University of New York, Stony Brook			Three-dimensional Voxel display with real-time rotation	

*Also called AIX Visualization Data Explorer.

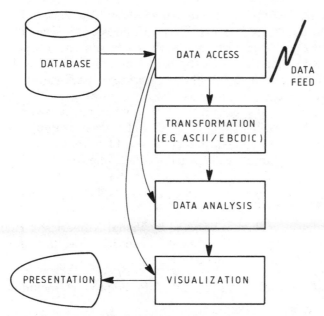

Figure 9.1 Work flow in a PV-Wave application, with possibility to bypass the main procedure.

Professional versions of all of them are running on most popular personal computers, workstations, and supercomputers. Among critical applications in both science and banking are regression and curve fitting, fast Fourier transform, differential equations, and the calculation of nonlinearities.

AVS and PVS differ from these four options for a number of reasons. They are both much newer constructs; they feature object orientation; have an end-user-oriented, modular parametric approach; and can run on parallel processors.

- AVS was originally developed by Kubota Pacific, a Japanese firm, but is now an independent company.

- PVS comes from IBM. It has been a research project at Yorktown Heights, NY, and is AIX-based.

Originally designed for CAD environments and volume data, next to its strong visualization features (graded as number 1) AVS emphasizes on-line data acquisition—but it is still relatively weak in analysis and simulation. The same is true of PVS, although the latter presents a good database bandwidth, as it can access up to 100 Mbits/s.

These are relative strengths and weaknesses. They don't diminish the fact that all six shells help with three-dimensional visualization as well as visual programming. Though many of their applications and their vendors' thrust have been in CAD, other domains, too, are open to implementation.

There exist other VP shells which have not yet established themselves in the market. As seen in Table 9.2, examples are VoxelView and apE III. Voxel

Visualization is a shell by the State University of New York at Stony Brook. In Europe a shell has been designed by the University of Bern. There are many other university-led VP projects, as we will see in subsequent sections.

Note that SAS, popular with the mainframers, is missing from this list. Apart from the fact that it is mainly a statistical package, it is one born for mainframe applications, and dinosaurs have nothing to do with interactive visualization and visual programming. Even when packages are squeezed into workstations, this is the wrong culture—not a good example to bring to the reader's attention. (The same argument is valid for transactional routines such as CICS and for a voluminous, expensive DBMS like DB2.)

9.4   Solutions Provided by PV-Wave

As we have seen, PV-Wave (marketed by Visual Numerics of Houston, TX) is one of the most agile tools for on-line data capture three-dimensional programming and visualization. Among its features:

- Easy-to-use approaches to enter data into the product, including information from databases
- Interactive graphics at three and higher dimensions, at user's choice
- Numerical analysis functions and the coupling of technologies such as data analysis, data management, and visualization
- Subroutines and utilities, packaged to minimize application development time and user training

Applications range from mathematical statistics to numerical analysis, signal processing, data handling, and visualization functions. Other applications involve linear and nonlinear equations, differential equations, eigensystem analysis, approximation, quadrature, correlation, and regression.

A graphical widget toolkit allows one to quickly create custom interfaces and application prototypes. Through a set of low-level tools, a family of high-level tools can be generated; and the same is true of means to connect the interface to the application. The shell provides a means of selecting and handling different views (an example is provided in Fig. 9.2) and makes feasible the manipulation of parameters such as axes, labels, line styles, and annotations.

Colors applied to images help extract features and present patterns and trends in complex, technical data sets. Both three dimensions and color can serve as discovery tools, to supplement the analytical side of the discovery process. Outside engineering and basic science, among applications areas which are more recently benefitting from visual data analysis are

- Risk management of financial products
- Foreign exchange
- Securities trading

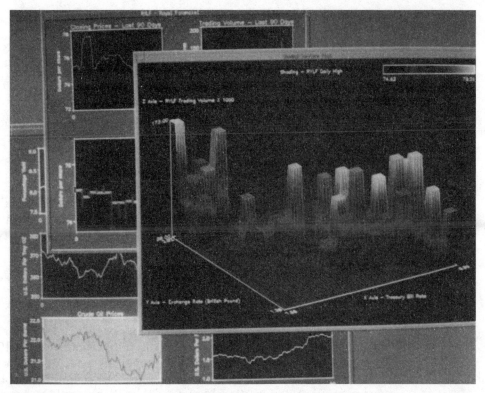

Figure 9.2 Three-dimensional presentation substituted for three different two-dimensional views of time series.

- Treasury management

The more classical application domains where PV-Wave has been primarily applied so far include

- Support for design and engineering
- Interactive experimentation and analysis of results
- Quality control in manufacturing and the service industry
- Remote sensing and signal processing

Still other application domains which are typically part of any list of pioneering departures are aerospace research and engineering; electric energy production and distribution; atmospheric research, weather prediction, and pollution studies. More recent applications are medical imaging and exploration of health factors.

Because of their welcome flexibility and ease of use, PV-Wave and its likes are valid tools in visual data analysis throughout the domains which we have considered. Users can explore visual programming capabilities with a fair amount of ease, as well as manipulate and analyze information elements in an ad hoc manner.

The solution provided in the majority of cases permits one to access, analyze, and visualize information elements in many formats; identify important features and trends; and treat multimedia information both computationally and graphically.

- Rapid prototyping and development of custom-made visualization of applications is feasible.

- This significantly improves the supported facilities, and so does the user choice of interface styles.

The system also features a context-sensitive, hypermedia capability which permits one to navigate through documentation to needed information. There are numerous integrated procedures that support the user's ability to quickly build his or her own functions and programs.

Data import and export are executed with a variety of industry packages, such as spreadsheets, word processing, data files, and databases. This leads to flexible input stream handling which, as stated in Sec. 9.3, is one of the shell's competitive advantages.

Contrasting all six shells which we saw in Sec. 9.3 to the naive routines of Cobol and other old programming languages, a learned observer will be tempted to remark that visual programming languages have been developed to exploit the volume of the human brain, while Cobol, PL/1 and other obsolete constructs are designed to use the size of a rat's brain. SQL tends to fall in between. The aim of Fig. 9.3 is to bring this distinction into perspective.

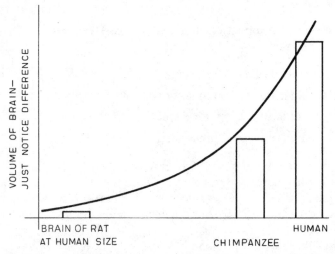

Figure 9.3 Visual programming languages exploit the capacity of the human brain while the obsolete Cobol and SQL address themselves to rats and chimpanzees.

9.5   Three-Dimensional Solutions with MatLab and Simulink*

Among the applications in visualization and visual programming realized with *MatLab* are parametric plots of cube root function in complex space, geographic information systems (GISs) with an image display of elevation, mesh plots with color, and visualization of slices through a volumetric data set. Other implementations include three-dimensional shaded surface graphs, three-dimensional contour plots, combinations of surface and contour plots, and a variety of image displays.

- The functionality embedded in MatLab helps to integrate numerical analysis, matrix computation, signal processing, data analysis, and graphics presentation.

- Solutions are visualized just as they are written mathematically, without traditional programming chores, which is true of all the six shells selected as a reference.

At the bottom line of the described solution is an interactive system whose basic data element is a matrix that does not require dimensioning. This makes it feasible to solve a variety of numerical problems in a fraction of the time that it would take to write a program in a third-generation programming language.

Matrices can be real or complex, and MatLab uses them to hold objects as diverse as images, polynomials, time series, signals, multivariate statistical information, and linear and nonlinear systems. The shell is endowed with a library of 500 mathematical, statistical, engineering, and other scientific functions.

- Fertile implementation areas include numerical methods, applied mathematics, simulation, optimization, as well as automatic control systems.

- The shell's power for matrix operations can be appreciated only by users who have struggled with arrays while programming in a procedural language.

As a visualization environment, the construct makes it feasible to create three-dimensional color graphics, such as surface rendering, contours, image display, wire frame, pseudocolor, and light sources. There are as well facilities for animation, volumetric visualization, and three-, four-, and five-dimensional presentations to gain insight into massive data sets.

The underlying graphical framework is based on an object-oriented approach and provides a valid way to represent, customize, and modify many aspects of the plots. The user can open multiple graph windows simultaneously, place axes in a window, and control the presentation specifics.

Another interactive product from the same vendor is *Simulink*. An extension of MatLab, it addresses itself to specific classes of usage such as process con-

---

*By MathWorks, Natick, MA. As stated, the name of the tool, *MatLab*, stands for Matrix Laboratory.

trol, providing an environment for modeling, analyzing, and simulating a variety of physical and mathematical systems.

Advanced integration algorithms and analytical functions have been incorporated to ensure fast and accurate simulation results. There are available integration methods for fixed, variable-step, and stiff systems.

- Monte Carlo experimentation is supported.
- Models help to determine stable equilibrium points.
- Interactive simulations are done with live display.

A rapid prototyping tool, the C code generator, makes it feasible to implement designs without lengthy coding and debugging. Control, signal processing, and dynamic system algorithms can be handled by developing graphical block diagrams and then automatically generating C code.

The system allows the execution of continuous-time, discrete-time, and hybrid models. The embedded real-time control sees to it that once a process has been designed, code for real-time controllers or digital signal processors can be

- Generated
- Cross-compiled
- Linked
- Downloaded

Databases can be downloaded on-line onto target processing. The user can create and execute code for an entire system or specified subsystems, taking advantage of real-time model validation and testing.

9.6   Example of an Extended Utilities Library

In a nearly virtual reality mode, the MatLab pictures are alive. The user can reach in, grab an object, or control the attributes of a graph. She changes a color or font, shifts an axis direction, alters a tick length. She can define attributes when creating a three-dimensional graph, or she can do the change interactively once the graph is on screen.

The concept of using tiles of prefabricated software is a bigger program construction, developed in the 1950s with *open* and *closed* subroutines. Open subroutines which can be incorporated into the main program through a call, or macrooperation, assist both in programmer productivity and in the quality of the resulting program. Therefore, they are widely used.

More recently, the specialization of libraries of subroutines into *toolboxes* has been an interesting development because it permits a greater range of supported functions. Some of these functions are personalized to particular applications. When miniapplications can be standardized, such as in connection with numerical analysis, the programming job as a whole profits.

By means of comprehensive libraries of functions or routines that customize the application environment, the user can handle classes of problems which are analyzed into more elementary functions, some of which are already programmed, tested, and ready to be incorporated through a call. These toolboxes address themselves to fields such as

- System identification
- Image processing
- Signal processing
- Neural networks
- Statistical analysis
- Symbolic mathematics
- Control system design
- Optimization

The system identification facility includes means for parametric modeling; the analysis of time-series, state-space, and transfer function models; automatic order selection; recursive techniques; model validation; and so on.

Image processing is enriched with tools for manipulation and evaluation of images and two-dimensional signals; two-dimensional filter design and filtering; two-dimensional transform restoration and enhancement; morphological operations; and image analysis and associated statistics.

Signal processing tools are designed to serve in spectral analysis, digital and analog filter design and implementation, filter response simulation, spectral evaluation and estimation, modulation, and demodulation. Parametric modeling is also supported by the shell.

MatLab's neural network facilities are used as design and simulation tools. They feature associative and back-propagation approaches; feedforward and recurrent architectures; competitive, limit, linear, and sigmoid transfer functions, as well as performance analysis functions and graphs.

Available statistical tools address analysis, modeling, and simulation. They are GUI-based, work interactively, and support normal, binomial, chi-squared, Poisson, and other distributions; regression and analysis of variance; random number generation; box plots, quartiles, and other graphics; interactive contour plots; descriptive statistics; and tests of hypothesis.

The set of symbolic mathematics features integrated tools for logic processing and variable-precision operations. Among the supported features are symbolic calculus, linear algebra, equation solving, as well as symbolic evaluation of special mathematical functions. There are as well a linear algebra package and a complete set of specialized functions.

Another set addresses itself to spline approximation and modeling tools. It includes curve fitting, smoothing, piecewise polynomials, B-splines, and spline construction and manipulation. Function differentiation, integration, and evaluation are other features.

Control system design and analysis tools incorporate classical and modern techniques; system interconnection; continuous- and discrete-time evaluation; state-space and transfer functions; model reduction; transformation between models; the Bode, Nyquist, and Nichols criteria for frequency response; root locus and pole placement; and *time response,* impulse, step, and ramp.

Finally, there are a range of optimization tools for general linear and nonlinear functions. They include constrained optimization for goal attainment, linear and quadratic programming, functions to determine minima and maxima, minimax and semi-infinite problems, nonlinear least squares, and multiobjective optimization for goal attainment.

The open-system approach followed by MatLab provides access to toolbox source code, so that the user can inspect, customize, and extend the algorithms and functionality of the toolbox to suit his or her needs. All subsets of the toolbox are available on the computer platforms on which the main program runs.

Because they all have a common basis in MatLab, these toolbox subsets can be used together in a seamless way. In theory, the user can apply system identification and optimization tools to solve a complex problem and can display the results as interactive three-dimensional graphs, without bothering to provide for interfacing and integration. In practice, system integration of software modules takes much more effort than the incorporation of automatic tools.

9.7 Tools for Visual Programming, Program Analysis, Animation, and Debugging

As stated in Sec. 9.3, PV-Wave and MatLab are not the only tools for visual programming. They are only two of the best. Since 1987 a horde of software development constructs have sprung up, each addressing visual programming and/or program visualization domains. Like the examples we have just seen, tools directed at program visualization typically include testing and debugging. Many of the new constructs, however, try to cover the whole range from VP to PV—and they do so rather successfully.

As expected, when a large number of new developments originate in university laboratories and address parallel programming as well, there are differences in design, and there is also going to be significant mortality.

- Many of the new VP tools will never get a market test.

- But the new concepts which they bring to the foreground will surely find themselves in a whole generation of commodity products.

- Visual programming and program visualization will flourish, but not necessarily under the currently available shells.

The majority of the programming tools which we discuss in this section are written in C and use XWindows. Evidently, they run on workstations, not mainframes, which all serious software development tools should do.

A *parallel flow graph* (PFG), from the University of Maryland, is a tool for visual parallel programming, program analysis, and debugging. Developed in 1988, it features hierarchical graphs used to represent and analyze concurrent, time-dependent systems. Structurally it has three parts:

- Data model
- Static program model
- Control flow model

The data model addresses the structure and interrelationships of collections of data that will be transformed through the shell. The static program component consists of a set of operations on the data, given as nonoverlapping basic blocks. The job of the control flow model is to express possibly parallel threads.

The University of Texas at Austin developed in 1989 *Code and Rope,* for program creation through visual dependency graphs. Its target is portable specification of parallel programs and the provision of reusable software facilities to assist in repeated usage of components.

Software development proceeds by visually creating high-level dependency graphs with visual semantics for nodes and arcs. Interfaces include a visual canvas for constructing a dependency graph, with text menus and icons serving to specify features of graphs. The construct maps and partitions the computation to a user-specified architecture.

Axe is a predictive software development tool created by NASA Ames Research Center. A 1990 product, its target is algorithmic development, partitioning, and mapping. It is designed to facilitate research for concurrent systems.

- It uses discrete-time simulation, instead of complex instruction-level simulation.
- It analyzes concurrent computational models on various architecture configurations.
- It can be useful in organizing and planning the early stages of software development.

In about the same time frame, the Argonne National Laboratory produced *Shmap,* whose aim is the visibilization of machine activity, particularly the study of memory access patterns in connection with parallel algorithms on shared-memory multiprocessors. This can be a considerable aid in the design, development, and understanding of programs and programming features.

Shmap analyzes performance bottlenecks of an algorithm before actual implementation, as well as the effect of different cache configurations. It permits one to study strategies on the access patterns of the algorithm by representing central memory and cache as two-dimensional grids with read accesses. Each access is colored in a way which reflects its origin.

Another tool for algorithmic development, visibilization, and debugging is *Tango,* created by the Georgia Institute of Technology. Built in 1990, it provides a flexible algorithm animation platform with semantics and models, assisting the user in understanding the behavior of an algorithm, hence expediting algorithmic design and the analysis of the resulting implemented program.

Tango displays a smoothly changing animation consisting of moving and interacting objects. This conforms to the direction that other visual programming tools have taken during recent years.

- Images move across a canvas and change features to represent the dynamic behavior of program modules or abstract objects.

- Animation is controlled interactively through graphics with views constructed from four object types.

These examples of new approaches, which espouse visual programming as their base technology, reveal the nature and extent of new developments. Yet, rather than capitalizing on the software potential which exists at the fringes of virtual reality, the large majority of computer user organizations have stuck themselves in the paleolithic and inefficient environment of Fortran and Cobol, paying the price in costs, delays, and low quality of deliverables.

9.8 Artifacts for Efficient Parallel Computer Programming

Visual programming and program visualization can be instrumental in helping to solve the software bottleneck which exists all over the world. The current huge backlogs in programming needs cannot be addressed through existing languages, and it is indeed surprising that people who should have known better cannot appreciate this simple fact.

Even if stand-alone monoprocessor computers, from workstations to mainframes, could be efficiently programmed through the old languages, this is absolutely impossible with regard to parallel computers. For high-performance computing, VP and PV are the pillars whether we talk of massively parallel processors or of the new generation of desk-area networks (DANs).

The University of Illinois in 1990 developed *Hyperview* for Intel's iPSC/2 hypercube. The goal is performance enhancement and visual assistance in debugging. The tool organizes and massages the large amounts of performance information obtained from distributed and parallel computing systems, and provides an integrated environment for analyzing the behavior of parallel programs.

Multiple window interfaces include bar charts, meters, topological displays, and graphs. Performance metrics are simultaneously displayed in easily understandable visual formats. Available routines

- Expose messaging and interaction bottlenecks.
- Analyze traffic patterns.
- Examine utilization of resources to improve efficiency.

For distributed computing rather than for massively parallel engines, the Technical University of Munich in 1991 developed *Topsys*. It is a program partitioning, mapping, performance tuning, and debugging tool based on program visualization.

The artifact aims to provide an integrated environment for instruction analysis, specification, and dynamic load balancing. It includes an animated performance metric addressing task interaction and behavior, and it permits automatic replay of program traces at variable speed. The possibility of manual scrolling forward and backward is also provided.

Performance tuning and debugging are also the goal of *IPS-2*. It was designed to provide feedback to the user, rather than to assist with visual programming as such.

- IPS-2 targets the execution of a parallel program and guides the user toward performance bottlenecks.

- It helps to analyze existing parallel programs to improve performance, by eliminating inefficient portions.

- Visualization is employed to enhance understanding of data and to emphasize critical areas.

Like other program visualization tools, this artifact provides an animated call graph and numeric plot windows which include text and tables. Critical path information is provided on call-graph display, with execution times and utilization information also shown graphically.

Faust was designed in 1989 by the University of Illinois at Urbana-Champaign to assist in performance tuning and debugging of implemented computer programs. This, too, is an integrated tool for parallel programming, expediting performance enhancements through analysis of parallel program behavior and the control of utility functions.

The *eXPlicit Algorithm analysis Tool* (XPAT), developed in collaboration between Purdue University and the University of Iowa in the late 1990s, is a visual parallel programming tool addressing

- Program simulation

- Analysis of behavior

- The definition of specifications

XPAT uses Petri Nets formalisms with transition graphs and enabling functions. It associates a predicate with each transition, and, through Petri Nets, it can do Markov chains, leading to an analytical study of massively parallel computer behavior. Code generation is not the primary target, although the Petri Nets can be analyzed and converted to programs for execution.

XPAT elicits user interaction and aids by providing program visualization capabilities. The construct includes a visual editor augmented with analytical modules. An interactive editor helps to eliminate syntax errors in the visual Petri Net syntax. In terms of programming methodology,

- Nodes represent program predicates or program states.

- Transitions emulate user-specified actions that occur during execution.

- Actions may modify network marking, therefore altering the control flow.
- Subnetworks can be grouped in a macro (closed box), leading to reusable software.

There is a simulation interface that helps to animate program execution by showing transition firings. Animation speed and detail connected to this facility are selected by the user.

The user can also specify the initial state of simulation, with program execution starting from any state. The user can also experiment with "what if?" scenarios and analysis modes. For instance, compute invariants and attempt to determine the mapping between them and the actual code.

The user can specify combinations of markings that are illegal, therefore helping to prune large trees; she can interactively query for reachable markings, specify forbidden accesses to shared variables, and handle timing information. Simulation provides insight to the system's operation, and embedded tools permit program modifications as necessary.

All the examples we have seen are based on new, knowledge-enriched visual programming and program visualization tools. Each one assists in the development of performance-efficient parallel software and provides considerable system support. Typically these tools

- Incorporate modular paradigms for parallel programming
- Integrate analysis tools and allow coherent development

Graphical interfaces underpin the process of analyzing information captured at run time. Program module execution is efficiently displayed, permitting one to visually analyze program behavior and verify correct operation and performance. Many of these modern development platforms allow zooming in and out to perceive high- and low-level details, with scrolling along the time axis. All are user-friendly, and many have adopted object orientation.

9.9 Management Systems for Distributed Databases

Even the best visual programming language will perform in a suboptimal way without the proper database management system (DBMS) support. Only object-oriented and relational solutions satisfy this characteristic, and as we saw in Sec. 9.3, the newest VP shells feature object characteristics.

While object orientation is the target that the foremost industrial and financial organizations have recently set for themselves, these applications are not yet generalized. Even relational implementations, which started a dozen years ago, do not dominate the landscape. Only an estimated 20 to 25 percent of all data is currently under a relational DBMS.* The balance is nonrelational:

---

*These are industrywide figures. With workstations, however, both relational and object DBMSs have a significant advantage. Under Unix the most favored relational DBMSs are Oracle (about 50 percent of all cases), Sybase, Informix, and Ingres.

- Hierarchical
- Networking (Codasyl)
- Simple file management
- VSAM and so on

All this is old stuff, very inefficient and strangling the company in a database management sense. But it is there and has to be accounted for in terms of the need for change and renewal of DBMS practices. It serves precious little to alter programming tools but leaves database management in the mess it is today.

Some of the queries that management poses when confronted with these issues are as follows: How will object technology provide our company with flexible, responsive information systems? Will it be able to tightly integrate the software and hardware we now use? Can we be sure such integration will take place?

The answer to these queries is that integrative solutions do not happen by miracles; neither do they come simply because of adopting a certain DBMS. They require a great deal of skill and effort as well as attention to detail, including

- A thorough study of prevailing conditions and needed solutions—also management control
- The development of an in-house architecture (since no vendor architecture fits a company's specific requirements)
- Lots of systems know-how as well as database expertise, persistence, and patience

The analysis of prevailing conditions calls for a thorough cost/benefit analysis of the strengths and weaknesses of object technology. This should lead to the establishment and documentation of a concrete plan of action for integrating object DBMS with relational DBMS and legacy applications. We should be able to measure benefits in terms of

- Quality of results
- Flexibility
- Productivity
- Cost

As has happened with many companies, this cost/benefit analysis will show that migration from our installed base to an enterprisewide integrative information system is not only possible, but also achievable with object technology. New solutions enable a better, more efficient model of corporate database and computation, starting with the renewal of the software development strategy through visual programming.

Chances are that a well-done, objective study will document the wisdom of distributed information systems and client-server solutions over centralized

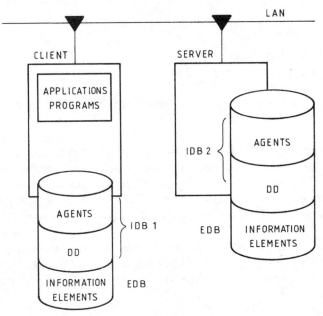

Figure 9.4 An approach to database intelligence distinguishes between intentional and extensional structures.

approaches.[2] Companies which wisely choose to capitalize on rapid technological advancements reached the conclusion that *intelligent databases* are the best solution.

Reflecting the implementation of a client-server architecture, Fig. 9.4 provides an appreciation of what it takes to implement an intelligent or expert database at the client and server levels of reference. The important systems layers are

- *Intentional database* (IDB) software, hence knowledge-enriched, including agents and data dictionary (DD)

- *Extensional database* (EDB) components which include the information elements under object or relational DBMS

Expert database systems represent the convergence of research in artificial intelligence and database management. They support efficient user interfaces and natural-language question/answer facilities and endow database systems with reasoning, planning, and justification capabilities, which are needed for visual programming.

9.10 Obstacles to the Implementation of Object Solutions and Intentional Database Management

If object DBMS and intelligent database management approaches offer many competitive advantages and are the wave of the future, why do companies not accept them outright? Why do they forgo the opportunity to prune their system and establish effective specifications on database usage through prototyping? Why don't they make available to themselves testing facilities for complex database applications?

The answer to these queries is precisely the same as that to why only the leaders take advantage of sophisticated tools to support software development. Only cutting-edge organizations know how to simplify the job connected with the evolution of large databases and programming libraries. The others face obstacles which are motivated by the following five reasons:

1. Cultural limitations lead to a most regrettable nonutilization of visual programming and object database possibilities for reasons of inertia, resistance to change, maintenance of the status quo, and fear of new technology.

2. A curious favoritism exists toward old mainframes and their vendors. Technology moves fast with an evident obsolescence in machines and in skills. But many companies don't see things that way. They try to avoid what they call the "bleeding edge," while in reality those bleeding are the laggards.

3. A defective technical update has happened often in the past, and it has curious results, such as creating a small "select group" for new technology rather than educating all systems specialists to the newer and upcoming tools, which is a rather common failure.

4. Lack of methodology and its inverse—conflicting methodologies—are nothing new in data processing. They happen all the time from the old, legacy programming procedures to the plurality of incompatible computer-aided software engineering (CASE) approaches.

5. There is a heterogeneity of installed DBMSs and languages. This is precisely the residue from data processing experience, characterized by failure to choose among alternatives and stick to the choice once made.

The confusion which today prevails in many aspects of legacy data processing does not provide the peace of mind necessary to sort out the priorities. Yet those information technologists who have been able to do so have found out how profitable it is to renew and restructure their systems, including

- Data organization

- Knowledge associations

- Processing rules

- Various kinds of constraints

The schema of a deductive database, organized into the two portions we saw in Sec. 9.9, EDB and IDB, should contain the general information about data solutions, ephemeral hierarchies, and knowledge organization. While IDB may be object-oriented, EDB schema definitions can be stored and accessed by using the well-developed relational technology.

As we saw in Fig. 9.4, IDB has two parts: IDB 1 is in the inference engine of the workstation associated with the user application programs, and IDB 2 is part of the database server, constituting its knowledge management layer. It contains data for

- Shared user knowledge
- Control knowledge (metaknowledge)

Metaknowledge and *object knowledge* ensure knowledge management. The relational database system in the EDB is integrated into the logical programming language. Knowledge and data are treated in the same manner.

This is, in a nutshell, the framework which can support visual programming and program visualization in the most efficient manner. *Virtual integration* of distributed heterogeneous database resources requires an integrated (but not unique) schema, which consists of the definition (header information) of all the EDB and IDB components and integrity constraints.

- The IDB is the rule base (knowledge bank) for deductive purposes.
- The EDB is the database for storing information elements.
- The data dictionary includes the directory, security control, data definitions, and object relations.

A deductive database is instrumental in promoting visual programming and virtual reality solutions. It can be constructed incrementally on top of an existing relational database. An elegant systems design not only provides a clear conceptual view of knowledge bank and database contents but also facilitates the organization of knowledge and information for efficient storage and accessing.

References

1. See D. N. Chorafas and H. Steinmann, *Virtual Reality—Practical Applications in Business and Industry,* Prentice-Hall, Englewood Cliffs, NJ, 1995.
2. See also D. N. Chorafas, *Beyond LANs—Client-Server Computing,* McGraw-Hill, New York, 1994.

Hardware and Software Issues Underpinning Visual Programming

The sophisticated use of computer software and hardware helps make a business more competitive and more comprehensible. It is therefore important to study the alternatives with which we are presented today, examine the more likely evolution, and bet on what may constitute a winning solution. Part 4 examines concepts, tools, and supports underpinning the applications in Parts 1, 2, and 3.

Network Appliances, Desk-Area Networks, and the Asynchronous Transfer Mode

10.1 Introduction

Visual programming technology cannot be effectively studied disjoint from the supports on which it runs. Because both computers and networks are in full evolution, this necessarily influences quite strongly the choices which have to be made to gain and maintain a competitive edge.

- As a matter of principle, no technology should be adopted because it is in vogue.

- The reason for investing in high technology—and visual programming is an example—is value differentiation.

The technological solutions offered to companies must be both *sophisticated* and *low-cost*. This is doable, and as a result, the advanced approaches utilized by tier 1 companies not only are cost-effective but also are changing over time to remain competitive. The goals are to

- Steadily improve revenue and profits
- Gain in market appreciation
- Provide for product innovation and the swamping of costs

Tough choices are necessary not just in technology but in any domain which is critical to the survival of an enterprise as a competitive force. Therefore, it is legitimate to ask, What kind of devices should be attached to the network? On which machines should visual programming artifacts run?

An issue which was brought into perspective during Comdex 95, and now pits one computer company against another, is whether the solutions for the late 1990s should be *network-centric* or *workstation-centric*. My answer is: both. The use of Internet underlies this choice:

- The pros of network-centric approaches promote the so-called *network appliances,* thought to be inexpensive machines.

- The pro-workstation camp sticks to the personal computer and its upgrades as the workhorses of the future.

Both are right, and both are wrong. Rather than inexpensive appliances and PC concepts of the late 1970s, the solution for the future should be multiple processors per workstation. That's the desk-area network (DAN) concept discussed in Chap. 8. Remember, however, that this bifurcation is a political issue and opinions cannot be fully objective.

Capitalizing on the high power but low cost of the microprocessor, some of the chips on a DAN will specialize as gateways, others in managing databases, still others in graphical rendering. DANs will be self-inspected by dedicated processor(s) rather than needing human maintenance groups. The concept is to better utilize available computer power, at an affordable cost.

10.2 Concepts behind Network Appliances, and Internet Users

The current market evolution sees to it that with privatization, innovation, and globalization the competition in business and industry intensifies. Nothing is spared to gain a competitive edge. Therefore, positioning your company against the forces of the 1990s is a challenging task which requires

- Strategic thinking

- Management ingenuity

- Advanced technological solutions

The choice of hardware and software to be networked on the Internet, or on any other communications system, should be examined from this triple perspective. The salient question is, Which investment will give your company the upper hand against competition? Network appliances might cost less money, but what kind of results do they get?

The notion of bare-bones network appliances versus desk-area networks was introduced in Chap. 8 in connection with Java. Because, however, its impact can be enormous, it is proper to take a much closer look at the arguments for and against each of the alternative solutions. While the market will be the final critic, what is the market telling us today which may be important in the future?

If current responses are any guide, the market for Web technology and for visual programming solutions, like those we studied in Part 2, will be bigger than the Internet, even if this has been the starting point. No doubt, as Internet rapidly develops, its existence will bring great changes in computing; but, in my judgment, the whole concept of relatively dumb network terminals is absurd.

- Using a dumb terminal and depending on a central software server are not much different from what we had in the old days of mainframes.

- As technology developed and new horizons opened up, this proved to be a mistake, and there is no reason to make the same mistake twice.

Where will the multimedia supports be? The graphics processors for visual programming? the database management system? The real-time processor for interpretation? The transaction processing monitor? The chips to enhance security? In short, what are we getting by paying the $500 for an appliance which has no monitor and no hard disk?

The market is motivated, and up to a point underwritten, by the demand for ever more powerful computers to run diverse and fairly sophisticated applications. Such computers consume an increasingly large amount of microprocessor cycles and central memory chips. Visual programming, three-dimensional graphics, teleconferencing, and multimedia applications also require specialized microprocessors for many functions. Neither are computers the only consumers of chip technology. Nowadays, more and more electronics are being stuffed into products ranging from cellular telephones to automobiles and house appliances.

Chapter 8 stated that while paleolithic mainframes had (and still have) one processor to serve hundreds or thousands of users—and neolithic workstations, as well as appliances, brought to 1-to-1 the user-to-microprocessor ratio—desk-area networks are a different ballgame altogether.

- By capitalizing on the very low cost of the mass-produced microprocessor, the goal is to serve the end user through n processors rather than one.

- This fits well not only with power requirements but also with solutions such as caching and multithreading which have entered the World Wide Web.

Caching is a technique applied to the Web that emulates the use of cache memory as a performance booster in a computer. For instance, browsed and visited documents are retained on the local workstation. Thus, time-consuming reloads over the Internet can be avoided.

Used in a networking context, this caching strategy goes well beyond the services that appliances can offer. Yet, its implementation is particularly important with some applications such as image handling, because images are a great time drain. Technically, there are two variations of caching.

- *Soft,* which stays alive for the session

- *Hard,* which stores the cache on the PC disk

Depending on the application run on the end user's computer, hard caching may be preferable, but it often results in major housekeeping chores at the end-user site. As for multithreading, because it supports multiple, concurrent Web accesses, it needs multiple windows within a Web terminal session. Therefore, it requires considerable computer power.

So much for processing bandwidth and database bandwidth. But let's not forget the requirements posed by telecommunications in an Internet setting. Time and again I hear this argument from Internet users: "The transfer rate broke down many times during the session, though my modem supports a 14.4 kbytes/s stream." This problem is not related to any single language, for instance Java. Rather, it is a general problem encountered on the Internet.

Remember the reference in Chap. 8 to the time it takes to load a WallStreetWeb applet: It can require 60 seconds or more. To emulate a larger communications bandwidth, some applications use small Java applets to reduce the transfer rate between the client and the server. For instance, miniapplets are a better strategy for updates than changing the whole page. But this needs hard caching, hence disk.

Either the end user stays at the bottom of the food chain by sticking to network appliances, or, if she graduates in her applications, she has to equip herself with appropriate software and hardware. The new release of the World Wide Web browser Netscape Navigator 2.0 requires a 14.4 kbytes/s modem, and as the foregoing reference stated, this too may not be enough. But even 14.4 kbytes/s changes quite a bit the requirements of communication channels as we knew them.

The upgrade in necessary communications bandwidth is important for practical reasons, as Netscape is the closest thing there is to a de facto market standard. It has even created its own norms regarding HTML, apart from the fact that, in February 1996, Netscape announced an agreement with 10 other Internet technology companies to create norms for audio and video over the Internet.

In conclusion, the supports which we use must be able to match the software industry's development of new and interesting applications addressed to end users. Already some of the packages which are in the market make Web sites lively with interactivity. Today and tomorrow, end users rather than professional software developers are setting the new programming style, and the choice of investments cannot be made dissociated from this fact.

10.3   Thrift Is a Virtue, but Don't Underestimate the Total Costs

Internet is a cross-database facility, and growing database-to-database communications pose challenges in regard to both channel capacity and local resources. Not everything is in the processors. Even if most PCs were equipped with fast modems, such as 28.8 kbytes/s, downloading even small programs is still a time-consuming job.

- From a communications viewpoint, there is a cost to access the Internet, and it is per hour of service.

- In the United States, it is very low—about $3 per hour—but in Europe and elsewhere it is much higher.

Although there are some regional on-line services that charge a flat monthly fee with no hourly charge, there are no national services with a competitive price structure. Until there is no cross-border marginal cost, surfing the Net can be prohibitively expensive. The lower the MIPS of the workstation (and of the vendor), the greater the need for communications—hence the cost.

Even if zero marginal cost is not forthcoming, the cost to the user for communications can be small compared to that for the use of central computer resources. IBM and other proponents of network appliances make the same mistake as the PTTs and other telecommunications companies did in the early 1980s by overcharging with Prestel. This killed the Videotex services worldwide.

With computers, communications, and software, as well as in any other business, what is most important is not what the vendor says—particularly the vendor who failed to keep its market leadership—but what the market thinks of products and services. Computer-literate end users need their PCs to continue to create.

- Creative work calls for more user-level features than are available as the least common denominator of a dumb appliance.

- During the last 10 years, users were happy to get the 1000-lb gorilla of the mainframe industry off their backs. Why should they now return to it in the form of an Internet superserver?

The hype around network appliances looks like the case of the unable who has been asked by the unwilling to do the unnecessary. The smoke and mirrors blind even some specialists who fail to address crucial technical and user-oriented questions. For example, will most computer users really prefer scaled-down generic software that must be retrieved from Internet each time it is used?

- Will a pay-per-use system requiring Internet access ultimately be cheaper for the consumer over the long run?

- What sort of fees will the new software providers charge, and how often will they recharge for the same services?

Here we are talking about a large and diversified population of users from managers and professionals to consumers. I make only one exception: kids playing Pacman or tic-tac-toe. Companies that fail to gauge the market fail in business. An example is Thinking Machines, the massively parallel computer pioneer that sought bankruptcy protection from creditors in mid-1994. In November 1995, it filed a plan to reorganize as a software company, because in its years of prosperity it relied on only one client: Defense.

This does not mean that there is no market for networked game machines, but it's a different market. Exactly because there may be a business opportunity, in January 1996 Compaq Computer and Fisher-Price announced a line of new *computoys* that could turn an aging home PC into 1996's successful toy story.

- The computoys aim to give Compaq a way to fight Packard Bell Electronics in home PC sales.

- That's part of Compaq's strategy, and the company aims to be twice the size of its nearest rival by the end of this decade.

Computoys, however, don't have the features that Internet users increasingly need or visual programming technology demands for its sustenance. In any computer system, including a network of computers, the input/output (I/O) subsystem is hard-pressed to meet the needs of applications.

- Multimedia implementations involve large transfers in a burst mode of 14.4 Mbytes/s or much more.
- Satellite data acquisition frequently requires data rates of 1 Tbyte/s or, most commonly, gigabit transmission (gigastreams) and megabit transmission (megastreams).

There are a proliferation of satellite communications projects, and these address, as a prospective clientele, both companies and consumers. With multimedia, the consumers' common denominator in channel capacity will be megastreams, while companies will go for gigastreams. Both will work on DANs, not on network appliances.

Terastreams may not remain for long as the higher unit of measurement. Scientific computing on massively parallel machines calls for terabytes of data per run, at the rate of 1 Gbyte/s to secondary storage and 100 Gbytes/s to archival storage. Eventually, this, too, may be narrowband.

Secondary storage devices are necessary because it is not practical to build central memory with infinite capacity and single-cycle access time. Increasingly, this secondary storage is the desk-area network; and considerable research is involved in managing the availability of information as if it were implemented as virtual memory across a network, rather than within a single computer. We look at this issue in Secs. 10.7 to 10.10.

10.4   The Business of $500 Network Appliances

Network appliances, or network computers (NC) are supposed to be cut-down computers, with limited memory and storage facilities. Some lack monitors, and the vendor advises to "plug them into your old PC or TV set." But they use embedded modems to dial into the Internet through a phone line. Once logged on, users can send and receive E-mail. However, the machines' limited capabilities will not permit the user to simultaneously surf the Net and do other conventional applications.

There is a great deal of hype connected with appliances, while very little is said of hidden costs. The argument that almost all data and documents created by users will be stored on the network, saving on the manufacturing cost of the terminal, is pure nonsense. The cost of the network resources will be a high multiple of the PC's cost—and it will be a repetitive cost running all the time.

- There is also the very critical issue of security and privacy, which would inhibit users from choosing a data warehouse hundreds of miles away.

- Few people would agree to have their files stored at a network node in the care of the information provider and pay the costs.

The $500 Internet machine could be the ticket for Net beginners, assuming that data connections into the home become faster, cheaper, and more reliable and that the Internet offers new content that appeals to people who do not yet own personal computers. It might also serve in schools for teaching, but in *intranet* solutions, not on the Internet.

Furthermore, no matter what these appliances are, they will need operating systems. CEO Lawrence J. Ellison says that Oracle has developed an operating system that takes up just 1 Mbyte of main memory versus 8 Mbytes for Windows 95. Short of having produced any miracle, it is correct to assume the facilities that this new OS provides are proportionally less.

Ellison thinks his program will be given away by Internet service providers, or built into computers and consumer electronics gadgets, and he adds: "I really think that Windows 95 marked the zenith of the personal-computer industry." After that, in his judgment, it was downhill for the PC.

But a 1-Mbyte central memory just for the OS is not what one would expect of a network appliance either. Recall that these appliances are less powerful than PCs, sacrificing the ability to work with a lot of available peripherals and software programs.

Two goals are indirectly implied by high-technology projects

- To swamp costs

- To provide sophistication while controlling complexity

But usually even the best project can attain one of the goals, not both. Therefore, no vendor dares explain to clients and prospects that the appliances they buy will be dumb. This is contributing to the free-lunch syndrome.

Are there lessons we can learn from developments in the 1990s which can be useful in the network appliance versus workstations controversy? One lesson is that during the last 10 years, computing is being increasingly seen as a network challenge.

- But this does not mean that the machine at the user's desk, laptop, or palm of the hand gets dumber.

- To the contrary, in the next few years, users may be much more interested in the services that desk-area networks provide, rather than appliances.

This concept is explained in Sec. 10.7, when we talk of MIT's ViewStation project. But in a nutshell, the attached device(s) may be not only new machines but also old PCs which can still do a useful job. Or they may be machines with specialized software.

By extension, automotive appliances and other gadgets from home electronics can be components of a DAN. The latter are closer to the notion of network appliances in the sense that they are specialized. They can do just one job—the job for which they have been designed. An appliance may run, for instance, a refrigerator. But it cannot run a refrigerator, an oven, and a TV set at the same time. In this sense,

- The concept of a low-MIPS network appliance is more for the home, the automobile, or other specialized device.

- This notion is principally consumer-oriented, not professional—and even that needs to be qualified.

In mid-1996, Compaq, IBM, and other vendors brought to the market for professionals some ultraportables at very reasonable prices. Compaq's Armada, for example, costs $2699 and features a 100 MHz Pentium processor, a color monitor, 8 Mbytes of central memory, 810 Mbytes disk drive, and a battery. These 810 Mbytes, which can grow to 1.1 Gbytes, are a bigger database resource than many companies featured 10 years ago with their multimillion dollar central computer installation.

The problem with $500 network appliances is that some users see them as low-cost general-purpose machines. They believe that a few hundred dollars can buy a complex array of applications, three-dimensional color graphics, and sophisticated visual programming tools. For selfish purposes vendors reinforce that hype.

A different way of making this statement is that in the years to come, successful network appliances will be mini-programmed. Most of their commands will be in firmware because they will be designed to do at low cost just one job. An appliance may be a facsimile machine, a car, or a handheld device designed for a specific purpose. But this handheld device should not be seen as another general purpose type of solution. The fact that the market did not espouse General Magic's broadly targeted solution is a fact which provides food for thought.

Though the concept of using agents in a sprawling communications environment was good, the reasons for the failure were multiple. As stated, the most important issue has been that the technology was not mature and the product had rough edges—but other reasons also contributed to General Magic's downturn.

Magic Cap is not the only product tested by the market and rejected. Frustrated from losing PC market share, because of its high prices which opened the market to a host of IBM-compatible PCs, in the mid-1980s IBM has introduced the PC Jr. Not only did PC Jr. fail to stop the erosion of IBM's PC market share, but the product itself was a dismal failure.

To paraphrase Abraham Lincoln's dictum, you can fool some of the people all of the time, or all of the people some of the time; but you cannot fool all of the people all of the time. Fooling all the people all the time is essentially what the $500 engine tries to do. The exercise will end by disappointing everybody, both its users and its makers.

10.5 Looking for Value Differentiation Rather than Reinventing the Wheel

One lesson which should be learned from the failure of PC Jr., the Magic Cap, and so many other products or projects is that it is impossible to build market leadership without having a solution clearly in mind. Solutions which are not cost-effective, modular, and expandable do not satisfy current requirements and have no market appeal worth talking about. No wonder that cognizant people in Silicon Valley were not impressed with what Oracle, Sun Microsystems, and IBM had to say regarding the future of network appliances: "We do not view it as a significant issue," said one of the experts. "It's a niche market."

Another of the better-known specialists in communications and computers added during the Palo Alto meetings: "I see myself using these appliances. But I will not get the PC off my desk." This meeting centered on advanced network applications with particular emphasis on visual programming. Consensus has been that you cannot do much with a $500 machine:

- VRML will require much more horsepower than what Oracle plans to offer.

- But Personal Digital Assistants (PDAs) may be served through an appliance.

Oracle worked with an Olivetti subsidiary in the United Kingdom to develop its network computer. But experts in Silicon Valley challenged the notion that anything consistent can be done for a sales tag of $500. The monitor alone costs $200. Oracle said that its computer will not include a monitor. It will be plugged into the monitor of another PC or a TV set. As Videotex has demonstrated, this is not an elegant solution.

- Why, if you already had a PC, would you want to pay another $500 for a half-baked engine with an incompatible OS?

- Who is going to write applications for a new OS which does not even have the slimmest chance of carrying the market?

- How is it that Oracle, Sun, Sony, Phillips, and other fans of network appliances don't remember the failure of AT&T and Knight-Ridder?

When, in the early 1980s, Videotex was going strong, and it looked as if it could carry the market, the telecommunications companies got greedy and overcharged for Videotex services, killing them in the process. The majority of services used the plain, old TV box, but some even developed their own appliances for Videotex.

The idea that a vendor can take a long shot at the clients and strike gold does not really correlate with serious thinking. Those who understand the evolution of the computer industry appreciate that whatever new we get in terms of computers, communications, and software has to

- Present a tangible added value

- Present competitive advantages in functionality

- More or less integrate with what we already have

The question has been asked, Why not use a $500 computer with an existing high-quality TV? There are three answers which strike down the $500 argument.

The first answer is functional, and it comes from Videotex times (late 1970s to early 1980s). Videotex was indeed implemented on a TV set, and it gave alphageometric representation while the terminal itself was dumb.[1] AT&T and Knight-Ridder Enterprises developed, at that time, a $500 black box (what a coincidence!) with keyboard and processor to make the TV set smart. Businesswise, the whole thing was a flop and cost the two partners a rumored $100 million.

The second reason is economics. Anyone who buys the reincarnation of the $500 black box will not use his or her high-quality digital TV set to play with the computer. The high-definition TV is for the other family members. Probably the old TV set nobody wants anymore would be used—and we are back to the alphageometric presentation. Matter of fact, I would rather use a digital computer monitor for TV, than the other way round.

The third answer is purely technical. Unless we talk of playing games, the integration of even smaller systems—a PC, workstation, or DAN—is an art which has its norms, rules, and software. Bigger systems are not made of dispersed components which grew up. *If* the architectural sophistication is taken out, *then* what remains is a stupid terminal.

Value differentiation is not being provided through dumb terminals. In fact, a significant number of computer wizards now think that even at home the low-MIPS network appliances will be no success story. In a few years, at home, there will be a 10 Mbytes/s cable feeding information. People will not tolerate low-MIPS devices with substandard services and a 5-min wait.

If appliances are to have a future as pagers, PDAs, and traffic information controllers in cars, then they must have a number of mass market characteristics. Experts at the Silicon Valley meeting suggested that they must

- Cost less than $100 each
- Have seamless integrative capability in a networking sense

Under these conditions there will be not one but *n* specialized appliances, each appealing to a niche market. But this is not what their promoters have in mind—at least not at present.

By contrast, the examples in Secs. 10.7 to 10.10 have these prerequisites. While these examples have been chosen from confined-space computing, they are just as applicable with mobile, nomadic computing. Solutions have to be found beyond PDAs, however, for instance, for the *Visual, Intelligent and Personal (VI&P) Services* which Nippon Telegraph and Telephone (NTT) suggests will dominate the beginning of the 21st century.

NTT is currently studying the VI&P technology and its applications as well as the social and other consequences of *visual databases* which will become possible with gigastream networks, permitting to service on-line

- Any client
- At any time
- With any program

For this to become a reality, many things will need to change, among them the way we look at computers and communications, from basic software to visual programming and program sustenance.

In essence, there are no big jobs; only small machines. The Suez Canal and the Panama Canal were big only because they were measured by mules and hand shovels, which were the "appliances" of their time.

The Hoover Dam and the Bonneville Dam, which broke building records when they were undertaken, were doable because of both the will of men who launched themselves into construction with resolve and dedication, and the huge machines which were used. The same principle is valid for the computing and communications systems to serve the society of the late 1990s. You cannot do anything valuable with a $500 engine in terms of

- Communications-critical
- Compute-intensive
- Memory-bound applications

Something might be done as an exception with limited functionality, but it will not last for very long. Fisher-Price may be right in coming into the network appliances market; but IBM, Oracle, and Sun Microsystems are wrong.

10.6 Client-Servers Changed the Way We Look at Systems Solutions

First, in the early 1980s, we had local-area networks with personal computers (PC/LANs).[2] Then, in the late 1980s, these developed into much more robust client-servers.[3] Now technology moves beyond client-servers into desk-area networks, but this transition further underlines the top five characteristics of client-server implementation.

1. The new *cultural* solution, free from bureaucratic EDP practices
2. The *low-cost* pattern, at 10 to 20 percent of mainframe costs
3. The *flexible* approaches, with small incremental costs
4. The enhanced ability to sustain *fast development* timetables
5. The agile *end-user orientation,* with visual programming, three-dimensional color graphics, and efficient protocols

During the 1990s, the client-server tide has been rising on both sides of the Atlantic. Until now the number 1 reason has been much lower costs in raw computer power. By 1995 this difference had mushroomed to 4 orders of magnitude, as can be seen in Fig. 10.1.

Because user organizations appreciate the effect of lower client-server costs on the bottom line, leading database companies such as Oracle, Sybase, and

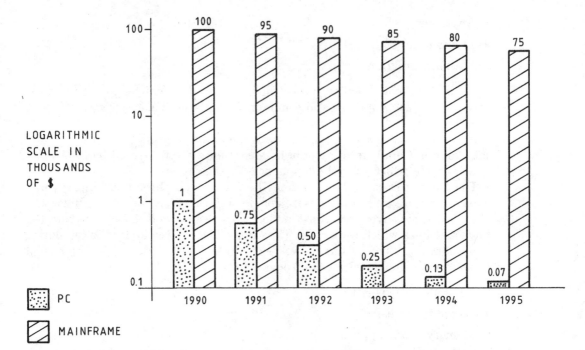

Figure 10.1   Dollars per MIPS: PC versus mainframe. In 1995 the difference was 4 orders of magnitude.

Informix, whose products are at the core of most client-server sites, are growing some 40 percent per year. Applications development tool editors like Powersoft (now owned by Sybase) and France's Nat Systemes are doing even better. Sales of Borland's Delphi—the company's answer to Microsoft's Visual Basic—are also rapidly progressing.

By contrast, with the exception of IBM whose stock has partly recovered because of marketing its DB2 as a data warehouse among its still loyal customers (a shrinking breed), the other mainframers go from bad to worse. For years the French government had hoped that Groupe Bull would "blossom" into a Gallic IBM. Sadly, it has. Since 1989, Bull, a state-owned computer maker, has lost more than $4 billion. Not only is the French taxpayer getting tired of footing the bill, but also the European Commission launched an antitrust inquiry into another $500 million of new capital approved by the French government.

- The idea that the money will help a mainframer transform itself into a profitable global computer services group is rotten.

- While Bull is angling for an extra $2 billion of state cash, government financing is throwing good money after bad.

The trouble with the management of mainframe companies is that despite overwhelming evidence to the contrary, they continue to believe that sales and profits in the mainframe business will recover. Even the network appliances they promote have, in the background, a concentration on mainframe hardware, software, and other centralized services.

Using network appliances as a Trojan horse, mainframers are advising their clients on how to best build networks around their huge and costly machines. This is a forlorn hope. According to a survey by Forrester Research, a mere 20 percent of big U.S. companies use mainframes in their computer networks. This picture is practically the same in England.

But as of 1996, costs are not the only reason why client-servers are in and mainframes are out. According to the Gartner Group, adopting the client-server model is from now on a management decision, not a technology drive. London's Ovum says that

- Companies that have successfully implemented client-server architectures are not simply interested in downsizing.

- On the contrary, they are doing so in pursuit of long-term goals, with *competitiveness* in the driver's seat.

Client-server computing gives the company's sales force more elbow room to adapt to the faster-changing demands of flexible manufacturing, rapid innovation, and huge distribution chains. It also has similar salutary effects on marketing and sales.

A limiting factor with client-server technology is skills. There is a shortage in the United States of computer-related jobs, such as rocket scientists and the new breed of programmers. Also managers needed to run sophisticated client-server networks are in high demand.

Starting a couple of years ago, companies such as Georgia-Pacific have been turning over rocks to find experienced people for distributed information systems.[4] The new technologists are in high demand. This is a challenging market because everybody is competing for the same people.

But don't count on companies which are lean and mean to turn back the clock to mainframes, dumb terminals, and appliances. Value differentiation is their guide, and this goes well beyond client-servers into the benefits which can be derived from visual programming and desk-area networks.

Perhaps the most pervasive of all reasons behind the major change which characterized top management policy, during the last 5 years, is networking. Regardless of their other assets and liabilities, Internet, the World Wide Web, languages like HTML and VRML, as well as virtual engines like Java are instrumental in changing—in the most radical manner—the way we look at communications and computers. Let's see what this means in terms of the new systems coming onstream.

10.7 The Concepts Underpinning MIT's ViewStation and Desk-Area Network

At MIT, a distributed multimedia solution known as desk-area network, VuNet is a 1 Gbit/s asynchronous transfer mode (ATM) system which interconnects general-purpose workstations, multimedia servers, and bridges to other networks. Media streams are exchanged between interconnected workstations and servers in a seamless manner.

The DAN architecture has several advantages over traditional client-server approaches, including the ability to share multimedia devices, thereby reducing the burden of multimedia tasks on the workstation. The new solution aims to ease the problems arising from the fact that the current generation of workstations are not well adapted to multimedia jobs because of their intensive input/output.

Part and parcel of the DAN concept is the ViewStation (VuStation). To increase the flexibility of the system and its performance, the designers have seen to it that multimedia devices are taken out of the workstation and connected directly to the network.

- Workstations access these servers over the network and coordinate the movement of information streams among the different parts of the system.

- This presents several advantages over the more traditional workstation model, including a better ability to share network-based resources.

- It also permits access to nonlocal devices and relieves one's workstation of a portion of the I/O work.

The strategy which has been adopted is quite different from multiprocessing because of the barriers that the latter presents between network and processors. DAN takes a simple approach to interfacing which permits flexible integration of more processors and workstations. This makes it feasible to

- Attach heterogeneous workstations to the network
- Target a specific performance upgrade

These heterogeneous workstations use the same bus and rely on asynchronous transfer mode for high-speed information transfer. Figure 10.2 shows the architecture of the desk-area network. The switches typically operate from 500 to 700 Mbits/s but can run at 1500 Mbits/s.

Much of the design effort revolves on the idea that allowing multimedia information to reach the application requires the channeling of significant bit streams to the workstation processor(s) rather than bypassing it with specialized hardware. This permits a greater variety of multimedia applications, allowing computer-based extraction of information at the workplace level. Software supports

- ATM adaptation layers
- Link table setup
- Flow control

By pushing these functions to the edges of the network and *into the clients,* the chosen strategy simplifies the design of network hardware and permits signifi-

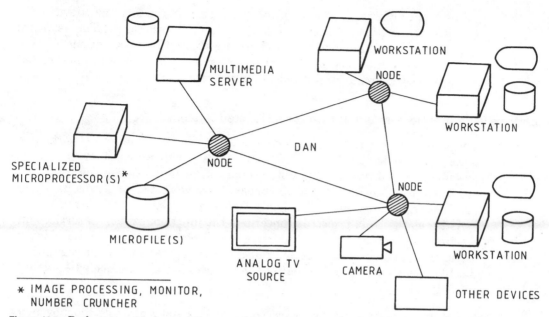

Figure 10.2 Desk-area networks permit one to increase functionality, specialize the off-the-shelf processors, and offload workstation-based functions.

cant flexibility in handling multimedia streams. It goes without saying that this job cannot be done through appliances.

In a way, the desk-area network can be seen as a *personalized Intranet*. Its design strategy replaces the traditional bus structure of the workstation with ATM interconnecting a variety of multimedia devices on a fast communications substrate which is internal to the workstation. The interface resides between the processor and its memory hierarchy.

The attention paid to flexibility and openness to future evolution see to it that the chosen approach can support different types of clients and servers. Three classes of devices are currently being integrated into the system:

- Workstations
- Specialized multimedia servers
- Internetwork interfaces

General-purpose workstations are connected through a host interface while specialized multimedia devices can be designed to link directly to the network. Account has been taken of the fact that offices are equipped with network switches which interconnect workstations and multimedia devices.

The current implementation provides for local- and wide-area links. At the prototype level, four nodes in Boston have been interconnected to another ViewStation unit installed in New Jersey. Each of these nodes can be dedicated to different jobs.

One of the significant aspects of this project lies in the fact that ViewNet is a 1 Gbit/s network using a modern communications technology. The asynchronous transfer mode is a new approach to interconnecting workstations, servers, and other network-based multimedia devices, as well as bridges to other networks. Also, the architectural choices make sense.

10.8 ViewNet's Architecture and the Sense of Trusted Systems

The ViewNet architecture supports the ability to easily share network-based devices, access nonlocal resources, communicate with workstations in a seamless manner, and treat remote units as part of the desk-area network. In a way reminiscent of the early years of Arpanet, no workstation serves as a focal point for organizing communications over the network.

As far as the DAN project is concerned, the functionalization of services and resources was necessary because currently workstations are not well adapted to multimedia tasks with input/output-intensive operation. Therefore multimedia I/O operations are taken out of the workstation and connected directly to the network.

- Using DAN, workstations access these devices and coordinate the movement of data streams.

- This is a flexible architecture with advantages over classical models.

The chosen solution provides a uniform interface to peripherals. Offloading the workstation from I/O functions, networking the latter through local ATM gigastream, leads to the rethinking of several design issues already known from LAN, MAN, and WAN. Solutions can be user-centered.

The network appliance fans may say that this is, after all, what they are suggesting to do with Internet. If they think or say so, they are wrong. Internet is a *public* network. By contrast, DAN is a *private* network which will be increasingly dedicated to one person.

- It is likely that IBM, which participated in MIT's ViewNet/ViewStation project, will use DAN software over the Internet.

- This will defeat the DAN concept which, in its fundamentals, aims to increase dependability and lead to *trusted systems.**

The researchers who participated in the MIT meetings did not fail to underline that the primary issue in connection to ViewNet is trust. Emphasis on trust and dependability, not only on reliability, is necessary because networks contain many unknowns and may be approached by potentially hostile users.

---

*For a number of years, the U.S. government has established *TCSEC: Trusted Computer Systems Evaluation Criteria; TDI: Trusted Database management system Interpretation;* and *TSIG: Trusted Systems Interoperability Group.* TCSEC identifies security requirements. TDI interprets TCSEC for different DBMSs.

The original DAN is a dependable network because it addresses the office space and working environment of the user. A private environment somewhat eases the trusted systems norms which, in wide-area networks, pose heavy requirements in terms of resources.

Because trusted desk-area networks can be designed and implemented much more simply, security is enhanced as the DAN workstations can be made aware of access control restrictions at the edges of ViewNet. At MIT, this function is implemented through software, within DAN's software-intensive design philosophy.

The MIT researchers think that moving network security into the end nodes provides a higher degree of protection. This, however, means that at the point near the end user a significant amount of computing power is necessary to handle in real time both security and other tasks. When this is done in an able manner, the trust boundaries of the network are essentially redrawn.

- In large networks, the infrastructure generally provides the necessary controls and other complex functions.

- With ViewNet, the host workstation software is trusted to run the network's protocols and security measures.

In terms of flexibility in operational execution, network functions such as routing and topology discovery are software-based. The ATM adaptation layer and flow control can also be in software. As a result, a more sophisticated process scheduling can be implemented.

10.9   The Able Management of Video Traffic*

One of the basic architectural features of DAN regards video traffic. Video traffic can be directed to compression servers programmed to deliver digital information directly to a DAN-based storage device or to a metropolitan-area or wide-area interface or bridge.

Incoming multimedia streams can be channeled to the appropriate ViewNet processor in compressed or uncompressed form. This traffic flow can be directed by agents or smart video boards. Design solutions can be locally applied in observance of several important factors.

- Available versus required bandwidth

- The specialization of attached processors

- Projected versus present traffic

- Wanted degree of resource sharing

- Cost factors affecting the solution

---

*See also the discussion of multimedia databases in Chap. 11.

Flexibility is enhanced by means of intelligent software and through interoperability. An ATM-based platform permits one to interface to a variety of other systems, providing a seamless connection between the desk area and the other network domains.

The infrastructure provides low-level media access, serving video traffic purposes from capture to display as well as other communication services. Audio acquisition and rendering are supported through commodity software and hardware, which is a plus.

A browser program is provided to look through the results of other applications such as the Office Monitor, Whiteboard Recorder, and Television News Agent. The first two function as video trash compactors that throw away frames but save important clips or other objects that merit the end user's attention.

Flexibility is ensured through knowledge-enriched routines. These permit one to port the system to higher-performance workstations as they become available.

- The main job involves porting the device drivers and associated software to the newer or faster platform.

- Because there are no complex functions in the input and output ports of the network, it has been possible to design much simpler interfaces.

A great deal depends on smart software and the flexibility which it affords. A critical goal in the design of ViewNet hardware has been simplicity. As already explained, sophisticated network functions were pushed to the edge of the network and became the responsibility of clients.

An asynchronous client interface has been chosen because clients should not be slaves to the network clock. Instead, DAN supports various input and output port rates, depending on the ATM to handle this well, with its small cell size and variable cell rate.

- Since sources and sinks of video and audio information must be able to handle data in bursts, DAN and its devices support bursty traffic.

- Network communication and its interfaces are transparent to the application, which is the way systems should be designed.

Among supported devices is a ViewNet video capture and processing board. It captures video frames from an NTSC source, packages them into ATM cells (if necessary, after processing), and transmits them across the desk-area network. The design is characterized by closed-loop control and temporal decoupling of the camera and the application.

- The workstation-based application software communicates with a video agent running on the video capture board.

- The closed-loop nature of this communication provides the feedback path that is essential to the support of a *perceptual-time* model.

Video streams can be generated with a variety of presentation and network characteristics. A rather simple set of cell-based commands is used to configure and control the programmable video capture and processing board.

The ViewNet project takes a software-oriented approach to video handling. The rate at which video frames are processed depends on the computational resources available to the workstation. Applications must be capable of varying the frame rate to

- Match available resources
- Avoid saturation
- Present a graceful degradation

Each workstation in ViewNet is responsible for opening, maintaining, and closing its own connections. This is done in a *wormhole* fashion by way of ATM control cells embedded in the data stream.

The wormhole is a concept from the physical sciences. Wormholes become possible because modern physics brings time and space together as aspects of a single framework, called *space-time*. This contrasts to the newtonian view of space and time as absolute and uniform.

Technically, *wormholes* are putative shortcuts between points in space. They join two places without visiting all the points on the straight line between them that theoretically is the shortest route.

- In the higher dimension, a wormhole is the hyperspace which envelopes the universe.
- It pinches two bits of something together to make contact across the gap.

Local distortions in space at two points narrowly separated in hyperspace cause them to bulge out and connect. Something could then travel down the wormhole to arrive farther away without traversing all the space in between. In the MIT solution,

- Daemons embedded in the allocation algorithms prevent nodes from stealing other nodes' connections.
- Processes run in the background verify link tables and refresh connections if necessary.

To maintain table consistency when the network is reconfigured, topology discovery daemons run on the workstations. Connection management gets pushed to the edge of the network. Each attached processor must be able to discover the network topology and initialize each link along the path.

The experience gained so far with the ViewNet environment demonstrates the relevance of the architectural choices which have been made. The flexibility of the chosen software-intensive approach became more apparent in the presence of concurrently active applications.

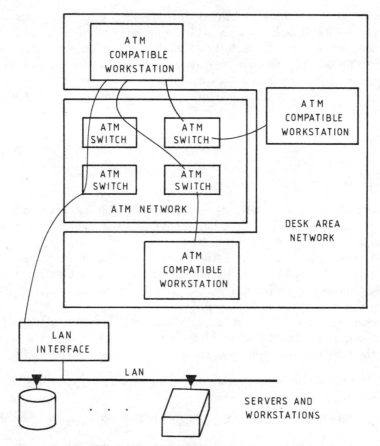

Figure 10.3 An ATM, DAN, and LAN interconnection architecture.

10.10 Why an ATM Protocol Serves Desk- and Local-Area Networks Well

Desk-area network and local-area network connections based on ATM involve hardware components which consist of microprocessors, memory units, switches, internetworking devices (such as routers and gateways), and other interfaces to the public network. Each of these elements can be interconnected in a variety of ways within the more general architectural concept shown in Fig. 10.3:

- A microprocessor unit in a DAN may be connected to one or more ATM switches provided it has more than one ATM interface.

- An ATM DAN would use a mesh or hierarchical topology, high-speed cell switching, and standard ATM protocols.

Besides gigastreams, hence bandwidth, one of the major benefits of the ATM DAN solution is its scalability. The concept of local-area networks is by now 20 years old, although applications really took off in the early 1980s. The elder protocols outlived their time. They are not really fit for the coming communications and computer environments. Are there alternatives to ATM? Yes there are, but they are not exciting.

- Fast Ethernet
- 100 Any LAN
- FDDI

Fast Ethernet is carrier sensing multiple access with collision detection (CSMA/CD). Back in the early 1980s, MIT had done a study which proved that collision detection (and collision avoidance) protocols reduce the bandwidth by almost an order of magnitude—and anyway are not fit for voice traffic. Neither are they fit for multimedia. Video will saturate Fast Ethernet.

Another problem of Fast Ethernet with multimedia is that it is nondeterministic. Other weaknesses characterize the 100 Any LAN, which is pseudodeterministic. Its protocol is poll-based, and to my knowledge poll selection is the eldest protocol with multidrop lines on record. It is more than 30 years old, revamped with Token-Ring, re-revamped with 100 Any Lan—but not changed.

As for FDDI's two versions, I see them as nonstarters and will not bet on them. Some years back because of a network project with a major financial institution I met with cognizant people at Bell Telephone Laboratories. They advised me to keep out of FDDI. Over the years never did I have a reason to regret this advice. FDDI has problems which make it unlikely to be implemented at the desktop in competition with ATM.

Tomorrow's computing and communications systems will operate in an environment in which hardware devices are so inexpensive and readily available that there are thousands in a typical office. Therefore, attempts to interconnect them with megabit stream shared-media LANs would be impractical.

Although classical LANs have performed very well from 1980 to 1995, and they have led to cost-effective client-server solutions which made mainframes obsolete, times have changed. Nothing says that LANs as we know them will live forever.

- Within a fast-moving technological environment, the limitations of existing bus and ring LANs have long become apparent.
- Demands for greater bandwidths and more sophisticated user populations are steadily pushing for new solutions.

DANs and LANs will have protocol support for a mixture of high-level communication services. They will, as well, be used as backbones to interconnect existing networks. The mesh-star, which we saw in Fig. 10.3, provides digital transport connections between one transmitter and one or more receivers. It is doing so in real time.

To ensure instantaneous transport facilities necessary for future multimedia applications, it is necessary to have DANs and LANs with high bandwidth and low latency. Distributed management principles must be fully observed because congestion control will be easier to handle when all traffic is under local authority.

Transmission latency and its effect on the underlying communications protocol(s) are a lesser problem in distributed desk-area and local-area environments than in centralized solutions. ATM architectures are well suited to this purpose, because the network will have relatively few switching elements and associated hierarchies, allowing simpler routing algorithms.

Another plus with ATM solutions is that the network may carry many different kinds of traffic—synchronous, asynchronous, and isochronous. But there are many problems still to be addressed, for instance, how applications programs determine their expected work and indicate it to other routines or devices. As the implementation complexity increases, applications must be able to specify parameters such as maximum delay, peak and average data rate, and cell-loss probability. Then the network should allocate its resources to satisfy the application's requests.

Another reason why the ATM protocol fits well the DAN architecture is that its network intelligence is located at boundary nodes while transit nodes provide data transfer along preestablished paths. This open-loop strategy sees to it that information may be carried in different paths in the network.

These are some of the foremost aspects of the new architectural approaches which are by now well advanced to influence systems design in the years to come. A DAN is not attempting to micromanage its resources. It offers them a fertile domain in which to operate. Other contributors are the object-oriented solutions which we discuss in Chap. 11.

References

1. See D. N. Chorafas, *Interactive Videotex: The Domesticated Computer,* Petrocelli, New York, 1981.
2. See D. N. Chorafas, *Designing and Implementing Local Area Networks,* McGraw-Hill, New York, 1984.
3. D. N. Chorafas, *Beyond LANs—Client/Server Computing,* McGraw-Hill, New York, 1994.
4. *Business Week,* June 20, 1994.

Object-Oriented Software
and Multimedia Databases

11.1 Introduction

Since Chap. 1, reference has been made to object-oriented applications as one of the competitive developments in information technology. In Chap. 2, in connection to programming in the large, we have seen a solution by Citibank which used objects to restructure its retail banking software. This is further elaborated in this present chapter.

Object orientation is not so much a new idea as a concept whose time has come. As we have already seen, it has its roots in Simula, the simulation language of the late 1960s, and in notions embedded in artificial intelligence and the theory of abstract data types.

Objects have semantic meaning, and the present visibility of this approach started with linguistic constructs such as Smalltalk-80. Object languages help to create a complete programming environment[1] characterized by

- *Active objects,* which include information elements and commands

- *Passive objects* with only information elements which, however, may be multimedia

The object paradigm can be applied in principle to any of the traditional tasks of computing, but there are some specific areas in which its application promises significant advances. Among the implementation domains where object-oriented database management systems (DBMSs) are particularly suitable we distinguish

- The implementation of agents

- Computer-aided design (CAD)

- Computer-integrated manufacturing (CIM)

- Advanced financial applications in derivatives, securities, Treasury, and Forex

- The new wave of office automation (OA)
- Computer-assisted software engineering (CASE) tools
- Visual programming solutions

Other application domains where object orientation presents significant advantages are geographic information systems (GISs), image processing, cartography, and a number of cases in knowledge engineering including the practical implementation of expert systems.

In the background of the interest in object-oriented solutions lies the fact that an able response to database and programming requirements can no longer be provided by traditional models: hierarchical, networking, or relational. For many applications with complex requirements, hierarchical and Codasyl solutions are inadequate, while relational approaches lack semantics.

11.2 Basic Concepts Underpinning Object Solutions

Objects can be ideas or entities from the application domain being modeled. They have their own identity in the database and can be referred to independent of their attribute values. As we will see in this section, an object-oriented solution rests on a number of basic concepts which have become prominent because the evolution in programming and database management is propelled by the growing requirements of the users.

- The objects of the new sophisticated environments need flexible internal structures with semantic meaning.
- This is in contrast to the simple database contents characterizing traditional data processing and to the legacy-type applications of the past.

Emphasis is increasingly placed on structuring a system around the objects that it manipulates rather than the functions it performs on them, because these functions change over time. A further goal is to reuse whole data structures together with some of the operations associated with them.

At the level of programming in the large, object-oriented notions help us get away from isolated procedures by describing objects as instances of classes consisting of abstract data types (ADTs). This means data structures which are known as a *class* from an established interface rather than through case-by-case representation. The class is a basic modular unit which describes the implementation of an abstract data type, though not necessarily the ADT itself. Classes may be reused in many different applications, with system construction viewed as the assembly of existing classes and of their instantiation.

Abstract data types are not the exclusive province of object-oriented applications. They can also be found with some relational DBMSs. Beyond ADT and the databases' *referential integrity,* however, there exist other basic concepts characterizing an object solution. Of these, seven are the most important:

1. Class
2. Encapsulation

3. Constraints

4. Inheritance

5. Metalevels

6. Polymorphism

7. Semantics

Classes are named collections of objects. Objects belonging to the same class share common functions. Computations are defined on a class and are applicable to the *instances* of this class and the associated constraints. Classes are organized into a hierarchy with inherited functions.

With *encapsulation,* under a shell which becomes the unit of reference, objects hide the internal structure of their data and the algorithms characterizing their functionality. Instead of exposing the contents of the capsule to implementation details, objects present interfaces, keeping their abstractions clean of extraneous information.

Constraints identify the permissible functions that can be applied to an object of that class, creating a system which makes it feasible to support generalization and specialization. A class type may be declared to be a subclass of another class. In that case, all instances of the subclass are also instances of the superclass.

- This is a good example of what is meant by functions inherited by the subclass.

- The notion of inheritance is very important in object-oriented solutions.

Inheritance sees to it that an object features characteristics of the class to which it belongs. (See also an applications example in Sec. 11.5.) This feature is a main contributor to the increased programming productivity through object orientation. Inheritance allows developers to reuse preexisting code, by deriving behaviors from classes which can belong to *ephemeral hierarchies:*

- A class provides specifications that describe the data model and the operations that can be performed on a given information element.

- An object is an example of a particular data structure constructed according to a plan; but while the solution adopts a hierarchy, this is *ephemeral,* hence very flexible.

A basic concept from knowledge engineering which can be found in object orientation concerns *metalevels*. A metalevel is a higher level of reference which sets behavioral characteristics and constraints. It also makes it possible to implement multiple inheritances. Etymologically, the prefix *meta* indicates a definition and a constraint.

- Metaknowledge is knowledge about knowledge.

- Metadata is data about data.

- Metarules are rules about rules.

Polymorphism is the process which enhances flexibility by handling many shapes through one interface. For instance, a software component can make a request of an entity or another software component without exactly knowing what that other party is.

The component receiving the request interprets it and determines according to its parameters, variables, and data on hand how to execute the request. Polymorphism gives the developer flexibility to create multiple definitions for functions, permitting classes to be more general and hence more reusable.

Semantics is the branch of linguistics concerned with the nature, development, structure, and changes of the meaning of concepts, entities, and forms. It is also the specific study of relations between signs, or symbols, and what they mean or denote.

- Hierarchical DBMSs support semantics because they are characterized by inheritance.

- But once set, this inheritance is inflexible while the inheritance of object approaches is perishable.

Objects are described by their behavior, and they can be accessed and manipulated by means of functions. As long as the semantics of the functions remain the same, the database can be physically as well as logically reorganized without affecting application programs. This provides a high degree of data abstraction and data independence. Handling objects within a networked environment presents major advantages over record-oriented data models. In an application sense, the objects represented as records can be referred to in terms of their attribute values. And, as we have already seen, encapsulated within an object may be only data (passive object) or data and commands (active object).

11.3 Object-Oriented Software and Corporate Architectural Standards

To design and build software through object-oriented approaches requires a foundation of languages, databases, programming tools, class libraries, and a methodology which sees to it that object-oriented systems coexist with investments made in classical languages as well as in relational, Codasyl, or hierarchical databases. Technically,

- A function may be applied to an object only if it is defined on a type to which the object belongs.

- Objects serve as arguments to functions and may be returned as results of functions.

A property of an object represents a function of one argument that returns a value when applied to the object. Functions that can be defined to include *predicates* and multiple arguments provide direct support of different relationships, therefore adding to system flexibility.

The integration of an object-oriented solution into *visual programming* affects more than just analysts, programmers, and database administrators.

Management needs to understand how the introduction of this technology changes the computing processes, thereby realizing business and technical benefits and reducing costs as well as timetables associated with software engineering.

The object approach can be seen as a natural outcome of historical developments connected to database management systems as well as of the transition which took place from a compute-intensive information technology to data-intensive solutions. Originally, which essentially means in the 1960s, the DBMSs have grown up from simple file systems storing an increasing amount of data, in association with a given program, to structures manipulating records through mechanisms that aid application-independent database approaches.

One of the most important issues to consider, as object databases get embedded in languages such as VRML and Java, is what a data manipulation language (DML) should be doing. The goal is to develop a means that fosters interoperability between software modules and applications, on one hand, and DBMS from different vendors, on the other. The goal is to achieve

- Greater operational efficiency
- A state of virtual (not physical) homogeneity

As multimedia information environments evolve, it is important to describe and define a DML whose syntax fits smoothly into the host language syntax. This requires a linguistic construct that takes full advantage of the strengths of the host language as opposed to competing with them, as does SQL.

- Able solutions will address at the same time programming in the large and programming in the small.
- They will also make use of agents as well as of interactive visualization, in order to promote greater end-user efficiency.

The Citibank example in Chap. 2 and the one which is coming in Chap. 13 focus on programming in the large. In connection to programming in the small, object orientation offers more promise as a method for developing computer software than alternatives such as structured, functional, or logic programming.

Supported by the object paradigm, software development and maintenance can benefit from code structuring and the sharing mechanisms which come into play. Data abstraction, for example, is helpful in ensuring the coexistence of many different internal data representations. Reusable modules could be encapsulated in objects whose interface would be the same no matter what their functions.

Changes could be handled by active objects. Constraints and a graph-based model could be seen as sets of objects connected in networks with message flows and activities associated with the connected objects. These objects can have implicit interfaces expressed by their

- Visual presentations

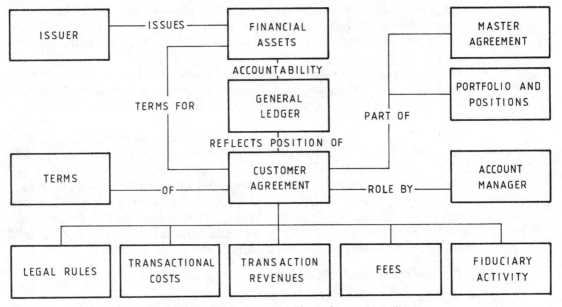

Figure 11.1 Programming in the large: business elements with an object orientation.

- Physical significance

A grand design would be a set of elements associated according to architectural rules. This can be accomplished in a part-whole ephemeral or permanent hierarchical fashion, with design rules maintained in an object dictionary. Such an approach simplifies the visual programming solution and serves the goals of a dynamic systems architecture.

Figure 11.1 presents an object-oriented application of programming in the large. It is based on a banking project. The whole scheme revolves on three objects, each of which can be taken as the kernel of an ephemeral hierarchy, depending on the application needs:

- Financial assets
- General ledger
- Customer agreement

Other objects in Fig. 11.1 are business elements entering into one or more of the principal flexible hierarchies. In connection with *customer agreement,* relevant objects for a specific transaction are the master agreement, portfolio, and positions; legal rules to be observed; transaction costs; and revenues.

If this is the high-level view, there are as well programming-in-the-small prerequisites implied by object-oriented software. Dr. John Pfaltz, of the Institute for Parallel Computation, University of Virginia, suggests that the power of object orientation is best exploited when the objects reside in main memory.

The use of disk storage reduces the effectiveness of object implementation since information elements must be brought into main memory as records, then opened up and exploited in an object-based manner. Hence programming in the small should pay attention to how objects are being handled, particularly in a distributed implementation environment.

11.4 Goals and Tools for Visual Programming Solutions

It cannot be repeated too often. One of the fundamental reasons why the software business is in crisis is that, by and large, developers are trying to solve the programming challenges of this decade with old, worn-out tools. Classical programming approaches are not nearly as sophisticated as the applications they attempt to build, resulting in an imbalance between the effort and the outcome. Aware of this, leading-edge organizations actively exploit the potential of object-oriented languages, and software design approaches based on visual programming are increasingly adopted. Much of the project success of VRML and Java is based on this fact.

Companies with experience in object DBMSs and object tools have found that their use has positive effects on the development of sophisticated applications. The same is true of visual programming solutions. Advantages are due to the degree to which object-oriented designs tend to be implementation-independent and the portability, adaptability, and scalability of solutions, while development time is reduced.

The combination of object approaches and visual programming permits the rapid delivery of modular business-critical applications, setting the stage for fast timetables. It also enhances the ability to identify important, visible projects that can be executed in days or weeks rather than years.

By enabling modularity and flexibility, visual programming and object technology serve to manipulate complex, highly interactive applications. Examples include risk management, treasury operations, and logistics management. All three cases involve a distributed implementation domain and have mission-critical requirements. By representing through objects the data, text, images, charts, voice, different annotations, and compound electronics documents, users can easily incorporate, exchange, and process polyvalent information elements.

As the example in Sec. 11.3 demonstrates, object solutions allow better integration among the elements entering into an application. For its part, visual programming enhances operating environments by making them more intuitive, and permits work to be done by moving the targeted entity on the computer screen. Therefore, users can focus more efficiently on the essential features of a problem.

- Object solutions make it feasible to effectively model real-life problems.

- Visual programming does not try to fit a problem to the procedural approach of a computer language.

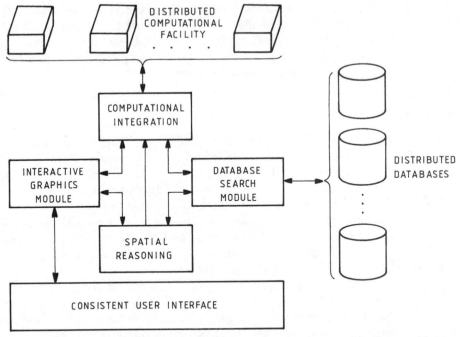

Figure 11.2 An object-oriented approach involving diverse computational facilities and heterogeneous distributed databases.

Figure 11.2 shows a modular object-oriented approach adopted by a manufacturing company to serve a computer-aided design strategy spanning two continents and five different countries. As with most similar systems, the component parts were heterogeneous, but an intentional database approach provided seamless access to multimedia resources.[2]

Class definitions adopted in this particular solution included common functionality, enabling developers to design programs by deriving subclasses. The chosen strategy has overridden existing methods by implementing new ones. The principle of encapsulation kept engineering designers from having to know all implementation details. As this experience demonstrated,

- Encapsulated objects effectively combined data and operations to be performed into a single entity.

- This helped hide the mechanics of an object from user-written applications that access the object.

The result has been a higher degree of data independence, as active objects encapsulated data with the procedures that can be performed upon this data. Typically each object carried a unique identifier designating the encapsulated object in the database.

- Pieces of code menus, icons, rules, forms, drawings, and bills of materials are examples of the wide range of entities whose attributes were represented by objects.

■ Procedures, referred to as *methods,* defined such operations as *copy, add, delete,* and *display,* essentially mapping an object's permissible behavior.

Methods were put into play by messages passed to objects by applications. The same message could be sent to different objects to trigger equivalent operations, but the exact details of how a message is realized were hidden from the person sending the message.

■ In the last analysis, complex concepts and structures were made more understandable by the removal of details.

■ This led to application independence which permitted the generalization of design factors.

The adopted solution capitalized on the fact that the process of abstraction is the antithesis of hard coding. If every detail were programmed, the program and the modules it contains would be inflexible and almost impossible to adapt.

By contrast, user-defined data types provided flexibility as well as a mechanism for associating greater meaning with the information elements. Object identity enabled users to distinguish two or more objects even when both had the same values for all their attributes except some particular, identifiable characteristic.

11.5 Exploiting the Capabilities Presented by Ephemeral Hierarchies

The concept of an ephemeral hierarchy is explained in Sec. 11.2. There we emphasized that metarules help to set both a reference level and constraints regarding the rules being used, while metadata provides information about the data we use. In this section we will see what can be obtained through the synergy of these notions.

In principle, synergy can be realized by programming in the large. Rather than addressing details at the coding level, programming in the large applies a knowledge-enriched approach which defines behavior and constraints at the *metalevel.* In an object environment, this metalevel is not necessarily hierarchical, but it has an impact on the levels below it.

In turn, metalevel solutions permit the implementation of an ephemeral hierarchy through an *inheritance* mechanism by which abstractions are made increasingly concrete, as subclasses are created for greater levels of specialization. Thanks to the principle of inheritance, developers can create a subclass to derive new classes from existing ones and provide the linkages necessary to add extensions.

All this is very important in connection with a business architecture because both metalevel structures and inheritance promote code reusability. They make it possible to create subclasses of new objects by adding or changing only those characteristics necessary to adequately represent the new subclass.

Attributes and methods associated with the parent class are inherited by the new subclass.

In a recent project on risk management executed in real time, objects were arranged in classes that addressed 15 different financial products, but shared common attributes and methods. Subclasses of objects formed out of other objects

- Inherited such attributes and methods from their ancestors
- Passed them on to their descendants

Certain attributes of lower-level objects were then defined through a series of stepwise refinements. The concept of *metalevels* made it feasible not only to implement ephemeral, hence flexible, hierarchies, but also to profit from multiple-inheritance possibilities, which added power to the system design.

- In a single-inheritance design, each class has one parent, leading to the tree structure known through hierarchical systems.
- Multiple inheritance creates networks of classes which are more difficult to visualize, but just as easy to traverse.

There are, of course, prerequisites. To face the complexity challenge, a solution must be able to resolve name conflicts in traits inherited from two or more parent classes which have properties with identical names. The interest in this approach comes from the fact that multiple inheritance has proved very useful in complex applications, particularly in parallel programming. (See also Chap. 12.)

Parallel programming, as well as the development of *frameworks* for all types of computers, can significantly benefit from polymorphism. As already explained, this is the process which enhances flexibility by handling many shapes through one interface. As a result of polymorphism,

- Methods can be written that generically tell target objects to do something, without requiring that the sending object know how the receiving object will understand the message.
- This permits one to provide in a seamless manner a significant portion of the functionality needed for a particular task, giving the designer a head start in software development.

In an implementation sense, polymorphism is associated with the process of message passing to trigger operations, one message initiating different processes—as demanded by the application—while maintaining as gateway a unique interface. This approach has a number of advantages:

- It facilitates visual programming.
- It provides a rapid prototyping capability.
- It makes feasible the use of a parallel compiler.
- It can function as a framework, as we will see in Chap. 12.

The application which we examined in Sec. 11.4 capitalized on all these advantages. Rather than attempt to micromanage the details of the different incompatible CAD installations used by the company at home and abroad, it addressed the programming-in-the-large requirements of the complex global CAD system.

Other implementations can evidently benefit from this experience. Care should, however, be taken to avoid biasing tool choices and applications results toward any one of the alternatives presented by vendors. The wise organization will keep the necessary choices to itself and develop the potential to deploy object technology broadly within its operations—through *its own* business architecture.

11.6   Why Object-Oriented Approaches Can Promote the Use of Agents

As we have seen, among the applications for which object-oriented solutions are ideally suited are computer-aided design, computer-integrated manufacturing, and computer-aided software engineering as well as imaging and multimedia applications and the implementation of complex systems in finance.

The common thread throughout these references is concurrent work. Object orientation provides an effective means for dynamically sharing records among multiple users, over the network. Some of the objects being shared may be *agents*; others use agents for message passing and for control reasons.

- Objects facilitate the use of help features.

- They also make feasible the implementation of daemons. (See also Chap. 10.)

Introduced as one of the characteristics of Unix, daemons are supervisory processes. Unix itself is not object-oriented, but the concept of daemons proved to be most valid in a networking environment, where supervisory processes must be universal and it is most advantageous to handle them as objects.

Also, the database-oriented applications of modern business and industry impose greater requirements on computer storage than fast reading and writing of simple records. Applications for knowledge workers are *event-driven* and need immediate traversal of thousands of objects within complex data structures, in fraction of a second.

- Object-based solutions provide a way to interact with databases in rapid access.

- It permits one to use transient data structures temporarily created by and for the application.

This ephemeral characteristic opens up new possibilities for human-machine communications, which are work group-oriented but perform as single-user programs when appropriately assisted by agents. Most of the tier 1 companies which today use object languages and DBMSs, capitalize on the described facilities.

One of the better-known financial institutions has used agents in an object environment, to help its executives and professionals pose an effective response to queries. This project capitalized on the fact that among the most interesting features of the visual programming language adopted were

- Object graph matching
- Attribute pattern matching
- Nested attribute pattern recognition
- Nested attribute access at large

Object-based agents have therefore been designed with features that ease database access and make query evaluation easier and more efficient for the end user. In turn, this has been instrumental in promoting mental productivity.

The adopted solution makes it possible to access complex objects for query purposes in an ad hoc manner. The implementation permits one to handle different variants, retrieving the latest version of an object as well as its predecessor version(s).

A similar project has been undertaken by an engineering organization, and it has given just as good results. This project features some more functions such as integrated archiving facilities which have been provided for large data items, such as

- Two-dimensional specifications
- Three-dimensional models
- Digital images
- Animation sequences permitting walk-throughs

The project has established a metalevel to the query language, which sees to it that the user is free to move objects, object clusters, or whole databases to the media of choice. Multimedia transfers take place from optical disks and from remote locations to local servers and personal workstations.

- It is possible to access, archive, and retrieve complex objects piecewise as well as to distribute one compound object among several media.
- Access to all objects is done through one uniform set of operations, and no application needs to know about the physical location of an object.

Assisted through knowledge artifacts, the system provides seamless networked user access. It operates in parallel, and it looks after transaction security. Privacy and security can be effectively supported through the use of agents.

In conclusion, as the examples in Secs. 11.4, 11.5, and 11.6 suggest, the solutions to important database problems are not known a priori, but they can be researched and developed. Significant software and hardware advances in this decade do not make brute-force approaches attractive, let alone economical.

- The scale of the prospective applications is too great.

- Their complexity is beyond what we have known so far.
- The new generation of applications call for departures from the beaten path.

To ensure that sound design prerequisites are observed, we need to learn more about user-centered approaches moving database management toward object orientation enriched with knowledge engineering. Competitiveness requires the discovery of appropriate characterizations of system properties, going beyond formalisms to capture essential structure.

11.7 Why Object-Oriented Solutions Can Improve Program Maintenance

Life-cycle solutions connected to software are today at a premium, not only because of the polyvalence of the problems we are confronting but also because the ongoing combination of different talents has produced some interesting results. The advantage of high-performance, object-oriented software is that

- It can create a flexible, responsive, and integrated implementation.
- It permits one to revamp the whole issue of program maintenance.

Object technology changes our perspective concerning what we can do in terms of maintenance. Software constructed from an object-oriented basis benefits from rapid development capabilities, flexibility within a distributed database environment, and higher programmer productivity.

At the same time, the more consistent product quality provided through visual programming and object orientation leads to a dynamic maintenance capability. It also makes feasible the design and sustenance of user-friendly human windows as well as the integration of interactive database functions.

Figure 11.3 shows an example of this last reference. The block diagram describes seamless data transfers between end-user functions, databases, and software packages over local-area and long-haul communications facilities.

- The core structure is a platform for integrating heterogeneous databases.
- The homogeneous interface is provided at the workstation level.

A steady preoccupation of users, and therefore of the more clear-eyed vendors, is the ability to integrate object-oriented databases with the existing conventional databases into a single, unified information system. The goal is to have component databases in a distributed environment operate in client-server mode, sharing information elements on a companywide basis.

- Applications should be accessing any number of distributed databases in a way that is seamless to the end user.
- These will typically be running on a variety of incompatible hardware and software platforms.

Because transparency has to be implemented through software, the use of

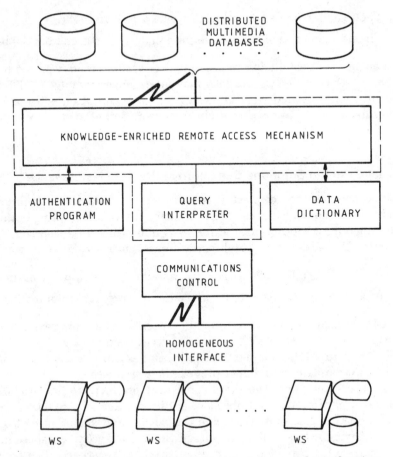

Figure 11.3 Object-oriented multimedia transfer between end-user functions, databases, and software packages.

agents should see to it that differences across systems are of no concern to the end user or the application. As far as the user is concerned, there must be

- One information system to understand
- One place to turn for answers to queries
- One virtually unified database structure

This is doable because object-oriented approaches help meet the needs of a variety of interactive users in different programming environments. Prior to the advent of the Internet, they were designed to work with industry standard C and C++ compilers. Today they increasingly use the World Wide Web and its tools.

As Part 2 explained, while VRML and Java offer the user-comprehensive visual programming facilities, they also contribute to changing the software culture. In turn, this has the positive effect of shortening development time, improving quality, and reducing costs for design-intensive implementations.

- Through visual programming, many components can be projected to integrate smoothly into an existing environment.

- A good deal of these components are reusable, easing both the development cycle and system sustenance.

- More benefits can be derived from an open architecture which is extensible and forms a solid base for transition to newer paradigms.

This requirement is particularly important as applications become increasingly interdisciplinary, solving problems in an ad hoc manner rather than in a fixed, unalterable frame of reference—hence, the wisdom of using perishable hierarchies, in the way discussed since Sec. 11.2.

Let me, however, add a note of caution. Not everything in our discussion is straightforward or fully proven. In its current form, object-oriented technology has not been around long enough for one to be able to point to a wealth of references—and users with successful cases prefer not to be named so as not to wake up competitors.

But the real-life examples given in this text point to a dramatic reduction in development and maintenance costs. Some companies that participated in this research talked about a reduction in life-cycle maintenance costs, for medium to large applications, of 80 percent or more. If this level could be sustained in the longer term, rather than devoting some 75 percent of human capital in systems specialists for maintenance reasons (which is an aberration), this could be cut down to 15 percent.

11.8 The Use of Multimedia Databases in Interactive Development Projects

Multimedia databases are a relatively new concept. One of its prerequisites is the effective integration of traditional data, text, voice, icons, graphics, image, and animation. Compound electronic documents are an applications example requiring a multimedia structure. In a business environment, teleconferencing and corporate memory facilities provide other examples of multimedia implementation domains.

All this is relevant to this chapter because the best approaches to multimedia databases are object-oriented. They are also open-ended and extensible. Assistance by knowledge artifacts is given to queries made networkwide, which often implies both qualitative and quantitative references. In terms of business and industrial use, the requirements for multimedia database manipulation include

- Flexible solutions to cognitive issues and semantics

- Synchronization of the different media, such as sound and images

- Enabling of modalities such as voice annotation of graphics and text

Supporting software includes hypertext/hypermedia for nonsequential document handling; speech command; augmentation of menu selection by spaceball

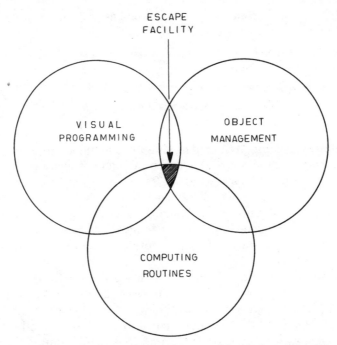

Figure 11.4 Agents can be instrumental in implementing an
escape facility.

or mouse and eventually through voice; as well as touch and speech commands
in a put-that-there form.

A valid system solution should provide for an efficient escape facility between
the different tools, computing routines, object management commands, and all
other entities entering into the human-machine interaction. Figure 11.4 shows
that this can be done very effectively through agents.

As we have seen in Chap. 10, the able handling of multimedia solutions is
feasible due to progress in communications at large, and especially wideband
optical communications. An equally critical role has been played by the implementation of new storage media such as optical disks and the fact that technology impacts on graphics through digitizers and generally digital models.

Semantics supported through object-oriented programming languages has
contributed a great deal, and the same is true of computer projects specifically
designed to capitalize on visual programming facilities. MIT's ViewStation has
brought innovative solutions to support interactive multimedia applications. As
already discussed, basic to this project have been these two premises:

- Architectural guidelines must be established to assist in the design of a
  media processing environment.

- Raw media data such as video pixels should be made interactively accessible
  to the application.

Chapter 10 has already explained why *perceptual time* is more important to interactive applications than real time. It has also outlined why the software approach adopted must be able to ride *technology's curve*, without upsetting the programming endowment.

The emphasis on perceptual time poses the challenge of identifying and developing algorithms that are computationally efficient. This can be achieved by taking an approach which, rather than attempt to mimic a human visual system as is done in computer vision, treats the camera as a sensor:

- Intelligence-enriched computer software is able to make sophisticated deductions without a full understanding of the images in the video stream.

- Such deductions are used to trigger some other action, for instance, recording a video snapshot in a file or sounding an alarm.

To reach such results, computation is organized around filters placed in the video stream. The ViewStation project has implemented a growing library of these filters which can be divided into two groups: stateful and stateless.

There are as well filters that do thresholding, match templates to images, take the difference between images, or perform other tasks. A basically object-oriented approach to media programming includes

- A set of conventions

- A collection of media processing modules

- An image processing library

- Necessary run-time packages

- A graphical user interface (GUI)

Old protocols, such as the 3270 and many others, have a character user interface (CUI). This is an aberration in a modern information environment. Not only should the protocol be designed for a GUI, but also it should be enriched with a growing endowment of functions, as shown in Fig. 11.5.

11.9   Network Protocols for Multimedia Applications and Wideband Channels

In Chap. 10 we discussed the choice of asynchronous transfer mode (ATM) as the line discipline for MIT's desk-area network and associated multimedia projects. Beyond this, other, more specific developments also proved to be necessary in order to establish and sustain an environment which is operationally sound.

For instance, the Media Laboratory has designed a number of network protocols for sending video from a programmable video capture board to a workstation. These protocols fall into three classes:

- Command

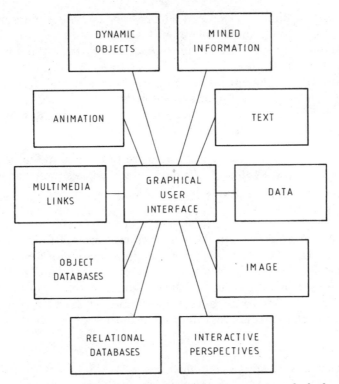

Figure 11.5 An application development environment can be both extended and enhanced through GUI.

- Video transport
- Video traffic

The command protocol makes the board execute a particular command using a single ATM cell, which is formatted into a number of fields. Command information is being carried by this shell.

To send video information from the video capture board to a workstation, the system uses a transport protocol similar to that specified by the ATM adaptation layer 5. Cells are grouped into larger packets—the transmission frames.

To avoid overwhelming the workstation's network interface with video data, the video capture board employs a network traffic protocol. Video is sent in small bursts separated by delays, during which the burst is processed by the workstation.

The message that these references bring home is that while the initial choice has to be factual, documented, and forward-looking, it had to be supplemented by greater detail, through other, more focused design characteristics. This is true not only of network protocols in a new domain, such as the handling of digital video streams, but also of all advanced applications of information technology.

What we classically call the basic software of a computer must be evaluated from a similar perspective. The operating system environment should be chosen to support multimedia all the way to the application programs—including *computer-mediated* and *computer-participative* video applications. There are two reasons for this statement:

- Even the best operating systems have not been designed for multimedia.

- The currently available operating systems are not optimized for use in a network-intensive sense.

Recall that when computer-aided applications were first developed, they were intended to support people working individually, stand-alone on distinct projects. This is the antithesis of the current trend, where groupware dominates and facilities already embedded in systems don't necessarily assist the implementation of multimedia.

- As their sophistication and complexity increase, applications need to support cooperative work by professionals.

- Team members must find it easy to work together in an interactive way and must have access to a growing wealth of multimedia database information.

- End users must be able to create new objects, or new versions of existing objects, without overwriting someone else's work.

Because the network is the computer, versatile network protocols must be designed and implemented. At the same time, every one of the goals described in these three bullets can be assisted through agents.

The synergy of agents and object-oriented solutions can effectively support collaborative work, allowing end users to have concurrent access to other professionals' ongoing work. It can also promote greater security, as Chap. 10 documented, using MIT's desk-area network as a background reference.

Users increasingly need to check out an object or group of objects, make changes, and bring them back into the main development stream. Engineering designers as well as rocket scientists[3] often wish to make these changes visible to other team members, notify them about milestones, and be notified by others when they contribute work. This is what makes concurrent group work a feasible and rewarding process.

References

1. See also D. N. Chorafas and H. Steinmann, *Object-Oriented Databases,* Prentice-Hall, Englewood Cliffs, NJ, 1993.
2. See also D. N. Chorafas, *Intelligent Multimedia Databases,* Prentice-Hall, Englewood Cliffs, NJ, 1994.
3. See D. N. Chorafas, *Rocket Scientists in Banking,* Lafferty Publications, London, 1996.

Frameworks for Multimedia and Parallel Computers

12.1 Introduction

A framework is a set of software modules that is expected to incorporate several program development tools. Engineering, particularly concurrent engineering, has made good use of frameworks; but in the general case, this is an issue more implicit than explicit in terms of programming approaches and of potential results.

The idea behind frameworks is that they help to normalize and package commonly required facilities. Therefore, they may help in the production of cleaner, more modular tools and packages, which can more easily cooperate with one another than those based on more or less incompatible technologies.

- Part of this definition is the *encapsulation* principle discussed in Chap. 11, but with a difference.

- The framework can be seen as a *reverse encapsulation,* where the environment supports the object.

Notice, however, that there is some hype associated with frameworks; therefore users have to be extremely careful with claims about tool integration. This is true because specific and explicit examples are still rare, particularly with the new framework announcements.

Some of the concepts coming into frameworks are known from other applications. For instance, as we saw in Chap. 11, object-oriented programming uses class concepts, inheritance, metalevels, and polymorphism. It has as well been explained that the practical implementation of these notions changes many things about the way users look at programming.

The object-oriented approach impacts on the development of libraries and the way software users employ them. We have spoken of class libraries to differentiate them from libraries that do not use object programming techniques. But class libraries are not static; they evolve.

- They no longer exist in isolation as simple development tools or aids holding open subroutines.

- But rather, they participate in the larger activity of creating modular applications, or subsystems of a larger implementation.

Indeed, some people in the computer industry look at these interrelated classes of objects that work together to form subsystems as software frameworks. This is not quite the definition given in the opening paragraphs of this chapter, but it is not much different either.

In an object-oriented sense, a framework can be just about any size, as long as it provides an organizing structure for class libraries. The resulting facilities see to it that software frameworks can be used, and have been used, with good results; but not all cases are really successful, as already underlined.

12.2   From Systems Concepts to the Effective Integration of Software Tools

The concept underpinning the approach discussed in Sec. 12.1 is that an object framework can stand alone or work in combination with other frameworks. The facilities that a framework provides help developers seek solutions for problem domains; the framework can also assist in program maintenance.

- Such general statement might, however, be considered misleading and therefore it should be looked at with care.

- There are frameworks and frameworks; and there are no universally defined features or requirements.

Starting with the fundamentals, what was said about facilitating solutions in a given problem domain is true only *if* and *when* a framework approach is used in connection with *rapid prototyping,* under stringent development timetables. With rigorous management of the software development process, an object framework could contribute the means for a well-designed infrastructure so that better software is created.

Good management practice will also see to it that a framework is used as a catalyst in taking a *life-cycle* view of the software. What this means is explained in Fig. 12.1, which identifies the main phases of development from conception to implementation and *sustenance.*

It is wrong to believe that, within this life-cycle context, tools would create miracles. A sound methodology is a prerequisite. Programming in the large must support a view architecture with command handling, saving distributed files and providing interactive documentation. Some, but not all, commodity frameworks have these features.

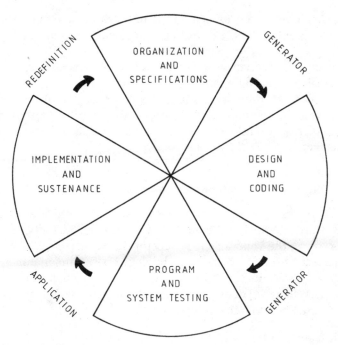

Figure 12.1 Opting for the implementation of life-cycle solutions.

While tools are an enabling technology, as with all created systems, project, management and grand design skill make the difference. Software developers must be able to look on-line at relevant source code. They should understand the calling sequences and the nature of the parameters as well as appreciate the framework's structure, facilities, and limitations, and ensure that the prototypes or modules they design produce the desired results. For instance, one of the frameworks currently on the market is said to offer novel software features able to monitor and control overall system behavior, despite errors in the application. Other goodies are "ingenious templates" for developing fault-tolerant replacement modules, integrating them into complex systems at run time.

It does not take an inordinate amount of experience to realize that these claims are from cloud nine. "There are no miracles," the physicist Dr. Rabii once said. "Only things we don't understand." Or things the vendors sell—either as hot air or because they do not understand what they are selling in the first place.

Developers using a software framework often find themselves in a "don't call us, we'll call you" situation. The object framework calls or subcalls into play subroutines. This, however, has prerequisites. It requires framework designers and implementers to clearly communicate the classes with their data members and method calls.

Software developers also need to comprehend and properly handle the overall architecture of the framework, when they are using it to accomplish their intended tasks. This is not as easy as it may sound, particularly with some frameworks available today. Be cautious concerning claims made by different vendors.

In conclusion, the transition from software development and applications involving classical linguistic constructs to an environment characterized by frameworks is not as simple as framework vendors say—but it is not that difficult either. Users will be able to get results only *if* they understand what they are buying *and* they are able to undergo a *cultural change*. But vendors rarely speak of this fact.

12.3   Can Frameworks Contribute to Software Integration?

It may sound ludicrous to ask, Can frameworks contribute to software integration?—given that integration is said to be the number 1 benefit of frameworks. But not everything the vendors say is substantiated by facts.

Let's assume that the information technology operations manager of an organization is really sold on the "integration" argument advanced by the framework's vendor. Which particular aspect of integration could, would, or should be supported the most (to name only three)?

- Linguistic constructs
- Database schemata
- Existing legacy programs

Figure 12.2 gives an example of the interaction between the first two items, and it suggests that the job to be done will not be easy, though it may be doable. Let's look separately at the linguistic constructs and database schemata included in this reference.

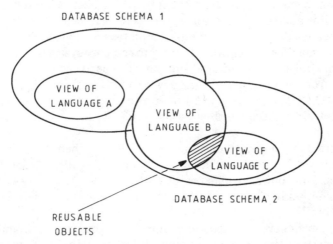

Figure 12.2 Integrating database schemata and language views.

The good news in this example is that language B, supported by the framework, works in synergy with language C, therefore leading to reusable objects. The bad news is that languages A and B are so different that they simply cannot communicate with each other. But there may be a way of doing so through encapsulation, rather than at an atomic level.

Only the proverbial long, hard look, based on detail and experimentation, can permit one to say whether a given framework might do what it promises. No two frameworks are the same; and while, in the general case, their use has shown merits in terms of certain applications, there are also a lot of false claims. These usually come in the form of

- New but poorly defined framework architectures and supported facilities
- Undocumented assurances that the framework lets users safely and reliably reuse most old software components
- Business failures hitting the software developers, which boomerang on the framework users

An example of the third bullet is *Taligent*. During a discussion with cognizant people in the Silicon Valley in January 1996, I heard the following comments:

- Taligent was a noble goal, but nothing has come out of it.
- The product was not dynamic enough to attract market interest.

One of the participants in this discussion compared the Taligent framework to VRML (see also Chap. 7) in terms of labor required for its development. He said Taligent employed 300 people for 5 years and got nothing out of it. By contrast, VRML was practically done by 1 person working for about 2 months—and it established a standard.

As for false claims, these typically follow the beaten path in respect to the goodies they promise. For instance, they suggest that users can incrementally improve system quality "in a structured way," or add new modules "without shutting down the system."

The more audacious undocumented offers "guarantee" a performance baseline despite errors due to bugs or change of old modules by new software components. Typically, they start by offering a methodology for computer resources, while the tools are promised at a later date. When that date comes, whatever tools are delivered prove substandard.

Claims and counterclaims about facilities able to integrate software tools are nothing new in the computer business. Nor is it any surprise that many of these claims are unsubstantiated. Rather, the surprise comes from the fact that in spite of such experience undocumented claims continue to be made, and many people believe them.

Quite often, user organizations fall prey to false promises because of the overriding need to acquire computer-based supports able to coordinate the efforts of a team of developers, including end users. In other cases, the reason for being taken to the cleaners is the unjustified hope that a framework will provide the ability to integrate routines from legacy applications.

This urge to find an integrative solution is understandable, and it has in its background the 20 or 30 million lines of code in the applications libraries of major companies. This will not be replaced overnight with new code—but neither is it going to be integrated through the false claims made by vendors. Hence, user organizations will be well advised to proceed with thorough tests prior to signing a contract.

12.4   Frameworks for Multimedia Applications: Microsoft's Active X

Microsoft's Object Linking and Embedding (OLE) technology—which has been recently renamed Active X—permits users to create compound multimedia documents consisting of objects such as text, graphics, charts, bit maps, and tables. It also makes it feasible for one application to drive another, through common macro programming spanning several applications.

Active X is essentially a serial processing object-oriented *framework* for modular software development, intended to be an open architecture for the Windows, NT, and Apple System 7 operating systems. The aim is to permit end users to create and manage compound documents that seamlessly incorporate objects of different types and formats, from spreadsheets to sound clips.

- Each object is created and maintained by its server application; but through the use of the framework, different features of the server applications are integrated.

- End users feel as if there were a single application, characterized by the functionality of each of these server software constructs.

The concept behind packages such as Active X is that while users used to buy software piecemeal, now they can get what they need through an integrated suite. This, it will be remembered, also happened in the mid-1980s when we moved from separate spreadsheets, word processing packages, time management, and other programs to an all-in-one type of integrated software. But now the level of aggregation is higher.

One of OLE's goals is to make it easier for users to seamlessly create compound documents employing multiple frames of reference. Other aims are to enable cross-application programmability by encouraging the use of component software modules and to permit new features and multimedia functions to be incorporated as they develop.

By this strategy, when an object is incorporated into a document, the document maintains an association with the server application that created it. In the OLE sense, linking and embedding are two ways to associate objects in a multimedia document.

- The differences between linking and embedding lies in how and where is stored the actual source data that comprises the object.

- This affects the object's portability, its methods of activation, and the nature of the compound document itself.

The framework takes care when an object is linked, even if link source data continues to physically reside wherever it was initially created. While in its current release OLE addresses serial-type processing, the concepts it incorporates can be extended to new structures required for parallel processing—evidently through the appropriate parallelization and optimization procedures.

For instance, the object linking approach to which the preceding paragraph made reference can be taken at different points within a document, within different document(s), or in remote servers. Only the link or reference to the object and appropriate presentation data is kept with the compound document. But the current solution has its shortcomings.

- Linked objects cannot move with documents into which they integrated to another machine.

- They must remain within the local file system or be copied explicitly, which is no longer a seamless approach.

The reason for proceeding through a linking strategy is its efficiency and the fact that it keeps the size of the multimedia document small. Furthermore, changes made to the source object are automatically reflected in any compound document that has a link to the object.

It is, however, possible to add complexity by nesting links and combining linked and embedded objects. With embedding, a copy of the original object is physically stored in the compound document, as is all the information needed to manage the object. Hence, the object becomes an integral part of the document.

Evidently, a compound document containing embedded objects will be larger than one containing the same objects as links. But embedding can offer advantages that may outweigh the disadvantages of extra storage overhead and the lack of simultaneous object update. For instance, embedded objects can be edited in place with all maintenance to the object done without leaving the compound document.

Depending on the sophistication of the software, in-place activation can include a variety of operations. Embedded objects can be edited, displayed, and recorded in place. Linked objects can be activated in place for operations such as playback and display, but they cannot be edited in place.

When a linked object is opened for editing, the server application is activated in a separate window. To return to the multimedia document, the user must either close the server application or switch windows. By contrast, with in-place activation,

- Users can interact with the document's objects right there.
- They do not need to switch to a different application window.

This is an important facilitation and change. To work on word processing, time management, spreadsheets, or database search, users typically open windows and switch between applications. Frameworks like OLE permit users to get away from that habit and make object-embedded solutions a fairly integrated approach.

As applications become more complex, these types of solution will necessitate not only frameworks but also very advanced linguistic constructs. They will require that the language used to control the multimedia implementation be comparable in a whole range of activities, from prototyping and code details to testing and sustenance, and that it operate in a cross-application sense and provide for parallelism.

12.5 Frameworks, Linkages, and Templates for Parallel Processing

In Secs. 12.2 and 12.3 we discussed what, in the general case, frameworks could and could not do. A good deal of their functionality comes from the concept of presentation objects. Concurrent applications capitalize on the sharing of information elements among many workstations.

- Object sharing becomes the basis for a flexible building of information systems, with each workstation displaying presentation objects to its user.

- But shared data objects must be protected via security, integrity, and transactional constraints, which not all frameworks offer.

The three main linkages employed between data and presentation objects are *value, structure,* and *transaction.* These linkages can be updatable, implying that values can be shared between presentation objects and information elements.

The value reference is important inasmuch as a linkage may be volatile, which means that a value can be changed by another application and that change is reflected in the presentation object. Therefore, a crucial consideration is the mechanism for resynchronizing the presentation and the data objects which it involves.

Structure linkages and value linkages resemble each other in terms of maintaining the necessary consistency between presentation and database information. But because structure linkages are active, scrollable, and updatable, they also affect the application design.

As their name implies, transaction linkages are associated with a transaction committed by the database system, with visibility perceived by a user manipulating presentation objects. One aim of this type of linking is to ensure that changes in data objects continually match changes in presentation objects. Another goal is to ensure an infrastructure on which novel solutions can be developed, such as templates and parallel processing facilities.

The term *templates,* introduced by the parallel processing community, is an evolving concept characterized by several definitions. The primary motivation for constructing templates is to rapidly infuse into common usage state-of-the-art algorithms in a form which can be adapted to specific application requirements.

- This implies that the template retains the desired numerical properties but is cast in a form which is independent of parallel architecture, data layout, and/or programming language.

- Many users, however, would like to see templates go beyond pseudocode, which can be found in textbooks and research papers, to become objects which are handled in connection with multiple architectures.

There are a range of issues involved in constructing an algorithmic template which is portable, scalable, and adaptable to different application requirements. One of the basic design constraints is that it retain the numerical properties which make the algorithm desirable in the first place. Some projects aim to do so through frameworks and agents.

The interest in finding a valid solution to this problem through agents, object-oriented approaches, and frameworks is not misplaced. The success of massively parallel computers depends on software flexibility, performance, and cost. Another "must" is ease of programming effort.

- A balance between these factors is required before massively parallel processing can become a success story.

- Some of the parallel programming projects currently in process talk of benefits to be derived without properly weighing costs and constraints.

As explained on a number of occasions, old languages, like the repeatedly rejuvenated Fortran, will not produce parallel processing results worth talking about. Hence the interest in new methods that use knowledge engineering concepts and tools.

Figure 12.3 outlines different strategies of effectively managing computer projects, assisted through knowledge engineering, regardless of whether these are new developments or a major maintenance job focusing on existing applications software. The choice of strategy is a function of two key factors:

- Complexity of the task
- Size of the project

A third key variable is the *available know-how*. Plenty of skill is necessary because it is a sound policy to start the study for a framework by looking at the broader implementation perspectives. As the field of parallel programming matures, the population of users will range from the occasional to the expert, encompassing both scientific and business routines within the same architectural solution.

The occasional, untrained parallel programming user will rely heavily on libraries of parallel algorithms and procedures as well as systems tools sup-

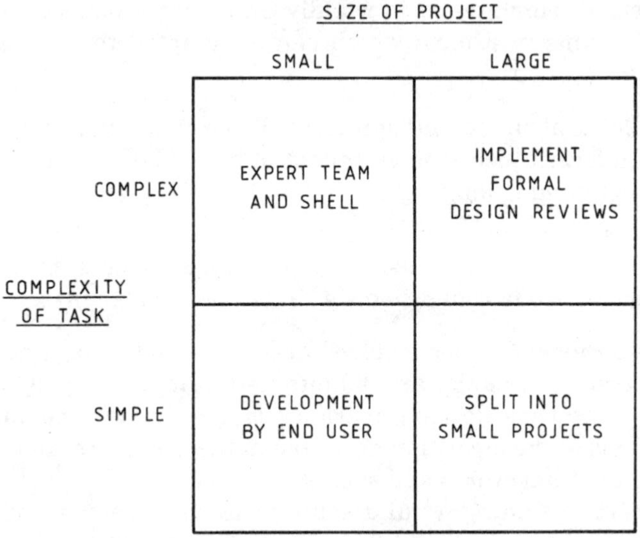

```
                              SIZE OF PROJECT

                       SMALL                    LARGE
                  ┌──────────────────┬──────────────────┐
                  │                  │                  │
                  │                  │    IMPLEMENT     │
                  │   EXPERT TEAM    │      FORMAL      │
        COMPLEX   │   AND SHELL      │  DESIGN REVIEWS  │
                  │                  │                  │
                  │                  │                  │
 COMPLEXITY       ├──────────────────┼──────────────────┤
 OF TASK          │                  │                  │
                  │                  │                  │
                  │  DEVELOPMENT     │   SPLIT INTO     │
        SIMPLE    │  BY END USER     │  SMALL PROJECTS  │
                  │                  │                  │
                  │                  │                  │
                  └──────────────────┴──────────────────┘
```

Figure 12.3 The best way to handle computer projects is through knowledge engineering.

posed to hide the details underlying the parallel architecture. The degree to which the end user will interact with parallelism depends on both the nature of the application problem and the available tools. Hence there is a need for application libraries of parallel algorithms, including software templates containing benchmark implementations.

By contrast, experts will use object-oriented methods in a parallel mode of programming, ranging from the development of special software to the building of libraries. In this, they may be assisted by genetic algorithms. (See also the reference to GMD-FIRST in Sec. 12.8.)

Much of the programming effort by experts will concentrate on the development of high-quality, parallel class libraries specialized to specific application areas. It is possible to write code that is close to the mathematical model behind a scientific or business application which either directly addresses this application or serves as a template and framework for end users.

12.6   Developing Frameworks and Application-Specific Software

As a general policy concerning software development in the 1990s and beyond, the focus must be on increased flexibility and functionality. We must be able to rapidly adapt applications to support a changing business environment as well as lower the sustenance requirements.

Chapter 11 has provided evidence that software reuse is one of the primary motivations for adopting object technology. Another key reason for using objects is the resulting flexibility which, in a dynamic market, is a long-term strategic asset. Ideally,

- For both expert and occasional programming, the architecture of the computer (hypercube, mesh, network, and so on) should be transparent.
- The computer should map its own characteristics. There is, however, a persistent lag in compiler technology which has to be overcome.

While parallel computers have been in scientific, commercial, and industrial use since 1986, the answer to the question "What kind of expertise is necessary to program a parallel computer?" has not yet been given in a factual and documented fashion. Besides this, this answer cannot be the same for end users and for systems programmers because the skills, goals, and priorities are different. For the expert programmer the priorities are

- An understanding of architectural prerequisites
- Algorithmic and heuristic expertise
- Good knowledge in the applications domain

By contrast, as seen in Fig. 12.4, the priorities run in a reverse order for the end user and occasional programmer. But there is also common interest in the solution procedure to be adopted.

Both end users and computer experts need to project the parallel processing application for portability, though the latter will do so in a more detailed form than the former. Both have to realize that in the years to come there will be many architectural changes, even within the product line of a given vendor.

Whether we talk of frameworks or of application-specific software, an important issue in the design of efficient algorithms for parallel systems is data dis-

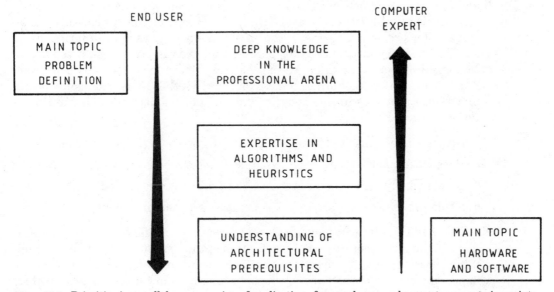

Figure 12.4 Priorities in parallel programming of applications from end-user and computer expert viewpoints.

tribution. Design decisions must include the mapping of data flows in a way accounting for the most likely changes in the expected *time to solution*.

A number of experts in parallel programming and in frameworks suggest that one of the handicaps currently characterizing software development lies in the fact that compilers continue to focus on code and not on

- High-level solution strategies, defined in this book as programming in the large

- Intermediate-level algorithmic descriptions, which interface between programming in the large and programming in the small

This lack of focus by compilers of current and future requirements is irrational because what is done now addresses only yesterday's problems—not those of tomorrow. Intermediate-level algorithmic designs, for instance, must incorporate alternative strategies for data distribution and make estimates of effective run times for critical routines, particularly those in class libraries.

Furthermore, a significant amount of the difficulties with the use of existing computer programming paradigms stems from a level of abstraction that is too low. Both the message passing and the shared-memory model reflect more the manner in which the machine works than the nature of the solution domain and the parallel algorithms being used. As a result, instead of helping, current linguistic and compiler scenarios are burdening the programmer with low-level details that should be taken care of by the basic software. This reference evidently includes all the different redefinitions of naive Fortran—so dear to backward-looking vendors and some computer "experts."

In connection to the message-passing paradigm, today every send and receive of a communication must be explicitly programmed. Since these sends and receives are synchronization points, the programmer is forced to explicitly synchronize a multitude of threads, thus micromanaging the application's code.

A similar problem arises with the shared-memory paradigm in terms of the weak consistency models used for performance reasons. As a result, the access to shared objects that must be explicitly synchronized becomes a burden. Another programming burden comes from the fact that there exist some poorly understood problems in the design of parallel algorithms and their implementation, such as how to

- Create a new concept of abstraction permitting one to think in parallel

- Parallelize computations with dynamic, heterogeneous data structures

- Access widely distributed databases which are not normalized

- Exploit reusable software in a parallel processing environment

Whether targeting frameworks or applications-specific software, programming in the large requires a valid definition of the computation domain, including a discrete point topology in which the solution is to be found. Equally important is the elaboration of the associated communications pattern, including the nodes that execute the algorithms.

A valid approach will focus on the selection of a synchronization scheme that coordinates the parallel threads but makes transparent low-level communication details. Data dependencies must be handled automatically by metaphors. Manual approaches make programming difficult to use and are error-prone—and this statement is just as valid with applications-specific software as it is with frameworks.

12.7 Evaluating Frameworks and Languages for Parallel Computers

Languages developed for massively parallel computers must be able to describe the coordinated operations of a number of processes. Typically such languages are based on paradigms, and the key problem is how to extract the *available parallelism* in the problem domain and execute it with as much *processing parallelism* as the underlying system can provide.

Some of the projects currently focusing on parallel programming underline declarative constraint-based approaches able to address layers of programming languages. The common-base framework targets a basic programming abstract of several high-level languages, introducing a description system which permits a certain decomposition of complexity. This involves

- The introduction of reflective functions for adapting and evolving objects in the applications environment

- A declarative description of object relationships expressed in an ephemeral hierarchy (see also the discussion of objects and ephemeral hierarchies in Chap. 11).

- A diversification of message propagation solutions, to be increasingly handled through the use of agents

A critical contributor to this process is the use of multiple paradigms which are understood in the programming environment. Employed in an able manner, they can give users the freedom to choose from various languages—but remember the constraints referred to in Fig. 12.2.

The requirements for system development addressed to parallel computers include two features different from those of serial machines. The first regards tools necessary to handle the *interconnection network,* including its topology, robustness, dynamic load distribution, and global synchronization mechanisms.

The second feature concerns the necessary support for the architectural development of processing elements. This brings into perspective the overall functions which contribute to the performance of the interconnection network—and it should be evaluated in advance, by means of system simulation. Experimentation is very important if we wish to be fairly accurate in terms of programming in the large, hence the grand design, and programming in the small, hence the detailed basic functions. It is wise to think of a functional assessment of the various components and subsystems entering the projected solution. This is a domain where object frameworks can make a contribution.

At the same time, no single form of concurrency is sufficient for parallelizing all applications. Because of the dynamic characteristics of the environment, parallel programs designed for portability among machines will need to exploit all kinds of concurrency.

- The challenge is to come up with a comprehensive model of parallel computing that is parametric in terms of paradigms.

- A knowledge-enriched parameterization allows programmers to express many kinds of concurrency within a given application.

Tools are therefore necessary not only for programming proper but as well for verifying the effectiveness of parallel computing. Optimization can be performed by means of genetic algorithms.[1] Simulation can assist in the prediction of future events from established models of operation.

- Simulation predicts macrobehavior by describing the pattern of interactions between microelements (examples are given in Sec. 12.8).

- Simulation foretells the consequences of complex situations presented by nonlinear problems.

Experimentation is necessary in parallel software solutions because the required programming-in-the-large approaches might be difficult to formulate because of the complexity of the phenomena being addressed or the incompleteness of information and knowledge regarding the description of such phenomena. Exploiting task-level concurrency is especially important in heterogeneous environments because of the need to match the execution requirements of different parts of the program with the computational capabilities of the different machines and their software. Therefore, not just object-oriented frameworks but also solutions involving agents and interactive visualization seem to be the best strategy. One of the current projections is that by early in the 21st century there will even be *intelligent materials* that incorporate sensor, programming, and effector systems.

12.8   Why Symbolic Problems Need Plenty of Imaginative Solutions

Like Alice in Wonderland who had to run fast to stay in the same place, the competitive markets of the 1990s demand lots of imagination and innovation just to stay in the running. In turn, this requires new competitive solutions which are a far cry from the hierarchical, bureaucratic, wasteful, and inflexible practices of the past.

Whether in the arena of computing or more generally in business, we must get out of the vicious cycle of limited vision with which most system designers, analysts, programmers, as well as computer vendors now work. The emphasis in Chap. 11 and this chapter placed on agents and object orientation should be seen from this perspective.

- Frameworks are only part of the solution, not all of it.

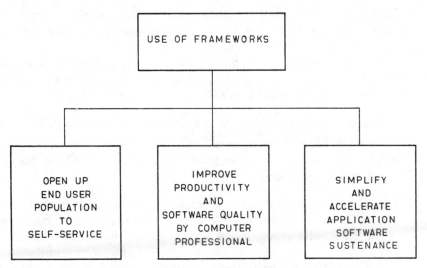

Figure 12.5 Goals targeted by framework solutions.

- As Fig. 12.5 suggests, they mainly serve three goals out of many which must be targeted.

The evolving information technology requirements point to fundamentally new approaches to characterize programming, but also raise the queries, How much do we know about parallel algorithms? and Can we really get results without knowledge-enriched software? Leaving aside the problem of algorithmic insufficiency which currently prevails, we can outline three classes of problems which are salient:

1. *Integrative algorithms* on which there exists very little practical experience at this moment. But agents are considered the best bet.

2. *Qualitative algorithms,* like fuzzy engineering, where substantial work is being done in connection with specific problems.[2]

3. *Major new application domains* such as image processing, two-way television, mobile computing, and so on.[3]

As we have seen on a number of occasions, a truly integrative software environment is still lacking although the need for it is becoming increasingly felt. Its evolution is seen as a very important contribution in closing the gap which today exists and tends to separate *symbolic* from *numeric* computation.

Usually, logic-type and qualitatively oriented applications do not exhibit a significant data parallelism, but there may be present a rather substantial program parallelism. The two issues of program parallelism and data parallelism may, however, be related, as path creation can depend on the actual data stream and can occur at run time.

A major difference between logical and numerical problems is that the underlying data structures are usually pointer lists, also created at run time.

Hence, it is necessary to recognize parallelism in symbolic processing automatically, as well as to develop parallelization settings in which the user can interactively work with the system.

An intermediate step to the attainment of this objective is semiparallel solutions in which, after being informed by the system, the user can indicate potential parallel paths in the program.

- Through agents and genetic algorithms the system will then allocate these paths to real processes.

- The use of an intelligent scheduler will help to distribute the processes over the available nodes.

Experts believe that this is the better course because, in many cases, the programmer does not have enough insight into the dynamic behavior of the program. Hence, he or she is not able to partition it appropriately. Knowledge-enriched solutions are therefore necessary to assist in profiling.

GMD-FIRST, the Berlin-based computer research institute of the Gesellschaft für Mathematik und Datenverarbeitung (GMD), has developed a genetic algorithm solution to parallelize new computer programs which have been written for parallel computers but in a rather serial fashion—or at least have not been optimized. This approach merits attention, because it documents that programmers can be assisted in parallelization through technology.

Only very exceptional individuals capable of parallel thinking might do the needed job all by themselves. For a few talented people, parallelism is natural. I already made reference to Wolfgang Amadeus Mozart who said that when he composed an opera, he would hear the instruments of the orchestra playing all at once. But Howard Hughes once commented that he himself had a one-track mind, and this is true of the majority of people.

In conclusion, the use of technology for parallelization of software is a promising concept, but it is not yet a generalized solution. Able solutions should see to it that not too many architectural details are brought in at the programming level, making it difficult to successfully exploit available architectural capabilities.

The challenge of responding to the programming requirements of new application domains must finally be appropriately addressed. This challenge primarily revolves on solutions to computing problems, both logical and numeric, and it has been brought to light because, today and in the future, the network is the computer.

12.9 Optimizing the End User's Return on Investment through Visual Programming and Visualization

Frameworks and other solutions which we have studied have been developed because the end user needs to interact with the system by "natural" means. Ten years ago this meant the mouse and the pop-up menus. Tomorrow it may be gestures, facial expressions, and spoken language.

Quite similarly, the end user must be able to receive information in the form of real-time three-dimensional images, including their interpretation and associated annotations. The end user should also be spared the effort of learning an exhaustive amount of technical characteristics, whether in serial or parallel applications.

A different way of making this statement is to say that end users should concentrate their efforts on more creative activities than low-level human-machine chores. To do so, they should be provided with powerful features through *visualization* and *visual programming,* an area where frameworks do not yet excel. Examples of possible applications include

- Cognitive and behavioral models including sensor fusion to understand the intentions of the other party
- Broadband multimodal interfaces particularly agile with visual patterns
- Information display solutions with virtual reality characteristics[4]

Since experience in these domains is still thin, it is advisable to proceed by means of simulation and experimentation, learning how to work with systems which not only are capable of real-time adaptation but also communicate their deliverables in the most effective manner.

A more sophisticated implementation of visual programming concepts will set itself the goal of predicting and controlling complex implementation environments. Rather than doing expensive and time-consuming physical experiments which may not be always precise, by means of visual programming the user should be able to

- Emulate a complex solution
- Predict behavior in a real-time sense

Prediction of lesser known phenomena, untapped resources, and future events is an integral and major part of the new application domains which provide a competitive edge. This already happens in financial environments where rocket scientists use learning genetic algorithms and other tools for market prediction reasons.

In information technology, some research projects approach this work through virtual processes in a given solution space. From the viewpoint of the application, the configuration of the processes constitutes a virtual topology to be mapped onto a physical and logical architecture.

One of the more advanced projects in this domain sees to it that the processes run in parallel under a synchronization scheme. The chosen approach involves globally alternating computation and communication phases.

- In the computation phase, the processes are agents performing the local operations autonomously.
- In the communication phases, the processes resynchronize and mutually observe one another's states.

One of the most critical challenges, which has not yet gotten the attention it deserves, is the solution of interdisciplinary issues which may involve incompatible or overlapping address spaces and/or have diverse synchronization requirements.

Both vendors and user organizations have started to realize that new technology changes the computers and communications ballgame as they knew it. Massively parallel computation, for example, is not just a matter of doing something faster. Rather, we should be looking at it as

- A tool for the solution of complex problems which could not be effectively approached through old technology and its serial computational processes
- A platform for knowledge-enriched software able to address in parallel combinatorial and interdisciplinary issues which cannot be handled serially

Programming in the large should be tuned to work in the way the user thinks and works, and this is one of the roles that object frameworks should play. Programming in the small should address program granularity and be provided with tools which are assisted in an effective manner through parallel compilers.

At the level of programming massively parallel machines, fine levels of granularity seem to offer the greatest potential for exploiting parallelism, but they also exhibit difficult compilation problems, particularly so when parallel processing is applied to solution spaces with hard real-time constraints. Hence the queries about

- Imperative timing and synchronization properties
- Trade-offs between run time and compile time
- Assessment of performance by component subsystems and in an aggregate sense

This is the context within which to examine the contribution of object-oriented software at large and most particularly frameworks. Not only run-time efficiency but also other characteristics should be used to evaluate performance. For instance, Oberon, a framework solution by Dr. Nikolaus Wirth, who developed Pascal in the 1970s, takes up less than one-fifth of the space occupied by a typical operating system and its supporting routines, and it also consumes less processing power than the corresponding elder software.

References

1. See D. N. Chorafas, *Rocket Scientists in Banking*, Lafferty Publications, London, 1996.
2. See D. N. Chorafas, *Chaos Theory in the Financial Markets*, Probus/Irwin, Chicago, 1994.
3. See also D. N. Chorafas, *High Performance Networks, Personal Communications and Mobile Computing*, Macmillan, London, 1996.
4. See D. N. Chorafas and H. Steinmann, *Virtual Reality—Practical Applications in Business and Industry*, Prentice-Hall, Englewood Cliffs, NJ, 1995.

Using New Software Technology as a Competitive Tool

Developing an increasingly more efficient software technology is a prerequisite to having a competitive edge in the marketplace, but it is not enough. We must also be able to implement in record time what we develop and do so in a way which offers visible advantages. The strong point of Part 5 is practical examples from finance and from a company's reporting structure.

13

Visual Programming Challenges and Managerial Needs of the Virtual Bank

13.1 Introduction

A fundamental concept in the financial industry whose implementation will be relatively long term is that of the *virtual bank*. Its infrastructure is provided by intelligent networks interconnecting any-to-any in an ad hoc manner the bank's channels with its clients, as well as with correspondent banks and other business partners.

This notion is an integral part of the virtual company and its culture. Whether we talk of the manufacturing, merchandising, or banking industry, the Alfred Sloan model of industrial organization—which promoted a decentralized operating system combined with central policy and financial control— is becoming increasingly irrelevant.

- We simply cannot afford to have inflexible, hierarchically modeled organizations running postindustrial business which requires fast response and flexible structures.

- But the virtual bank has prerequisites. The network is one of them; another is the online distributed databases and the fully personalized computing promoted through visual programming.

To survive, a bank must have a strong capacity to create and deliver value to its customers, and this requires high-technology supports. Another prerequisite is integration. Some money center banks have 200 different networks around the world, a number which has grown over the years. It is therefore not surprising that their management is dearly interested in their integration into one *virtual network,* supporting

- A distributed client-server architecture
- Local and long-haul communications links
- Deductive databases, many of which are heterogeneous
- Interactive interfaces for cooperative processing

Several banks are taking object-oriented approaches, handling business objects inside the virtual network. The principle behind this approach is valid both for the long and for the short term: "Everything we do must be technology-proof," says Colin Crook, chair of Citibank's Corporate Technology Committee.

13.2 Anticipating the Needs of the Coming Years; the Marketing Approach

The financial services industry has a wide range of public duties to fulfill in supporting the social infrastructure. In today's information society, one of the most important themes connected with the development of financial systems and services is the capacity to handle dramatic changes in products and markets, in spite of the uncertainty that pervades the business environment with ever-increasing frequency.

To achieve this goal, we need to do financial engineering, implement rocket science solutions,[1] keep our skills flexible and adaptable, and be careful about the return on investment. All these reasons suggest espousing a short software development cycle with visual programming at its core.

As Colin Crook suggests, the phenomenal rate of change throughout the banking industry among the banks, their customers, their product base, and their technology is accelerating. Therefore, we must anticipate a rapid evolution on every front and be ready to redefine both our company and our mission each step along the way.

The leading players in the financial industry have set their technology directions according to this principle. One of the success stories of the last few years involves targeting the *marketing* effort.[2] Market segmentation and targeting are relatively new concepts in banking. They have evolved by applying what has been learned from manufacturing—and they are technology-based.

- Geographic information systems (GISs) have proved a valuable method for segmentation purposes, and they are a good example of visual programming.
- GIS makes it feasible to develop customer clusters that are meaningful and actionable in a business sense.

Neural networks have been used for customer targeting in direct marketing campaigns and achieved higher performance in customer cluster identification than classical approaches such as linear regression analysis. Fuzzy logic and neurofuzzy approaches help in the study of patterns and make it feasible to configure services to the individual needs of customer and market segments.

But once market focus has been achieved, the results must be effectively visualized, and three-dimensional color graphics are the best way to proceed. Banks which work along this frame of reference get results. Typically such results are proportional to

- The ingenuity with which a bank manages its investments in technology
- The choices which management makes
- The priorities given to the different efforts

Some of the priorities are ill-defined or downright rotten. Every year the banking industry spends billions on technology, yet many banks are not even close to employing leading-edge tools. A survey by Ernst and Young and *American Banker* indicates that

- Over 75 percent of bank computer programs are still written in Cobol.
- 84 percent of banking software is designed for mainframes.

Moreover, 80 percent of the software used by banks is over 6 years old, and only 37 percent of their branch offices are networked. The same study reveals that most banks are simply not investigating new advances in computer applications.

Leading bankers who participated in this research suggested that today's challenge is the next wave of organizational and technological development, virtual offices, and virtual reality applications. Few financial institutions so far have taken the precautions necessary to meet the prerequisites and the results of this challenge.

The appropriate strategic plan is not in place, and issues of timing-specific implementations—and of studying their consequences on business—are not well understood. What is clear, Colin Crook says, is that a bank must address not one but three fundamental challenges:

1. The ability of its technologists to work in partnership with the bank's various businesses, in rapid response to market and client needs. Visual programming can be instrumental in this task, both for programming-proper reasons and as a communications medium.

2. The skill to navigate successfully through the inevitable changes and complexities that are occurring in the turbulent financial and technological markets. This skill does not come as a matter of course. It has to be developed through steady training—and it must be supported through real-space systems.

3. The wisdom to migrate effectively to the future technology model from the current installed base of applications, without upsetting ongoing work.

These three missions must be performed practically in parallel without disruption of operations, while at the same time providing the bank's managers and professionals with a global view of products, customers, and competition.

This is exactly where the marketing plan can have strategic importance. A worthwhile marketing plan should attack and challenge the "obvious." This means nearly every premise in sight and every classical way of doing things. There is a steadily decreasing role for vanilla ice cream banking.

To execute such a strategy in an able manner, a financial institution requires a well-coordinated, imaginative, and cost-effective approach to doing business. Virtual reality helps to provide this holistic approach and to increase the bank's competitiveness—because it modernizes the parts of the current system in sore need of improvement, the *input* and *output* ends.

13.3   Looking at the Bank as Networked Autonomous Channels and Services

Both the network and the banking services which it supports must deliberately be kept dynamic. The more successful financial institutions participating in this research gave plenty of evidence on the new management policies characterizing their operations. One stated, "Since we know that the banking business is changing, we must answer in an able manner five crucial questions." These questions are

- Where is our business going?
- From where will come the future profits for *our* survival?
- Who will be our "dear customers"?
- What kind of products and services will they need?
- What should we be doing in the next 5 years? In the next 10 years?

All five questions have to be asked and the answers must be focused, not general, because specific answers motivate people. It is precisely in this situation of growing challenge that market studies are now done involving the banks' most important customers.

Everybody knows that financing facilitates the movement of funds from suppliers to users. But not every banker appreciates that the identification of *suppliers* and *users* of financial services is no longer as clearly defined as it used to be. Neither is it common knowledge that the creation of financial products to satisfy customer needs now takes a lot of research, development, and implementation (RD&I).

One after the other, top-of-the-line financial institutions which are following the RD&I approach find out that what most of their customers really want is help in their own business. This means

- A stream of innovative financial services
- Steady enrichment with high technology

Bankers Trust has been emphasizing this dual issue for the better part of the last 10 years. Dr. Carmine Vona, the executive vice president for Worldwide Technology, stated that after study, top management decided that "If the appropriate advanced services were provided to the bank's clients, then return on investment was assured." Therefore, the decision was made to

- Link the bank more closely to the customer, using high technology
- Do so not only through networks but also by means of intelligent artifacts

This view of technology as a competitive weapon started in the mid-1980s but accelerated in the 1990s. American Express provides another example. This company was among the first financial institutions to deploy a large-scale, rule-based expert system, the *Authorizer's Assistant,* which is still in production. Since then, it has experimented with and deployed

- Visual programming solutions
- Genetic algorithms
- Neural networks
- Imaging solutions
- Speech recognition
- Scientific visualization
- Virtual reality

This new generation of tools has been applied to diverse domains such as automating service bureaus, matching sales to the customers' desires, and detecting fraud. The implementation has shown good return on investment and has had a favorable impact on the ability of American Express to face market challenges.

Contrast these highly efficient, customer-oriented approaches with the mainframes, Cobol, SQL, the 3270 protocol, and other absurdities—in short, the legacy applications on which many banks spend money and from which they suffer. Such nearsighted views result in spoilage of financial, human, and technological resources, and they serve badly even the very short term. As a result,

- Ill-conceived tactical investments multiply and become major constraints to strategic solutions.
- Having spent once and seen no deliverables, management is loathe to spend again.

Yet, the money has been ill invested in the first place, and it is useless to cry over spilled milk. At the end of November 1995, the Banque de France, which manages the account of the French Treasury, paid 10 percent of the French public employees twice. The reason was a computer error.[3] That's what one gets from using old technology.

In 1986, the Bank of New York suffered a major failure in its mainframes and could not deliver securities for 28 hours. This obliged it to borrow $20 billion from the Federal Reserve for 1 day at a cost of $50 million. The estimated cost of this failure was $0.05 per share in earnings in the fourth quarter of 1986.

Investors have been shocked by the fact that such huge risks exist in the banking business. Can this situation be changed? The answer is, yes, it could, provided that the proper emphasis is placed on leading-edge technology and on the return on investment (ROI).[4] The proper emphasis means

- A balanced approach between short-, medium-, and long-term requirements—in markets, products, human capital, and technology.

- Systems solutions which follow distributed information systems principles, but emphasize reliability, security, and ROI.

- Appreciation of the fact that medium- to long-term planning does not mean postponing decisions. It means calculating the long-term impact of the decisions which we make today.

The decision to use the advanced technologies of which we speak, including intelligent networks, visual programming, three-dimensional graphics, and virtual reality, has to be made *today*, not tomorrow. Such a decision needs to be made in view of the fact that current profitability from classical data processing is very minor, if not altogether nonexistent.

13.4   Successful Solutions in the Banking Industry and Intraday Financial Time Series

Many senior bankers find as an excuse for inaction that they understand precious little about technology. At the same time a large number of data processors in senior positions have chosen to live in the past. They fail to realize that a stubborn, inflexible attitude is a sign of weakness, not strength.

- Mediocre technologists are often macho types: "Nobody can tell me what to do."

- By their nature, they are drawn to the lost cause and will not turn from it.

A key characteristic of successful solutions lies in the ability to do things ahead of others. This may not always be recognized as a *virtue,* but in the military no general has ever been a success without having this quality. Information technologists, too, must look ahead and must be flexible in adjusting their strategies to the situation, and not vice versa. The same is true of bankers.

It is not always easy to be ahead of the state of the art or to see things well in advance of the majority. For instance, today many bankers and their technologists fail to realize the difference which exists between *continuous* and discontinuous, or *quantum,* process improvement. Yet, this distinction, which is shown in Fig. 13.1, is fundamental both in banking services and in technology:

- Continuous process improvement has to do with *current performance.*

Typically, it operates in a steady but rather slow manner and deals with predictable change. This is a type of incremental improvement which is tactically managed, and the benefits it produces tend to be limited.

For instance, in programming, changing from Cobol to Delta, the precompiler which gives Cobol code, is an example of continuous change. By contrast, in

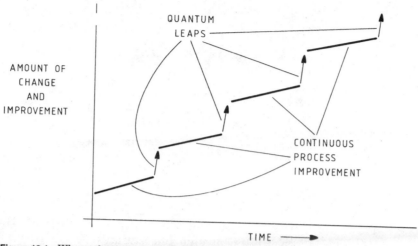

Figure 13.1 When a business process is improved through major changes, the result is a quantum leap forward.

adopting *visual programming* approaches, the change is discontinuous. It requires altering the cultural image of the past.

In most financial institutions, the management of change is a job given to the organization department. However, visual programming applications cannot be handled by organization departments because they know very little about visual programming. The work that the organization department does is focused on formal aspects of processes and procedures, which are often limited and under local sponsorship.

This type of continuous process improvement is necessary because management appreciates that the only things that evolve by themselves in an organization are disorder, inefficiency, and friction. That's what the second law of thermodynamics suggests. But the correction of local inefficiencies provides no quantum leaps.

- *Quantum process improvement* means rethinking key business operations and renewing them.

That's where visual programming and virtual reality applications come into the picture. Taking quantum leaps is a process of restructuring and revamping which brings with it discontinuous, unpredictable change. The aim is radical improvement, and the goals are strategically managed.

A valid solution would provide a balance between formal and informal aspects of the restructured process. We don't talk of minor beachheads but of *change*. Sponsorship of quantum change is by definition a process owner's responsibility—and he or she should be accountable for it.

A critical question management must pose is, Can we afford not to move ahead with technology and lose our market as a result? And the answer must not only be factual and documented, but also make good business sense—now and in the future.

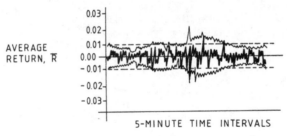

Figure 13.2 Intraday returns in the currency exchange: rate of Deutsche marks to U.S. dollars.

For instance, the adoption of a policy of *intraday* financial time series is a quantum leap forward. It is a value differentiation service positioning our bank against its competitors.

Figure 13.2 explains the sense of this reference. As with any commodity, 5-minute intervals provide traders and financial analysts with significant information about the pulse of the market.[5] The Deutsche mark/U.S. dollar foreign exchange, which is shown in this figure, is the most frequently traded currency value in the world.

- The classically used hourly and daily time series are too coarse-grained to give even a hint of the prevailing volatility or to help in prognosis.
- Yet profits are made by capitalizing on market volatility, and losses result from being insensitive to the changes taking place.

Not only does the modern bank need fine-grained financial statistics, but also it should be in a position to exploit the data stream which it obtains through 5-minute intervals and eventually at minute and subminute levels.

- This requires *ad hoc software* which is developed as the need arises.
- The only way to get it is through *interactive visual programming* by the trader and the financial analyst.

This is a cultural change which only the foremost banks and treasury departments comprehend. Figure 13.3 dramatizes the difference which exists in financial time series between daily, hourly, and 15-minute recording intervals. Five-minute intervals run 3 times faster than the fastest in this figure; and minute-level recording intervals run 15 times faster.

Dr. Carmine Vona phrased his thoughts in this way: "Because of high technology we are capable of doing many things our competitors cannot offer. The merger of technology and business is at the core of the solutions we seek." This is the spirit which moves a bank ahead of the industry and makes it a member of tier 1.

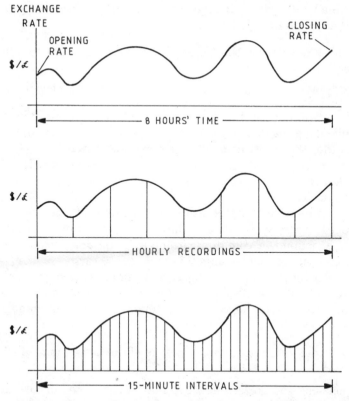

Figure 13.3 The amount of information provided by increasing the frequency of financial data is striking—even if between the first and third graphs the difference is only little more than an order of magnitude.

13.5 Advanced Visualization Research at Santa Fe Institute and at UCLA

"One of the crucial questions that are not appropriately asked, much less answered," said Dr. Judea Pearl of the Cognitive Systems Laboratory, University of California at Los Angeles (UCLA), "is where the information is coming from." What data processing has totally forgotten is that information which needs to be processed and then reported does not come only from quantitative data sources with a numerical input. This is only part of the problem. It comes as well, and most importantly, from persons and is characterized by approximations due to linguistic constraints.

Another key issue that has not been thoroughly examined, Dr. Pearl suggests, is what the recipients are going to do with the output from the computer system. To be useful, this output should be personalized—but prior to customization we must know its users and its uses.

Along this point of view, which is opposite to how data processors look at information handling, the Santa Fe Institute (SFI) of New Mexico is currently working on a joint project with the Human Interface Technology Laboratory, of Seattle, Washington.

- The goal is to increase the *bandwidth of financial data* to human decision makers.
- The SFI project uses and promotes visualization technologies in banking.

One of the approaches currently being developed centers on visualizing price movements along the line of the examples given in Sec. 13.4, and even goes further than that. Stock prices move in three-dimensional columns that the user can touch and feel for stimulus purposes. Sponsored by a leading financial institution as part of nontraditional research, this is a good example of virtual reality in practice.

The three-dimensional presentation in Fig. 13.4 is effective but static. Virtual reality goes further by providing an interactive sensation. Interactivity is basic to the enhancement of communications and the perception of sensitivities. Visual programming supplements this sense of interactivity.

Managing a pension fund, for instance, is an interactive process. Investment quality can be improved if we understand how an investment we plan to make relates to the others already in the portfolio. Pension fund managers are keen to examine

- How new commitments alter the nature of the investments already made by hedging risks
- How pension fund goals connect to not only finance but also demographics and retirement patterns

To improve a fund's performance, we need both processing power and the tools to study how small to medium-size investment groups interact—and what the outcomes of such interactions are. This poses further requirements.

SFI has steered two projects along this frame of reference. One is on virtual reality (VR), and the other addresses what it calls a *process gas*. The latter emulates the lattice gas findings by the research done at Los Alamos for nuclear engineering purposes.

- The idea is to divide a complex process into elements which interact with and impact one another.
- The goal is discover characteristics of turbulence which can be visualized through VR.

The processes in the lattice are *agents,* and each has its local laws. On these premises lie the foundation of *artificial life,* a process also known as *swarms.* "By generating artificial realities we create a basis for better understanding of real reality," said Dr. Chris Langton, a senior SFI scientist and principal investigator of artificial life.

- The term *artificial life* should not be frightening.

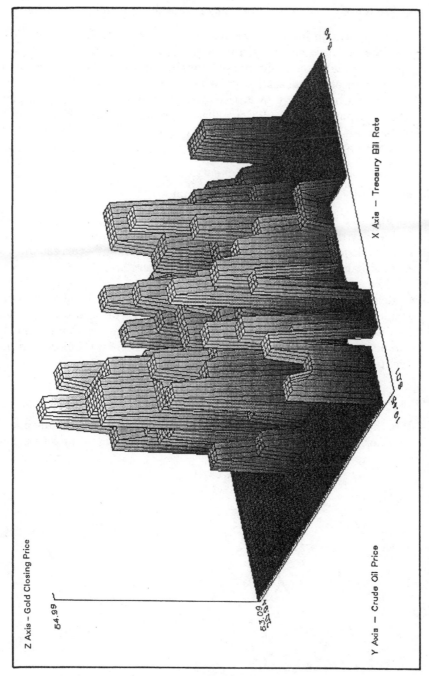

Figure 13.4 A three-dimensional presentation of gold price versus crude oil price and Treasury bill rate. (*Courtesy of Precision Visuals*)

- What essentially it means is algorithms for real-time simulation.

An application in virtual worlds in connection with the aforementioned project does not necessarily need data gloves and head-mount displays. It can be nicely executed in a nonimmersive manner and still benefit from the presentation powers of virtual reality artifacts.

Working by analogy to lattice gas, the *process gas* is a good paradigm of swarm behavior in populations. The approach is object-oriented and tends to emulate an ant colony with each object composed of smaller objects. As is the case with financial markets,

- These objects live in environments.

- Each environment has its own dynamics.

As Fig. 13.5 shows, there are many inter- and intracommunicating subsystems in the way this aggregate shapes up. The artifact features many semi-independent molecules which—in a financial environment—correspond to traders belonging to different schools of thought. Therefore, the overall structure constitutes a sparse communications network.

Most of the interactions in an artificial life setting take place in a distributed fashion. The underlying system rules may characterize an insect colony, birds in a flock, or buyers and sellers in the financial market. Comparable behaviors can be studied by analogy, as we saw in Part 1 when we discussed patterns of events and analogical reasoning.

13.6   Benefits Derived from Nontraditional Financial Research

Whether in finance, manufacturing, or any other domain, a real-time simulator or other modeling construct must be enriched with guiding rules, constraints,

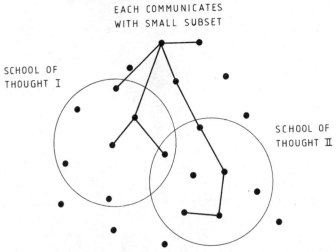

Figure 13.5 Swarm project system with lots of semi-independent molecules or traders.

and exceptions which might be even more permanent than the rules. It also has to be supplied with semantics for

- Better understanding of a given situation
- Effective linkages to the environment

In its more sophisticated version, visual programmers should operate within this enhanced, integrative approach to modeling. The Santa Fe Institute believes that virtual reality can provide a very effective nonimmersive approach to the visualization of interactions which are *nonlinear* in nature but exhibit

- Global dynamics
- Global patterns of activity

(See also Chap. 14 about programming in virtual reality.) A key part of the experimental focus is the interactively simulated real-time conditions, for instance, how the agents switch around rules and constraints. Current research has found that groups of semi-independent agents can be more adaptive than either of the following two limiting conditions:

- An environment with agents having fully individual behavior
- A system characterized by monolithic structures where every move is precast (as happens in highly hierarchical financial organizations with thick procedural manuals).

Along this line of reasoning, some of the Santa Fe Institute studies have focused on traffic jams (corks) and the saturation of telecommunications networks (Erlang units). In both cases, results are fairly conclusive in indicating how and why above a certain density of traffic flow bottlenecks form.

Based on the project he is conducting at UCLA, Dr. Judea Pearl advises to carefully examine mapping relationships between attributes in *belief networks* (not to be confused with Schaefer's belief functions). Fuzzy engineering can be instrumental in this connection because

- Many situations in finance resist analysis in deterministic and even in stochastic terms.
- But these can be attacked by fuzzy logic.

A virtual reality presentation can also be seen in this context. More precisely, it reflects the approach to be taken in moving from the abstract to the real, from the domain of the rocket scientist and the financial analyst to that of the manager.

As suggested in Fig. 13.6, such a transition from the idealized world to the concrete will never be linear. It may follow the path of curve *A,* or *B,* or *C*; or it may never reach the goal. Many representations of real-life processes fail because

- They are not able to abstract and idealize a complex situation, hence, to take off.

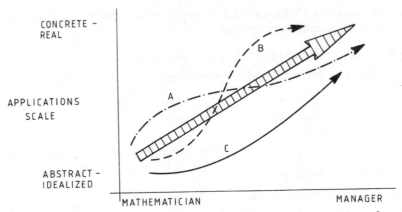

Figure 13.6   The quest of a transition from the abstract to the concrete, or from mathematics to management, is never a linear path.

- They have no concept of how to move from the abstract to the concrete.

Although it is in itself a sort of abstraction, virtual reality really aims for the concretization of output. As such, it does not differ so much from the goal of fuzzy engineering, which is in essence a quest for *defuzzification.*

At the Santa Fe Institute, the swarms project practically has the same objective: to make abstract things more concrete by studying the transition possibilities. Markov chains also address this process of transition and the associated probabilities.

- Colonies of insects are typically built according to migration phenomena.

- This is the way capital markets and money markets act.

The behavior of fish schools and that of insect colonies provide good examples of interactions characterizing the *move of capital.* One of the major contributions that rocket scientists bring to finance is this background, which permits one to think through this sort of analogical reasoning.[6]

Research has documented that in living quarters outside their nests, insects go on *random walks.* But after an ant deposits chemicals as a message for having found food, the system becomes a *tightly patterned* activity—all the way to controlling the speed for carrying food by keeping the procession steady.* Hence the pattern is

- Random

- Deterministic

- Random

Senior financial analysts who worked on the subject of similitudes between physical and logical systems suggest that survival patterns characterizing

---

*Ants seem to be able to judge the carried weight and add forces, if necessary, for steady going.

ant colonies can be found to work in a similar way in capital markets and money markets.

- Applying an outside force can destroy the colony's (market's) structure.

- But after some time recovery comes, and the colony (market) will be restructured.*

Interestingly, computer viruses also work in a similar manner. So do knowledge robots ("knowbots") which are now implemented in intelligent networks. Knowledge robots are also being used in programs for database coherency, broadening the implementation perspective of the artifacts but also capitalizing on processes learned from the physical sciences.

13.7   Visualizing the Results of Sensitivity Analysis

In its simplest form, sensitivity analysis is a *what-if* evaluation. It is made, for instance, to check the effects of assuming a larger company debt, effecting changes in a product's price, experimenting on different hypotheses regarding projected sales levels, and so on.

What-if evaluations are one of the first and best examples of visual programming. They have been greatly helped by spreadsheets, a two-dimensional visual programming tool. In fact, in the early 1980s sensitivity analyses done through spreadsheets were the reason for the marketing success of the spreadsheets themselves and of personal computers.

The study of sensitivities involved in a process can have many background motivations. It may concern balance sheets, profit-and-loss statements, or ways and means of confronting the increases in the cost of production or the cost of sales. The level of reference addressed through a sensitivity analysis may vary and usually does, from issues connected to product appeal, market forces, performance, and the level of technology which is necessary to the ability of management to keep costs in check or evaluate risk factors assumed by the treasury as well as their possible aftermaths.

Whether the bank gives loans to a company or invests in its equity, every inch of profit and loss, as well as of advantages and disadvantages, has to be thought out in both fundamental and business terms. But once the models used for sensitivity analysis have done their work, the outcome must be visualized in a comprehensive manner.

Experienced financial researchers appreciate that a great deal of sensitivity analysis is a matter of pattern recognition. For instance, what is the cost control pattern projected by the company undergoing sensitivity analysis? The sales pattern? The revenue and profit patterns?

- Are management policies geared to continue to reduce cost, without swamping innovation?

---

*An example is what is currently happening in eastern Europe as well as in Latin America.

- Is the company under study able to provide sophisticated solutions for its customers, keeping ahead of competition?

To answer these queries in a factual and documented manner, the financial analyst has to do a good deal of homework. This will invariably be done interactively through computers. Therefore, it requires of the analyst

- A fair amount of visual programming know-how
- Seamless access to public and private databases

Regarding bank loans, the ability of a borrower to service debt may be particularly *sensitive* to changes affecting a set of criteria that the credit department has prescribed for a given industry and/or a certain company. The lender bank needs to be aware in advance both of the sensitivities and of how their variations influence the risks taken with the loan—and no two cases are the same.

A commonly done sensitivity analysis in connection to loans and investments is the *worst-case* scenario. It shows what would happen to the borrower's ability to repay the loan under pessimistic assumptions. This is an exercise in risk management.

- Risk control is a domain where sensitivity analysis provides management with valuable information.
- This information must be patterned to permit walk-throughs and switching from one scenario to another.

Results can be mapped for visualization purposes on a radar chart; an example is shown in Fig. 13.7.[7] This radar chart identifies a six-dimensional domain of sensitivities in *off–balance sheet* financing, in terms of

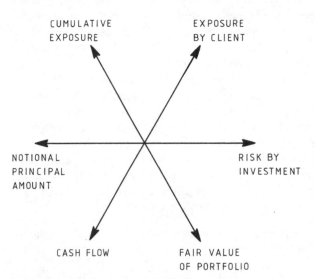

Figure 13.7 A six-dimensional presentation of exposure factors to be done in virtual reality (For a comparison, see Fig. 13.4).

- Exposure by client
- Risk by investment
- Fair value of portfolio
- Cash flow
- Notional principal amount
- Cumulative exposure[8]

There exist, however, degrees of sophistication in any experimentation. *If* the critical variables are changed one at a time, *then* a spreadsheet run on a PC can be the tool that the banker needs for a *what-if* analysis. But this is not true of more complex sensitivity analyses which reflect the effects of a joint variation of crucial factors.

- Complex evaluation methods require simulators which manipulate more than one of the initial assumption at a time.
- The solution we develop must be interactively visualized, preferably in three-dimensional color graphics or virtual reality.

These are cases which may go beyond the visual programming skills of the end user. He or she will need professional programming assistance, although the end user may do experiments analyzing covariance and other effects.

In a significant number of cases, the success of sensitivity analysis will largely rest on *database mining* and on *models*. The information in the database will provide historical relationships; management assumptions or forecasts; sales, pricing, and cost data; risk management considerations and related decisions; and other factors needed in the experimentation. This information has to be massaged:

- With database mining and computer forecasting models, sensitivities can and must be evaluated in real time.
- The interaction between the model and database information permits one to test existing forecasts and plans as well as develop new ones.

When in Chap. 4 we spoke of real space and real time in connection with the Internet and the World Wide Web, we said that in a growing number of cases on-line execution with ad hoc programs is not only the better solution but also the only one which makes sense. Real-time simulation contrasts sharply to the practice followed by many banks of laboriously making changes by hand and then waiting for the overnight batch to get numerical results—which is nonsense.

13.8   A Strategy Which Can Lead to the Virtual Bank

The more sophisticated the sensitivity analysis is, the closer a financial institution finds itself to implementing the virtual bank solution. Quite similarly, the better the visualization approaches, the virtual office setting, and the teleconferencing facilities, the more effective the distribution of banking services toward the client base and within the institution.

In Chap. 14 we will talk of *telepresence.* This discussion aims to bring home the fact that not only data but also people may operate in real space. Eventually, the second coming of the information superhighway—through solutions which go well beyond the current Internet—will require enormously more powerful visual programming paradigms than those we have today. The careful reader will pay plenty of attention to the *virtual dome,* because this is one of the earliest examples along this line of reasoning.

Stripped to its fundamentals, virtual presence augments the whole sense of visual analysis of multimedia information. Visual programming, virtual reality, and telepresence are not curiosities designed by eggheads, but are the very sense of *future competitiveness,* which essentially means survival. Just the same, client-server computing, distributed databases, and networking solutions are not done for the fun of it, but to serve one major goal—profits.[9]

Future competitiveness and profits are the two pillars of staying in business. During the middle to late 1980s when the efforts described in this chapter really started, the field of advanced, nontraditional financial analysis was dominated by proprietary projects developed in corporate research laboratories. But now commodity software products are available, assisting in visual programming by end users.

Financial institutions are increasingly using engineering visualization tools. One of these tools has been developed by Precision Visuals and is currently used by Nations Bank and Chemical Banking, among other institutions. During the meeting in Boulder, CO, with Precision Visuals management, it was mentioned that

- The financial computing market now comprises 20 percent of the firm's total revenue.

- This means a lot in terms of cross-fertilization of skills.

Even without the concept of the virtual bank, the collecting and archiving of text, data, and graphics becomes an enormous task. This makes it so much more important to have a way to dissect and understand financial information in an interactive, graphical environment.

- Because of the globalization of markets, banks are finding themselves in an ocean of information elements.

- It is simply not possible to proceed through classical means, no matter what the mainframers are saying.

A competitive banking environment requires facilities for image processing, animation, and customized applications development. This is not a "maybe." It is a *must.* It is competitiveness versus backwater.

Virtual banking will never become feasible without direct manipulation paradigms that permit the financial institution's professionals to directly interact with their data. Such interaction must take place in an ad hoc way very quickly, prior to making a commitment, which once again requires visual programming.

If some traditional-thinking bankers approach visualization software with a mixture of fear and doubt, their major clients, the institutional investors, are most eager to pursue technologies that could provide them with a competitive edge.

- Sophisticated investors see to it that visual data analysis becomes the alter ego of financial computing.

- Multivariant financial research on the transaction price, time, and trading volume reveals information that no classical tool can ensure.

- Three-dimensional plots can effectively show the tick-by-tick price of a stock—the pulse of the market—while the daily closing price with its high and low provides a very partial answer.

As we saw in considerable detail in Sec. 13.4, important financial information can never really be revealed in an effective manner by the classical time series published by Dow Jones. But a tick-by-tick pattern becomes complex because the same instruments are traded in different markets that do not behave in a similar way.

In these few paragraphs lies the concept of the virtual bank. The improving capabilities of three-dimensional visualization, combined with object-oriented techniques for the representation of information relationships, can substantially increase the strength of exploration provided by information systems.

Tier 1 banks have commented in the course of my research that graphics and visual programming play an important role in allowing them both to better understand large data sets and to explore a higher degree of selectivity. In terms of information relevance,

- To be beneficial to its user, the system should provide many different representations for the same data sets in order to address customized needs.

- Visualizations and representations should ensure analyses from a variety of angles for the same data set(s).

- Response should be ad hoc and in real space (defined in Chap. 4), providing graphical representations of the relationships among clients and financial instruments.

The solution which we adopt should also allow for an effective comparison of these graphical data representations. It should make feasible critical tests which are end-user-defined.

These issues constitute fundamental prerequisites not only of any bank but also of any other company. They are vital parts of an infrastructure which permits one to distribute products and services quickly to end users, leading to significant advantages in a marketplace that is more demanding than ever.

References

1. See D. N. Chorafas, *Rocket Scientists in Banking,* Lafferty Publications, London, 1996.
2. See also D. N. Chorafas and H. Steinmann, *Database Mining: Exploiting Marketing Databases in the Financial Industry,* Lafferty Publications, London, 1994.
3. *Nice Matin,* November 30, 1995.
4. See also D. N. Chorafas, *Measuring Returns on Technology Investments,* Lafferty Publications, London, 1993.
5. Dimitris N. Chorafas, *How to Understand and Use Mathematics for Derivatives,* vol. 1: *Understanding the Behavior of Markets,* Euromoney, London, 1995.
6. See D. N. Chorafas, *Rocket Scientists in Banking.*
7. See D. N. Chorafas and H. Steinmann, *Virtual Reality—Practical Applications in Business and Industry,* Prentice-Hall, Englewood Cliffs, NJ, 1995.
8. See also D. N. Chorafas and H. Steinmann, *Off-Balance Sheet Financial Instruments,* Probus Publishing, Chicago, 1994.
9. See also D. N. Chorafas, *Beyond LANS: Client-Server Computing,* McGraw-Hill, New York, 1994.

Programming in Virtual Reality and the Virtual Dome Application

14.1 Introduction

Chapter 13 has demonstrated how and why new, powerful visual programming tools are necessary in the banking industry. Competitive advantages obtained from well-designed visual programming approaches permit both end users and software developers to work out applications that are consistent with current needs and can be delivered interactively, rather than after months or years.

Not only the developers but the users of computer applications as well become more productive through agile and friendly visualization approaches that help them work faster in a comprehensive manner. Human-machine interfaces must be graphical, and they should be rich in programming paradigms. Emphasis must therefore be placed on

- Concepts which the end user can easily understand and apply without delay as the need arises

- Artifacts which are knowledge-enriched and effectively focus on the job being done

- Solutions based on industrywide norms and standards, at least infrastructurally, while the value-added tools are customized

The manufacturing industry and merchandisers and bankers consider short time to market as the cornerstone to business success. Yet, software developers often lag in terms of timely deliverables. They do so as if they do not understand that no product today can have a competitive edge in the market without agile computer support.

Visual programming, object orientation, and the use of agents radically influence the timetable of deliverables—and the quality of the applications. What is more, in the majority of cases visual programming, desk-area networks, and high-performance communications fit well together. A well-chosen and properly implemented visual programming tool will operate in a distributed environment, even if the latter is characterized by diversified, heterogeneous structures.

The goals of the last item in the preceding list are to make feasible the development of computer software without worrying about problems of suppliers and to protect existing investments. Key to this is the adoption of *open-systems* solutions, always keeping in mind that there are many red herrings in this business of open architectures.

The solutions which we provide must be able to integrate all the computer resources and other facilities which are available. They must also lead toward greater user interactivity based on the user's familiarity with the interfaces. These interfaces increasingly become three-dimensional. Sometimes they are remote, as we will see in the example of the virtual dome.

14.2   Thinking about the End Users' Viewpoints and Prerequisites

Forty-three years ago, with the advent of digital computers in business and industry, programming was a specialist's job, and it stayed so for nearly four decades. However, as Parts 1 and 2 have documented, the Internet, the World Wide Web, and the tools which they provide are radically changing the concept of how computers should be run.

The centralization of computer supports has proved to be wasteful, inflexible, and alienated from users. In its way visual programming by end users has many similarities to the cultural change which took place in the early 1980s with the introduction of personal computers at the workplace by the end users themselves:

- The PC knocked down the concept of centralized computer hardware.
- Visual programming does away with centralized software development.

Still, in a surprisingly large number of companies this old concept of depending on centralized programming has not yet changed. It is essentially in leading-edge organizations that end users have taken over many programming chores—and this self-service policy has produced very good results.

- When the end user gets so intimately associated with her or his own software, it is proper to ask what's really the user's *viewpoint* and how it can be observed.
- The answer has to keep in perspective the fact that technology has gone beyond the effects of serial programming, on which computers have revolved for so many years.

Today, we have more sophisticated languages and more complex applications than ever before. But at the same time, users are demanding a far greater degree of simplicity when it comes to putting these applications to work. This is an overriding concern which has to be answered in an able manner.

Users want applications that don't require advanced learning, and companies want software that minimizes the need for training. The divergent trends of greater sophistication in applications and greater simplicity for users mean that what looks user-friendly today is likely to incorporate complex and convergent technologies tomorrow—and these must be incorporated in a seamless manner. This is the first and foremost mission of visual programming.

The quest for excellence is never-ending. During the coming years, a great deal will be heard about more advanced types of applications which even the current visual programming and program visualization tools cannot support, for instance, *virtual dome* software and *synthetic sensations,* which constitute more advanced aspects of virtual reality, as the examples in Sec. 14.3 and thereafter document.

By contrast, current visual programming tools support well more basic end-user requirements. We saw a number of such tools and their well-founded applications in Chap. 12. For those who have not yet gotten the message:

- High technology has left the land of mainframes and personal computers, has traveled the domain of networking, and is currently exploring the continent of new software solutions.

- This points to a major directional shift, with the quest for new departures becoming much more pronounced.

At the architectural level, areas that were once labeled stand-alone are coming together. This is exemplified by the convergence of computers, communications, and multimedia. There are plenty of examples of this.

What we are seeing right now, and can expect more of in the years ahead, is that convergence is being experienced everywhere in advanced technology, spreading from its base in telecommunications into semiconductors and software. All industries will now have to deal with the changes created by the trend toward greater convergence.

- Many managers and professionals in different trades, that is, the end users, know and appreciate this fact.

- That is precisely why they need their self-developed software, visual programming approaches, and open systems.

Bluntly stated, information scientists have no business involving themselves with the applications software of the end users. Neither should they continue to lock themselves into operating systems as if they were cocoons. Rather, they should apply themselves to more demanding tasks such as *input/output* analysis and perception.

As Fig. 14.1 suggests, large-scale systems get easily saturated in terms of input/output. This is characteristic of all organizations and structures. The single person fares somewhat better, but here, too, there is an I/O saturation point;

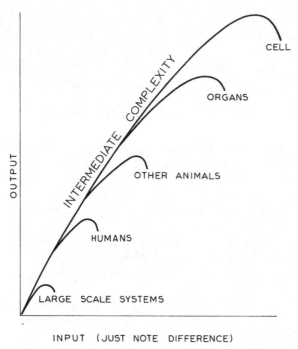

Figure 14.1 The complexity of an organism has a direct
impact on its ability to absorb input and give output.

after that point is reached, giving more in terms of input gives less output, not
more. Figure 14.2 demonstrates this idea.[1]

- Something similar happens with markets where information flows prove to
  be more effective in distributed environments than in highly concentrated
  monopolistic situations.

- Apart from the diseconomies of scale, there is as well inefficiency of size,
  which particularly shows up in fast-moving environments and in times of
  significant innovation.

Competent managers and professionals understand that the controlling companies of yesterday—those that set not only their own directions but also the
direction of others—have no more clout. The marketplace is teaching them that
incredibly rapid changes are now setting the direction for them.

These concepts are not alien to programming in a virtual reality setting,
because after all (with the exception of the entertainment industry) virtual
reality projects are not being done for the fun of it, but to answer specific engineering, marketing, financial, and other business requirements. This is the
managerial viewpoint to be respected in software development. We will return
to this issue in Sec. 14.4.

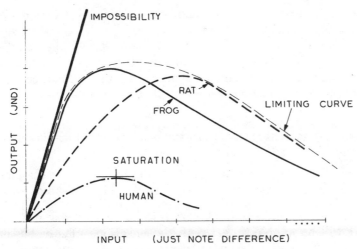

Figure 14.2 The study of the input/output function is very important in information technology, for reasons of optimization.

14.3 The Concepts of a Virtual Dome and Telerobotics

At NASA's Ames Research Center in Mountain View, CA, a virtual reality solution permits one to look around the surface of Mars, which has been recreated from satellite data. A motion sensor in the head-mounted display permits the user to look in any direction as the computer rerenders the scene to reflect fascinating perspectives on the Martian landscape. This is not a Mars exclusive.

Real-time simulations with a feeling of *being there* can be powerful. But they also present challenges beyond what has already been done with less sophisticated applications.

Professor Michitaka Hirose, of Tokyo University, aptly suggested that the ability to induce *realistic sensation* in telecommunications is rapidly becoming a key issue in many applications fields. A good example is space telerobotics. To address this problem, Dr. Hirose and his associates developed the *virtual dome* concept. It consists of

- A rotating camera head unit
- Communications gear
- Graphics workstation

As we will see in this and the following sections, the rotating camera head unit gathers the complete image of the surrounding area from a remote location. The graphics workstation generates the virtual spherical screen inside of which the user can experience the visual sensation of being in the remote location.

Among the programming challenges is the fact that the two subsystems work asynchronously. To experience better realistic sensations associated with being in a remote place and looking around, the time delay between head movements and the displayed image must be minimized.

One of the important factors associated with providing visual sensation is the dynamic field of view which changes interactively according to the user's head movements. This means overcoming a bottleneck in conventional tele-communications regarding the effect of time delay caused by transmission time. In principle,

- As long as the distance between the head-mounted display and the camera head is small, the lag is not so perceptible.

- But when the camera head has to be located in a remote place, the time delay between head movements and displayed images becomes significant.

This is causing a number of problems. If the time delay exceeds a certain limit, the user will be unable to feel realistic sensations. She or he could lose the sense of orientation or even suffer from a seasickness syndrome.

To address the time-delay problem at the level of programming in the large, Japanese virtual reality researchers advanced the concept of the virtual dome. The principle is to separate camera head movements and the user's head movements. In this manner, the time delay on the communication line does not directly affect performance in looking around in an immersive VR environment. In the project conducted at the University of Tokyo, four subsystems contribute to this solution:

- Camera head unit
- Communications channel
- Image display system
- Sophisticated software

The camera head unit is located in the remote place, as shown in Fig. 14.3. This device steadily scans the surroundings to capture a complete image of the area. Images are transmitted to the display system by telecommunications.

The image display system consists of a graphics workstation and the head-mounted display with position sensor. Screen and images taken by the camera are texture-mapped onto the virtual dome, permitting the user to experience remote synthetic sensations.

- Because all the information is located in the graphics workstation, there is no time delay related to looking around.

- No matter how far away the camera head is located, the user almost never loses the sensation of "being there." (We will talk more about this issue in Sec. 14.8, in connection with telepresence in a business setting.)

Planning issues and technical problems are, however, posed and require an efficient solution. For instance, the physical characteristics of the system may inhibit the transmission of real-time information.

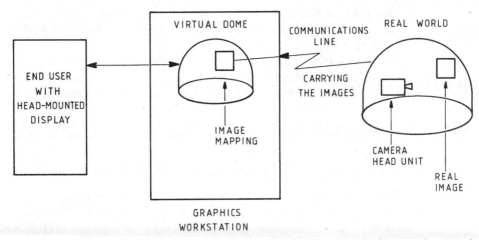

Figure 14.3 Programming-in-the-large system synchronization through the use of a virtual dome.

Interestingly enough, as we push the frontiers of knowledge, problems quite similar to those of the virtual dome will be encountered by business and industry in a more generic sense. These kinds of challenges will multiply in the years ahead. Hence we should be learning now from the most advanced experiences.

14.4 Learning How to Handle Complex Applications

The problems encountered with telerobotics and solved through the virtual dome should be seen as a challenge from which we can learn a great deal. Similar limitations may arise in other cases due to the time required, for instance, to scan complete images of the surrounding space and to draw a texture-mapped virtual dome in the workstation.

In this as in other applications, an efficient method for refreshing the images is needed, for instance, assigning priority to refreshing images in the direction in which the user is currently looking. This is what the University of Tokyo has done, but it entails programming-in-the-large requirements as well as coordination perspectives.

At Dr. Hirose's project, a solution has been implemented in which entire images of the surrounding space are first captured by the rotating camera head and sent to the workstation. Subsequent camera actions are *driven by the user's* head movements.

- When the user changes head orientation, he or she will initially see previously obtained images.

- But if the user continues to look in the same direction, images from the remote camera will rapidly refresh the old ones.

This permits the user to "be there" without losing her or his sense of orientation. To perfect the model, three-dimensional cues have been added which help present more realistic sensations.

Different computer vision software packages have methods to calculate three-dimensional information from two-dimensional data. The two-dimensional images gathered by rotating the camera head are projected onto an uneven virtual dome.

- Even if the dome is uneven, three-dimensional sensation for the user is significantly increased.

- The images appear proportional even at distances which may be very long.

The interesting aspect of this idea is that it matches quite closely requirements encountered in industry, particularly in the domains of transnational operations, two-way teleconferencing, concurrent engineering, and 24-hour banking.

These facts of business life permit us to merge what was stated in Sec. 14.2 about the observance of the end user's viewpoint with what has been learned through advanced projects like the virtual dome. There is a significant similitude between worldwide marketing challenges and applications in telerobotics— and a similar statement can be made about teleoperating in the world's financial markets:

- Competitive companies understand that they need to sharply decrease their response time to succeed.

- Their management must appreciate that modern industry is not going through transitions—it is going through cataclysmic transformations.

For instance, in the past, the information technology industry was directed from the top down. Now this industry is being driven from the bottom up. We have gone beyond the mainframe versus the PC. *End-user programming* is the new starting point.

In all industries which undergo such radical transformations, such as finance, skilled management appreciates the depth of the ongoing changes and demands real-time services to face the challenges in an able manner. This is true not just in networking but in every aspect, starting with applications software development.

- The newer the company, the easier it is to meet those criteria, *reinvent itself,* and keep itself permanently in transition.

- Investors were once warned never to invest in a company in transition; but transition has become a necessity today.

Investors are now advised to target the dynamic companies where transition is a built-in culture because, like it or not, all successful enterprises really have to be flexible enough to deal with the unprecedented changes taking place today.

The example of the VR and visual programming implementation in the context of the virtual dome brings home the message that successful companies must operate as if they were research laboratories. They will need to steadily reinvent themselves, renew their cultures, drop old habits, and keep at the peak of technology. This message goes all the way down to the level of computer programming. Personal computer software should be done at the workplace by the person who needs it for visual solutions. Systems specialists should apply themselves to much more demanding tasks. Here again, the virtual dome is a case in point.

As a last piece of advice, the best solutions which develop along this frame of reference are object-oriented. Many projects integrate knowledge engineering artifacts, from rule-based expert systems to neural networks and fuzzy sets. The more advanced proceed through a *metalayer,* as is documented by the different examples we have seen. To do so, they utilize visual programming approaches.

14.5 Intelligent Software for Realistic Sensations

There is no exclusive way to ensure realistic sensations. One of the newest approaches, for instance, is the *virtual clay* (virtual holography) which we discussed in Part 3. Another, slightly more classical but crucial approach is the ongoing integration of visualization and acoustics.

As emphasized on several occasions, virtual reality sensations beyond strict visualization are very important. Hence, as an extension of the virtual dome, researchers at the University of Tokyo are planning to add an auditory channel. In the system under development, sound waves are analyzed by microphone pairs attached to the camera unit.

- The approximate direction of a sound source can be estimated from the phase shift between two sound waves detected by a microphone pair.

- By using at least three microphone pairs, the three-dimensional position of a sound source can be determined, and a more precise calculation can be done.

Once the source location is determined and the loudness of the source is known, the monaural sound and its location are transmitted to the user through the communications channel. The three-dimensional sound environment of a remote place is regenerated at the user's side. This approach helps to save channel capacity and is quite flexible because information is coded.

This and other examples bring into perspective the different types of coordination needed in sophisticated virtual reality environments. They underline the important role that control software plays in managing large-scale systems.

- The problem of software design for advanced implementations must be discussed from the viewpoint of developing needs.

- Time and again VR projects find out that a conventional methodology is not sufficient for realistic, complex virtual reality designs.

- The use of interactive multimedia and visualization technology can be a solution and can impose new demands on software.

In this context, the VR project of Tokyo Electric Power has developed a method of mapping from an originally logical representation into a virtual representation. Using VR technology, researchers developed a non-text-based programming approach which, as we will see in this and the following sections, presents fundamental innovations.

To understand the impact of the solution in question, it is appropriate to note that the type of networking of resources that an electric utility requires is not limited to the power supply. It is a much more general problem involving computers, communications, and software because it is full of advanced applications aspects. Two basic problems make themselves felt:

1. How to coordinate many computers and software resources through *programming in the large*

2. How to best program each computer in the VR environment, which is *programming in the small*

Part of the challenge today is that when information scientists talk about programming, they usually address the second, smaller and easier problem. Yet, even though this, too, has its challenges, it is the first problem which looms and can make or break the sought-after solution.

One of the reasons for the relative inability to conceive the first challenge is due to the classical training in information technology. Another reason is the fact that computer control for large-scale systems has developed rather recently. For nearly 40 years, research in programming focused on solutions for the individual machine. Very few projects addressed the systemwide perspective and its architectural implications.[2] Current programming approaches, including the more advanced, tend to become limiting and insufficient in the case of programming in the large, where the most important factor regards *total configuration* rather than a list of statements, as practiced in classical software design.

Systems solutions, such as the virtual dome or the VR power production and distribution network, typically address broad-scope problems with many unknowns, hence many degrees of freedom. They do not concern the more logical, exact issues. Hence,

- A global methodology is needed to guide in the overall architectural design, even though each individual subsystem may be known.

- Whether the goal is real-life systems solutions or VR, narrow-focus and narrow-bandwidth solutions pay no dividends.

The competitive advantages of a multimedia visual representation are due to its added value over data and text representation. Through images and pattern recognition we are often able to understand the total aspect of a system. This provides a broad-minded attribute which, nevertheless, has to be complemented by synchronization routines in order to support a multimedia environment (for instance, visualization and sound, as in the case of the virtual dome).

14.6 The Effectiveness of Visualization in Programming in the Large

Some of the best software researchers believe that visual programming plays an important role in facilitating systems understanding in programming in the large. A combination of graphics and text could provide a good solution, but an even better approach is object orientation, multimedia, and animation.

The approach chosen for programming reasons by the virtual reality project at the University of Tokyo is object-oriented but also incorporates a concept of *succession,* developed in the course of a parallel research project.

- Succession refers to successive message passing through several objects.

- One succession corresponds to one function of distributed computing over the network.

A *world mode* in visualization is followed for observing whole shapes of the software. This permits one to handle programming-in-the-large characteristics. The succession approach is chosen for editing message passing among objects. Each mode still has its own action menu.

The procedure chosen for making the transition from programming in the large to programming in the small is characterized by the following promises. Programming in the large corresponds to defining specifications of methods, objects, and messages systemwide and to establishing relationships among objects.

- A three-dimensional visual representation of complete software can be constructed by using a virtual three-dimensional environment (to be discussed later).

- This virtual three-dimensional environment can be considered as a sort of high-level source code where the architectural characteristics dominate.

By unbundling the visual representation, the objects, templates, and methods can be automatically extracted. After obtaining an architectural overview, the user can concentrate on defining the contents of each module, given that the consistency among objects has already been solved by the systems approach.

Better still, the conversion from three-dimensional visualization can be done automatically through compilers, as the preceding chapter demonstrated. The production of IF, THEN, ELSE statements as an intermediate level to object code is compatible with the suggested message-passing approach. Once established, the method of the object can be automatically activated at run time.

- Such an approach helps to provide a relative time concurrency control that is required by many systems.

- For absolute time concurrency, timer objects are necessary to ensure message transmission at specific milestones.

This is one of several solutions aimed to ensure that visual programming techniques can be exploited in a flexible and efficient manner to assist in programming in the large, programming in the small, and the necessary transition between the two as well as in the debugging and performance enhancement of software.

The goal is to achieve fast and easy development procedures, ensure straightforward and intuitive user interfaces, and provide for general applicability of the infrastructure. If it is designed in a parametric form and is knowledge-enriched, this infrastructure can be subsequently customized as the situation demands.

Another means of useful and meaningful visual representation of artifacts is through *metatools,* or tools helping to build other tools for visual programming and program visualization solutions. The aims are to

- Create highly configurable visual analysis capabilities
- Provide an overall generic tool structure
- Develop custom visualization approaches

Among the requirements are the introduction of custom definitions and the ability both to integrate an animated simulator and to drive simulation and experimentation through message exchange and traced events from actual program executions.

At the University of Tokyo, the basic part of the implementation of a visual programming environment has already been completed. The chosen solution displays the message flow between processes in virtual three-dimensional space, as shown in Fig. 14.4.

- A family of methods is a process carrier.
- A slab represents a method.

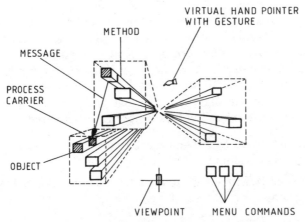

Figure 14.4 The three-dimensional visual programming environment at the University of Tokyo.

- A box represents an object.

- Three-dimensional windows and cursors are used.

Through the employment of a virtual hand, which works as a three-dimensional pointer, and an action menu which detects gestures, the programmer can handle virtual objects and messages in the virtual three-dimensional environment.

In this and similar developments, support software, incorporated in an interactive visual editor, assists in graphic object selection and placement as well as graphic object interconnection. The features identified in Fig. 14.4 make feasible a new concept of menu-driven attribute assignment. Collective object functionality dictates the semantics.

Knowledge-enriched software helps to display internal behavior of the objects as well as interactions among objects. Interactive examination of the internal object state is very important, particularly in cases of animation and sophisticated simulation procedures. The visual representation capabilities provide the added value.

14.7   Extending New Programming Concepts to On-Line Transaction Processing

Eventually, virtual reality worlds will be used to simulate business transactions from sales negotiations to financial issues. They may also help train workers for flexible manufacturing, for instance, by projecting job instructions in an immersive environment.

- In theory at least, this type of instruction can replace hours of training in which workers learn jobs and then must be retrained when the task changes.

- With interactive displays, a worker might assemble one product and then switch to another on the same day, with little loss in productivity.

In the same way, employees can learn to handle polyvalent transactions which would be automatically carried to their desks through networks. Virtual reality will assist by way of execution in creating a simulated environment for each type of transaction, including constraints and grids to capture handling failures.

Along this line of reference, a recent experimental project has focused on programming in the large, with the aim of supporting on-line transaction processing applications for distributed computer architectures. Its aim is to enable software developers to rapidly design, test, implement, and maintain client-server transaction processing applications in a way which is portable from one platform to another and without the need for specialized skills in either transaction processing or client-server technology.

The concept is to provide a system software environment for deploying new applications in a robust, predictable, and consistent manner. Account is taken of the fact that on-line transaction processing must meet stringent requirements for reliability, availability, performance, concurrency, and security.

Scalability and systemwide manageability are other important requirements to be fulfilled, and the uniqueness of programming in conjunction with virtual reality approaches lies in the fact that both scalability and manageability are better defined through visual inspection, hence more feasible. The user has an improved hold on transaction executions, which also makes the simulated environment a good ground for training.

Because of the design principles characterizing its development, a virtual reality orientation meets the requirements of modern on-line transaction processing applications. It also assists visual programming approaches through

- Graphical user interfaces
- Distributed management
- Multiple-database access
- Object-oriented handling

Because of the networked nature of programming in the large, the resulting artifacts can be easily deployed to multiple sites, with heterogeneous hardware and software configurations. This can be done without custom programming to account for differences in underlying hardware, operating system, database management system, presentation services, and communications protocols.

Software design at the aggregate level can nicely provide the necessary coordination among various database transaction managers on the network. Simulators embedded in the VR system will help ensure that component modules work together to complete a transaction or back out of a transaction if not all its parts execute.

Quite similarly, a virtual reality implementation can help in terms of reliability and availability as well as provide a testing ground for applications and data integrity—both being critical requirements. Such an approach substantiates data integrity by enforcing rules and constraints associated with application data.

Experimentation, conducted through visual programming and program visualization, helps to test for possible errors and evaluate cases of rollbacks of both the database and the state of the application to the beginning of a transaction. Classical solutions to transaction processing, particularly those that are mainframe-based, have proved to be deficient in managing error situations.

Testing a programming-in-the-large transaction management approach through VR makes it easier to confine systems in order to provide on-line installation of upgrades or new applications, without having to take down a running real-time environment. Applications are thus inherently more resilient to errors and can be more effectively managed.

14.8 Why Telepresence Offers Important Advantages with Queries and Transactions

Telepresence is a virtual reality term that refers to the remote participation in an activity by the user(s) of a system. Applications can range from a meeting

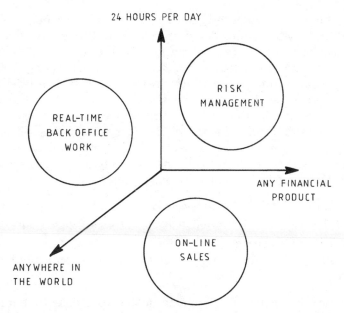

24 HOURS PER DAY

RISK
MANAGEMENT

REAL-TIME
BACK OFFICE
WORK

ANY FINANCIAL
PRODUCT

ON-LINE
SALES

ANYWHERE IN
THE WORLD

Figure 14.5 Telepresence can be instrumental in global financial operations, which classical data processing cannot serve.

to the manipulation of logical objects such as transactions or physical equipment. An example is provided by Fujita, a major Japanese construction company which built a VR solution that permits an operator to remotely direct earthmoving equipment. The operator views the site on a computer screen, then employs controls that signal the robot to do a specific job. With VR, the image is so painstakingly exact that the human makes no mistakes in directing the operation.

A metaphor can be drawn with the handling of financial transactions and queries. For the global financial institution and the global manufacturing organization, telepresence has become an important competitive advantage in their activities. As suggested in Fig. 14.5, the money center bank operates 24 hours per day, on any product, anywhere in the world. Typically, major transactions involving billions of dollars* are made between parties who never meet with one another. Transaction management is therefore a major programming-in-the-large problem which has to be handled all the way from the *risk management* aspects characterizing and dominating a deal down to the counterparty and accounting issues characterizing *back office* work. The unknowns in such large, complex transactions are so many that virtual presence can make significant contributions, even if the only effect is to provide a channel over which the people who trade get to know one another. There is, however, much more than that.

---

*For instance, in notional principal amounts and in off–balance sheet financial products such as futures, options, and swaps.

Security benefits become automatically available through telepresence. Authorization is better controlled with respect to the actions that a counterparty can perform. Access can be managed at the deal level, individual subtransaction level, and particular input/output characteristics. This is in contrast to traditional approaches which deal with access at a level that is less direct and obvious, such as read or write access to a file. Security provided through telepresence is in addition to the existing security mechanisms on a server machine—and this is just as valid for transactions as it is for queries.

By means of telepresence, participants in a deal are involved in a visual editing procedure, with a personal handshake simplifying the transaction process. Visual programming faculties are also being promoted:

- Once established, telepresence becomes a reusable application like graphical user interfaces, icons, processing logic, and transaction specifications.
- Developers can construct applications by tailoring familiar telepresence objects, subject to visual object editing designed specifically for a transaction type.

This procedure is not truly different from the work done by template-driven editors. During the last few years, since template-driven procedure editors became available, developers do not need to learn any syntax, even for specifying complex algorithms or database access.

With semantic checking performed immediately and automatically, application developers do not need to remember what objects have been previously defined. Transaction software provides assistance via a list of allowable values to be manipulated through visual programming means.

14.9   Training in Programming through Virtual Reality

Many practitioners think that in business education and job training the chief benefit from virtual reality would be lower costs and better performance. On this premise, in the United States, the Electric Power Research Institute has teamed up with MITRE to determine whether an electronic mockup of a power plant control room using stereo projection displays can be truly effective in training plant operators. The use of VR is considered, in principle, to be an improvement over currently used training rooms for fossil fuel plants. Other problems are seen in cost swamping, as a current type of training room costs up to $1,000,000 while with the use of VR the cost might dip to under $100,000.

For the same reasons, the Japanese government commissioned the Mitsubishi Research Institute to do a virtual reality study on the impact of VR on education. This particular project aims to go well beyond existing computer-aided instruction (CAI) approaches and to focus on multimedia.

It is expected that not only will virtual reality provide better solutions for learning and programming purposes than the already known CAI methods, but also it will make possible programming in the large of the training process as such. It will make it feasible to merge education and experimentation, making the educational process so much more interesting to the learner. As an example of what might come out of such a merger, using a workstation, urban planners in Los Angeles are building an 80-block by 80-block virtual model of renovation plans for riot-damaged areas. Virtual reality helps because it is hard for untrained people to read blueprints and understand them and the cost of physical three-dimensional models can be prohibitive. Yet, the Los Angeles urban planners feel that community involvement is indeed essential. Through VR users will easily learn how to drive through the streets as if they were in a real environment. They will also be able to fly over city blocks and walk through houses and alleys.

Both ease of use and real-life sensation count a great deal, and the aim is to develop an intelligent training system which integrates expert systems and agents with training and teaching methodologies. The purpose of any solution along an evolutionary line of reference should be to provide a bridge between the knowledge acquired from books and oral explanations and the procedural skills necessary for successful performance in increasingly complex jobs.

Some years ago, simulators of that type were relatively slow to develop, required significant contributions by way of skilled contributions, and were therefore very expensive. As a result, they were mostly limited to the Army, the Navy, the Air Force, and NASA. Today, virtual reality brings these solutions to practically everybody's reach.

Few people really appreciate that programming and executing training chores underpin any and every successful implementation of technology. Because of very rapid advances in science—and particularly in computers, communications, and software—virtually every practitioner today is a *lifelong trainee,* and for efficiency reasons

- Trainees must be exposed to realistic scenarios that evolve to higher levels of difficulty and provided with assistance tailored to their demonstrated skill levels.

- As a training device, virtual reality can serve to augment understanding, ensure high-quality training, and allow scarce expertise to be delivered to a large number of trainees.

Visual programming in a VR setting permits one to make the architecture of the training system both realistic and modular, one that can be adapted to a wide variety of tasks. Such a solution typically integrates

- *Domain expertise,* reflected through knowledge engineering
- *Object-oriented* databases and execution processes
- *Interactive three-dimensional graphics* put at the disposal of trainees
- *Agent* technology, as defined and detailed in recent projects[3]

Software is the cornerstone of what has just been stated, and, like training, software is an entrenched phrase that means many things to many people. Just like training, software is an intangible. Unless we use it, we do not know what it is. That is why many people find it hard to understand just what software and training can do.

Software is the critical mechanism that makes hardware productive. Computers are nothing without software. Just the same, training makes people productive. On the job, humans are nothing without training. Agents provide the missing link between software and the user community.

14.10   Expressing Some Realistic Expectations

The solutions which we have seen in this chapter are polyvalent. They permit both software designers and users to leverage work they have done in the past and allow them to evolve their systems over time. For instance, the able use of telepresence offers advantages all the way to the establishment of programmatic interfaces.

The contribution of telepresence to programming in the large is even more significant if we account for the fact that it enables developers to extend the system and its component parts with custom functions. In the financial domain, for instance, this will mean

- Better-focused global risk management
- Credit risk computations regarding a counterparty
- Market risk evaluation by financial product
- Authorized access to particular databases and gateways

This can be further enhanced through the construction and employment of reusable objects, a practice promoting consistency across applications. It is as well improving productivity in developing and maintaining software modules with predictable quality and performance.

Reference has been made to the fact that visual programming and virtual reality environments can be instrumental in improving configuration management and version control facilities. Developers can interactively define software and hardware structures as manageable views of large volumes of objects.

- Visualized interactive version control leads to better management of version creation and change propagation.
- For shared networks, telepresence ensures a common set of administrative facilities for deploying new applications.

Both approaches facilitate systems work, from development to production and maintenance. Also they make applications easier to install and test in a networkwide manner. When problems are discovered, personal contact through telepresence can ensure that queries are answered and that they are isolated and corrected, with the new version being quickly deployed.

Equally important is the ability to train developers and users in new concepts, features, and solutions. We spoke of the importance of this issue in Sec. 14.9; here are some further examples.

In one fairly recent application, the trainee model is an object data structure which contains not only the simulated environment but as well a history of the individual trainee's interactions with it. Another feature is an interactive visual report generator that

- Produces a formatted trace of each trainee session and its particular features

- Provides the trainee's supervisor with a high-level description of each person's current skill level and progress

All interaction takes place in the form of a nonimmersive virtual reality setting. The *domain expert* is in the form of a production rule expert system capable of carrying out the deployment process using the same information that is available to the trainee.

This module also contains a list of *mal rules,* that is, explicitly identified errors that novice trainees commonly make. In this manner, the trainee can be provided with feedback specifically designed to help overcome any anticipated conceptual or procedural problems.

The educational scenario generator is also an expert system enriched with a development database and assisted through agents. The mission of this module is to design increasingly complex training exercises based on:

- The current skill level contained in the trainee's model

- Any weaknesses or deficiencies that the trainee has exhibited in previous interactions

The on-line database serves as a repository for all parameters needed to define a training scenario and includes problems or abnormalities of graded difficulty and other in-training characteristics.

The functions of the educational session manager are also supported by means of interactive intelligent artifacts. One is the error detection component, which compares assertions made about correct and incorrect actions in a particular context. Another module, an error-handling component, decides on the appropriate method of guidance based on the trainee's skill level and the responses given in the training session.

The net result to be retained from all these references is manageability through automated facilities, including optimal use of system resources and dynamic approaches to databases, training perspectives, and controlled access to applications. The resulting interactivity is quite helpful for version control also in the sense of acquiring knowledge of technological sites and configurations. This is classically not part of the application definition, but it has now become a must.

References

1. Based on seminal research done in the 1970s under a NATO contract, at the University of Kansas.
2. See also D. N. Chorafas, *System Architecture and System Design,* McGraw-Hill, New York, 1989.
3. See also D. N. Chorafas, *Agent Technology in Communication Networks,* McGraw-Hill, New York, 1997.

15

News in the Future: The Personalization of Reporting and of Information Representation

15.1   Introduction

Every company needs to be vigilant of both its customers' requirements and the need for new sources of revenue, hence profits. Major players in business and industry have steadily searched in the 1990s to create strategies to provide tailor-made trading and investment opportunities, but only the best have appreciated the level of high technology which they need in this task.

To give the reader practical and convincing examples of what can be obtained through technology leadership, in this chapter, as in Chap. 13, I concentrate on banking and finance. But the examples are polyvalent, and therefore they can be used as well in other industries.

One of the pillars on which this chapter is based is the ways and means for navigating in a perilous financial environment through better visualization of information. This strategy is based on custom-made approaches rather than the more classical, slow-moving reporting schemes still dominant in many banks.

Dynamic solutions are doable through agents who understand their master's *personality profile,* then filter and edit information for her or his work, rather than offer lots of irrelevant references. Hence, the reader is presented with what he or she wants to read. Once established, a modeling system customizes the content and presentation, producing a flexible electronic newspaper and underlining the content of selected financial news and other items.

Practical examples dominate the references made in this chapter. The discussion presented in the text is based not on hypotheses but on real-life projects which are currently under way and are providing concrete results.

The other pillar on which this chapter rests is the quantum leap forward in news handling. Emphasis is placed on the Internet rather than broadcasting. It is the Internet—not CD-ROM or other optical storage media—which makes the end user aware that the printing press of Guttenberg may have become an outmoded way to convey news.

At the beginning of January 1996, the London Sunday *Times* launched its first Internet edition. This means that the newspaper came globally on-line. It can be accessed within minutes by anyone, anywhere in the world through a personal computer and an Internet connection.

At about the same time, *The New York Times* announced a similar strategy; it, too, now has an Internet edition. This is a database comprehensive coverage of news to which subscribers will have direct access. The printed word still serves a purpose, as long as it does not become sluggish and unimaginative. But a big share of the pie in news events will go to computers and the communications market.

15.2 Networking May Be a Better Way of Delivering Daily News

As the current offering to its readership stipulates, the Internet edition of the Sunday *Times* will be compiled on Saturday evenings, alongside the more classical printed alternative. The database news will be available to Internet users before the printed paper could be distributed to them. What is more, I suppose on a trial basis, the Sunday *Times* Internet edition will be free:

- The print and distribution costs of the paper edition are less relevant in the on-line environment of the Internet, the Sunday *Times* says.

- Alongside the editorial stories there will be hot links allowing Internet readers to refer to other related articles.

The more the end user cross-indexes, the more she or he will need visual programming. Yet, in both cases, the London Sunday *Times* and *The New York Times,* the technology will be the easier nut to crack. Much more complex are the legal issues, particularly those relating to copyright.

In the United States, for example, the 1976 copyright law attempted to resolve the debate about intellectual property rights by defining *how* it can be used and *when* users of intellectual property must compensate copyright owners. But the proliferation of on-line solutions greatly complicates things because it presents problems having no precedents.

In years past, the main challenge was photocopying, which is a simpler legal case than on-line access. Still, the 1976 legislation had to be clarified through litigation to adequately deal with photocopying, because unauthorized copying is easy to do and difficult to detect.

Now in the Internet era, copyright owners are finding it even more difficult to control the distribution and publication of their intellectual property. There are simply no checks and balances when a document can be transmitted from one computer to another and then laser-printed in seconds.

Other challenges relate to advertising and the legal risk involved. In the case of the Sunday *Times,* the current offering provides Internet users with *keyword* searching in each day's issue along with the opportunity to look back at the contents of previous Internet editions.

- Some material can be more easily classified and mined in the database than other material.

- Advertising is not that easy, because companies paying for it want it to be proactive rather than passively resident in the database.

Research material can be browsed on any subject in the news from more than 1000 news stories that will be posted on the Times newspapers' Web site each week. Internet users who register on the Times newspapers' Web site will also be able to surf through *Interactive Times*, shared by *The New York Times* and the London Sunday *Times*.

One of the innovative features of *Interactive Times* is *Personal Times*. This service allows readers to set up their own profiles of what types of story they wish included in their personalized newspaper edition. Advertising could be part of Personal Times. An on-line classified advertisement database covers a number of different issues, including travel, motoring, property, recruitment, lonely hearts, personal affairs, and business.

Interactive Times is an interesting restructuring of newspapers as we have known them for over 100 years, and the London Sunday *Times* is not the only editor of newsprint searching to reinvent itself. Another fairly recent example is R. R. Donnelley, whose executives have wondered whether their company, the world's largest commercial printing firm, is still relevant in its business strategy and product line.

In a world that is increasingly dominated by software, electronic publishing, and the Internet, R. R. Donnelley's management worries that traditional ink-on-paper printing might be facing a gradual but inevitable obsolescence. To meet the challenge, the company takes advantage of high-technology and electronic publishing tools to increase its share of the mature U.S. market and tries to bolster its position in the still-lucrative traditional print business in developing countries. This two-tier strategy makes sense, but it will not be valid for very long. The rise of software and other market trends propelled by technology make 25 percent of Donnelley's present business obsolete. But at the same time, the opportunities that high technology creates far outweigh the risks, once these business opportunities have been properly capitalized.

Book publishers, too, have entered cyberspace. As John Wiley stated in a recent newsletter,[1] through networks the publisher has a storefront that takes up no square footage but has unlimited shelf space for its titles. Internet is a world accessible with a computer and modem.

Wiley's first foothold in cyberspace was established in 1994 when its Direct Response Marketing department rented a storefront through CompuServe. Located in the CompuServe virtual mall, Wiley Bookstore features mostly business, finance, and computer technology titles. Shoppers can browse through them, decide what they want, and purchase. The publisher's marketing people also seed bulletin boards with press releases and sample chapters, using copyright notices. (However, this does not mean that the copyright problems described at the beginning of this section have been solved.)

As these examples document, Internet, America Online, CompuServe, Prodigy, and others are beginning to change the way publishers and booksellers promote and market their wares. The pioneers are learning from their own experimentation and their own mistakes, as well as from the examples of other pioneers. None of them, however, has yet found in cyberspace a way to make copyright laws foolproof.

15.3   What Is Meant by *News in the Future?*

Timely and accurate news is one of the requirements for better performance in any market. Better than timeliness, *prognosis* has been every banker's, treasurer's, or other investor's dream. Prognosis means reading tomorrow's newspaper today. But at what cost?

Being able to forecast future events helps to avoid the misapplication of complex financial instruments or the misunderstanding of their likely aftermaths. The real danger is that the forecast may go astray; or that while it is correct, its implications are misunderstood. Therefore, not everything is in prognosis. An equally important requirement is the customized way in which news and analytical results are presented.

News in the Future (NIF) is a project undertaken by the Massachusetts Institute of Technology aimed to be a pace setter. Its goal is to provide flexible, personalized presentation with multimedia content. A cornerstone to NIF is sophisticated software.

This and the next four sections examine what NIF means for industry at large and in particular for financial institutions. But a word of caution before we start. The goal of prognostication and of the personalization of news briefs and highlights is better comprehension of future events. Forecasts don't aim at future decisions, but rather at the future impact of current decisions.

As the MIT researchers commented during a meeting on NIF, the able use of technology can be of significant assistance in the perception of coming events. (See also Chap. 3.) A great deal depends on the ingenuity with which reporting formats are customized. Figure 15.1 makes a distinction between prognosis and personalization of reporting structures along a four-dimensional frame of reference; it emphasizes the ability to respond to opportunity and the associated risk-reward results.

The personalization of information is most important not only in connection with news items but as well in the domain of new analytical findings. These can be instrumental in altering old concepts; but to do so, they require a great deal of custom-made presentation. Prognosis, anticipation, and response to opportunity need a dynamic structure.

At MIT's Media Laboratory, the News in the Future research consortium explores the feasibility of a personalized newspaper as well as the means to offset customization costs. Since it started in October 1993, this project, nicknamed Fishwrap, is supported by a consortium which includes 19 founding

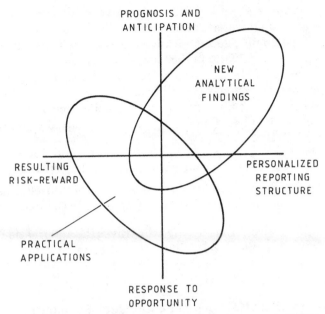

PROGNOSIS AND
ANTICIPATION

NEW
ANALYTICAL
FINDINGS

RESULTING
RISK-REWARD

PERSONALIZED
REPORTING
STRUCTURE

PRACTICAL
APPLICATIONS

RESPONSE TO
OPPORTUNITY

Figure 15.1 A competitive edge depends on the prognostication
of tomorrow's opportunities.

companies and 60 participants. And it has grown from an interactive video
guide to a full-fledged electronic newspaper.

The NIF effort rests on the premise that refashioning the news industry will
require a comprehensive look at not only content and its presentation but also,
if not primarily, the end user and her or his wishes. Researchers at the Media
Laboratory are exploring four fundamental areas:

- Automatic information collection
- Machine understanding of content
- Computer modeling of individual needs
- Customized presentation

A focal point is the comprehension of content of text and images, with representation facilitating a better understanding by the reader of the author's message.
The quest to bring a tailored newspaper, the *Daily Me,* to the marketplace
requires solution to two hard problems: figuring out what the news item, article,
or other feature is about and properly identifying what each person wants to see
or read. Personalization is the driving force. Automation does not necessarily
mean that computers can replace editors, nor does it imply interactivity at all
costs. The effort does begin with the end user and his or her wishes.

Presentation schemes currently under research and development tailor content—whether market data, editorials, or advertising—to the user's interests
and resources. Multimedia are employed to present objects through a variety of

modes—video, audio, and still. Context-sensitive media are seen as serving several purposes. A single presentation can be shown, for instance, to different professionals or age groups, automatically adjusting itself to each one's requirements. This is part of the effort of tailor-made applications.

In the background of the NIF study lies the fact that, as current market research documents, customization will be a key competitive advantage in the late 1990s and beyond—as fiber-optic connection of offices and homes will provide the input of not 1, 10, or 30 but of 100, 500, or eventually 1000 channels.

- Current research projects suggest that with 500- and 1000-channel cable systems on the horizon, television broadcasters will increasingly *narrowcast.*

- Customization will appeal to smaller and more specialized audiences. The same holds true for publishers disseminating news to their customers.

MIT's *Daily Me* projects that *agents* will travel the information superhighways and byways to gather and deliver all the news that fits a subscriber's world of interests.

15.4 Why Does Bit Radiation Affect Management Information Systems?

Managers able to understand the direction in which their business is moving will appreciate that bit radiation is both an opportunity for and a challenge to executive information. In banking, for example, customer loans and investment perspectives of interest to consumers as well as corporate treasurers and institutional investors can effectively use customization and narrowcasting.

As far as newspapers are concerned, the revolution in the making means that the entire paper, including its layout, becomes fairly easy to manipulate as long as it stays in digital form until the last minute. As the example with the London Sunday *Times* documents, these digital bit streams can be shipped around electronically, and in the future they may include audio as well as video information.

Financial institutions and manufacturing companies with experience in multimedia are planning a similar strategy. They suggest that home banking through Videotex and similar approaches has been a failure because it bet on too narrow a bandwidth—hence, it could not provide value-added services. This, however, is now radically changing with optical fibers reaching both offices and homes, supporting broadband communications, and personal computers with optical disks and multimedia switching from the office to the home, at price tags of $1500.

Projections and estimates, of course, have this particular characteristic: The hypotheses on which they are based may be overoptimistic and, therefore, the events they project may never materialize. But this is not an excuse for inaction.

In the 1970s when transmission costs were high, predictions about the percentage of text that would be computer-readable by the turn of the century advanced levels as high as 90 to 95 percent. But the mid-1980s saw a considerable slowing down of the growth curve in computer-readability. Today only about 1 percent of the world's information is in digital form.

This estimate, made by the *Economist,* appears accurate when we consider photographs, film, and video, all of which require so many bits. Such statistics, however, do not reflect the fact that many media are digital in terms of coding, even if they are not understandable by computer. For instance, an audio CD is digital, but is not structured data.

- A concert recorded and transmitted via digital or analog video has no structure. Each frame functions as a facsimile.

- The alternative is to capture the event as a model, with each member of the orchestra represented as a complex algorithm.

- The kinematics of the event can be derived by a sensor and transmitted to a receiver in algorithmic form.

At the receiver, not in the camera, the representation is flattened onto the screen and displayed holographically. As a current project at MIT demonstrates, not only can the concert be seen from any perspective, but also the computer is able to reconstruct plays as diagrams, compare the tactics of one play with the one before or after, and show it from the perspective of this or that viewer.

This is a bit radiation field worth lots of attention. Digitization with visualization makes it feasible to change the angle to draw attention to important information content, which is a process particularly vital in

- Geographic information systems
- Symbolic data representations
- Financial analysis and investment viewpoints

The more we customize, the more we need to program in an ad hoc way. Customization brings to the foreground the need for visual programming approaches. Among the applications to which reference was made during the MIT meeting are

- Airport control conversion of the radar chart into a three-dimensional representation of air lanes and ground

- The integration of two-dimensional representations into a three-dimensional framework, to better serve customization needs

Both examples are practical, and they help to emphasize the duality between real-time simulation and bit radiation. They also have a potential impact in that news can be perceived much more effectively than in classical newsprint.

Radical change means cultural change, and, therefore, it will not happen overnight. Our society has 500 years of experience with the typography, packaging, and delivery of printed matter that is not suddenly going to disappear.

- For a decade or more still, print will remain a vital ingredient in presenting information to mass audiences.

- But the wheels of change are already turning, and the first beneficiaries will be the information providers and the receivers of narrowcast information.

A number of cognizant people in the field now believe that both the way of exploiting multimedia bit streams and newscasting as such are in for thorough revamping. The new strategy is based on factors such as

- User-induced modeling

- Media manipulation

- Dynamic displays

Because the biggest challenge is tailor-made newscasting, the word *newsworthy* will be redefined according to not only the area where a reader lives but also his or her background and interests. This is what we have tried to do with management information systems.

15.5 Similarities and Differences between Management Reports and Newspapers

Not everything is the same in filtering and editing financial news versus other general-type information. But the flexibility of the method described in Secs. 15.3 and 15.4 is such that the process is easy to adapt, customizing the reported items to an intended population area for narrowcasting and personalizing them for each subscriber or reader.

One of the differences between financial information targeting an investor and more general newspaper style is that the former should be focused and concise. By contrast, a successful electronic newspaper must be able to store vast amounts of multimedia information.

Targeting can be done in several ways. The best today is graphics, a subject we addressed in practically every chapter of this book. Another is a dynamic matrix presentation, and Fig. 15.2 gives an example from reporting treasury information. This case is taken from an n-dimensional reporting structure which includes

- Different currencies and their consolidation into a chosen currency

- Dynamic estimates of currency exchange

- Country risk and restrictions on the outflow of money

- Money market rates by financial center and other selected criteria

In an application along the foregoing line of reference, agents see to it that the presentation is adjustable to the treasurer's profile and to the profile of each assistant. Each assistant has a dedicated knowledge artifact. Other agents look after database mining operations and the filtering of data streams from information providers.

```
                   INCOME (CASH) GENERATION
                   HIGH              LOW
              ┌─────────────────┬─────────────────┐
              │                 │                 │
        HIGH  │ HIGH CASH FLOW  │   NEGATIVE      │
              │                 │  CASH BALANCE   │
INVESTMENT    │                 │                 │
GROWTH RATE   ├─────────────────┼─────────────────┤
(CASH USE)    │                 │                 │
              │      CASH       │                 │
        LOW   │  ACCUMULATION   │   CASH DRAIN    │
              │                 │                 │
              └─────────────────┴─────────────────┘
```

Figure 15.2 A personalized high-low matrix for reporting available balances.

Database mining[2] is an example of the similarities which exist between the reporting of personalized financial information and that of customized general news of the London Sunday *Times* and *The New York Times* type. In both cases, the user should be able to retrieve both new and older references, as well as to add background and depth to the topic of interest. Such a solution, experts think, is quite feasible with

- Mining algorithms and agents
- Advances in compression technology
- The introduction of sophisticated software

Knowledge-enriched artifacts remove the barriers which existed before and help to manage the movement of electronic documents between computers. But an effective application requires efficient visual programming techniques for manipulation—numerical, textual, graphical, and pictorial information. Such information must be stored in a form that enables quick access and update by computers. It must be readily scanned and subject to quick and accurate access.

Under current technology, this task is feasible, although it is not always easy. Direct transfer of information from paper to computer-accessible media is usually difficult because of the presence of diverse types of information, for instance, textual and graphical, as well as

- The use of multiple sizes of fonts
- The existence of tabular structures
- The presence of handwritten material
- The nonperfect quality of documents

Current research in video coding increasingly emphasizes structure as a means of leveraging. At MIT's Media Laboratory, image understanding, machine vision, and a priori knowledge are used to produce video representations in terms of component parts—actors, backgrounds, and moving objects—and to generate content annotations for story construction.

Forms of coding under current research have implications for production, postproduction, distribution, and viewing. The goal is to script, produce, and work with a story represented as a structured video database in order to examine diverse issues including

- Script annotation
- Storyboarding
- Camera design
- Production techniques
- Data formatting
- Viewing paradigms

Another major challenge lies in the fact that today multimedia is to a significant extent a fax-type of process, particularly in connection with raster scanning. Very few projects currently undertaken in the financial industry appreciate the challenge posed by this reference, yet it can have a long-range impact in terms of cost-effectiveness.

15.6 Exploiting the Potential of Layered Image Presentation

One of the imaginative projects at the Media Laboratory is the layered image representation. Image sequences are decomposed into a set of layers ordered in depth. They are enriched with associated maps defining their motions, opacities, and intensities, which aid the process of comprehension.

This strategy makes it feasible to synthesize the image sequence by using available techniques of *warping* and *compositing*. The challenge is to achieve the targeted description starting with an image sequence from a natural scene. MIT researchers suggest that rendering is easy but vision is difficult. Solutions must account for the fact that image coding contains a model as well as an implicit vocabulary. Taken together, these offer a way to describe images as, for instance, a sum of cosine functions which forms the implicit image model. This, too, can be seen as a visual programming approach.

If motion compensation is used for moving images, then regions in the image model move coherently across time. The design of an image coding system has three interrelated parts: encoding, representation, and decoding. The choice of representation determines the nature of the solution, while encoding converts the representation to an array of pixels for the display. These processes are underpinning the now-popular multimedia solutions.

With an image sequence represented as layers, it is possible to perform flexible editing and postproduction operations that would not be feasible with more classical solutions, where the content of one frame is estimated by applying a spatial transformation to the content of a previous frame. By contrast,

- In a model based on image layers, the image consists of a set of levels, which are ordered in depth.

- Such a representation is used by cell animators, who paint a set of images as a way to produce the final image sequence.

The cells contain areas of varying color and transparency, emulating image formation of objects in the natural world. This is also the approach used by computer animation programs, in which image layers are defined and each layer has its own

- Motion

- Depth

- Pattern of color

- Intensity

- Pattern of transparency

The information stored in a layer can extend over a larger visual angle than is presented on a given image. When data is accumulated over frames, the model considers how the individual samples in the frames are to be mapped into the accumulated layer. The latter has a sampling lattice, and the incoming images generally present samples that may not align precisely with those of the layer.

In some cases, different images in a sequence may have different degrees of resolution. When this happens, a laplacian pyramid is built to combine the information from each image, with pyramid coefficients forming the different images being compared. The coefficient with the largest deviation from zero is retained.

By itself the layered representation does not necessarily offer data compression. To achieve compression, representation is used in conjunction with other image coding techniques. Each of the maps in the layers can be compressed by using standard image coding such as transform coding or subband coding.

Analysis of a scene into layered representation requires grouping the points in the image into multiple regions where each region undergoes a smooth motion. The motion model used in the analysis will determine the quality of the representation.

The MIT researchers have chosen to use an affine motion model to describe a wide range of motions commonly encountered in image sequences, which include translation, rotation, and zoom. The analysis of an image sequence into layers consists of three stages:

- Local motion estimation

- Motion-based segmentation

- Object image recovery

The motion segmentation algorithm is divided into local motion estimation and affine motion segmentation. The images of the corresponding regions in the different frames differ only by an affine transformation. These examples help explain the depth of necessary research to make news in the future and personalization viable propositions. They also explain some of the major changes taking place in the use of technology.

15.7 The Need for Semantic Image Modeling

From powerful algorithmic representation to very effective visual programming visualization solutions, the paradigms embedded in the examples which we have seen in the orbit of the News in the Future project are portable to other application domains. No field of endeavor has a monopoly on the able use of new technology.

Finance can benefit a great deal from the personalization of reporting and of information representation. No bankers, traders, treasurers, or investment advisers can function properly without knowing in a factual and documented manner where they have been and where they are going. This is particularly true in a dynamic financial market of currency exchanges, derivatives, and other complex financial products which offer significant benefits to writers and buyers but can also cause great problems in terms of the real-time management of risk.[3]

The means which we put at the disposition of bankers, treasurers, and investors must permit them to analyze in real time the risk of complex derivatives instruments such as path-dependent and -independent options, inverse floaters, discount swaps, and circus swaps among many others. They must make it feasible to

- Visually program risk control strategies and algorithms
- Interactively apply multidimensional what-if scenarios, well beyond spreadsheets
- Calculate the prevailing risk-reward parameters as well as deviations and exceptions
- Present the results in a personalized form through interactive visualization

This polyvalent approach to financial analysis is particularly vital for products which are new to the market or have been designed ad hoc to meet specific needs, whether such customization involves adapting existing instruments or starting anew.

Bankers can profit in terms of experience from lessons learned from computer-assisted engineering, particularly the concurrent solutions of the last few years. These largely rest on semantics modeling which can be instrumental in appreciating counterparty default and structuring image representation in an interactive manner. In both cases, exploiting the semantic value of the context makes the interpretation not only easier to comprehend but also flexible in terms of mapping. The models are available; but to be effectively applied in banking, they also need a new culture, which during the last few years has been known as *interactive computational finance*.

The pillars on which rests interactive computational finance are models, communications, and computers. Intelligent software is as much at a premium in banking as in other industries. For this reason, one of the research projects at MIT has set up a two-way interaction between available contextual information and the models used to represent visual information. The ultimate goal is to put semantic meaning into information theory. According to this project, the effective execution of semantics requires real-time modeling, which becomes feasible as computers begin to approach gigaflop speeds at an affordable cost— and data networks feature gigabit per second bandwidth.

With this type of technological support, it is possible to interact in real time with fairly complex quantitative and qualitative models such as those required for the control of complex financial instruments. In an information-rich environment where data, images, and sound are readily accessible and digitally communicated, the issue of semantics and content-based search is important. One of the projects at MIT is developing a repertoire of graphics that will allow computational assistance in the expression of dynamic interactive design. This is based on the premise that an electronic information environment needs new graphical principles, tools, and editors which are suitable to the intelligent representation of information.

The graphical set under development will be integrated with real-time design assistance systems, in order to cope with the magnitude of visual complexity resulting from multiple data streams, which today deluge the user. Breakthroughs are necessary that bridge the gap between the hands-on world of designers and the more abstract, symbolic world of programming. Therefore, knowledge tools are developed that explore spatial, temporal, and relational rules and methods which

- Rank information for the viewer
- Influence the responses which she or he gives

Depending on the application, real-time semantic image modeling may imply an extremely demanding environment that requires the integration of multiple degrees of freedom of input/output, coupled with state-of-the-art computational processing. Effective interfaces must sense user activity on a wide range of length scales, ranging from less than a millimeter for stylus input through centimeters for gesture sensing, to meters for local tracking, and to kilometers for navigation. In finance as in engineering, these measurements must increasingly be done in three dimensions, must produce images as well as metrics, and automatically must maintain the required spatial and temporal resolution. This is a technological world of compound requirement.

Such facilities must be supplemented by the integration of landscapes with pictorially convincing virtual environments, enabling a multimodal natural language communication with the virtual environment display and its contents. This can be done through combinations of multimedia output channels.

At the output end, there is need for development of intelligent visual programming and graphics representation tools to support the interactive creation of symbolic information landscapes. Finally, comprehensive research projects should investigate

- Perceptual issues in synthesizing a coherent scene from disparate parts
- Social issues in the visual depiction of a community
- Technical issues in the integration of live and processed video

At MIT, a Meta-Media project aggregates a rich set of graphic tools and editors with searching, browsing, linking, scripting, and visualization capabilities. The aim is to research new design perspectives emerging from real-time, multi-layered information in an electronic communication environment.

15.8 Using Graphics with Simulated Financial Markets

In scientific visualization, complex mathematical equations translate to images that reveal new meaning to the knowledgeable end user. As we have seen in Part 2 on the Internet, the World Wide Web, VRML, and Java, cruising through a database the end user not only retrieves information but also can test models through market simulation or investigate behavioral patterns.

Computer-generated images of a market response can be easily displayed for the analyst's perception to help create a realistic training and trading experience. Hardware devices and software routines technology makes available help to measure responses to conditions, such as changing liquidity and volatility, that would be full of risks in actual circumstances.

The ability to foresee a product or a market before a commitment is actually made is an invaluable tool for financial analysts and new product designers. Rendering software makes it possible to create a realistic picture of a product automatically from three-dimensional models, so projects can be optimized and feedback can be taken into account early in the design cycle.

- Rendered images can be used by marketing and sales personnel to sell an idea to a potential customer.
- Photorealistic image of a product or project makes it easier to communicate investment intent.

These references are the alter ego of the personalization of reporting and of information representation which we have examined in connection to news in the future. They are, as well, a great leap forward from the static use of signs and symbols. Fixed symbols are a different ballgame.

Because the model resides in the computer, changes induced by feedback are done easily and quickly. The next is animation. The ability to display the evolution of three-dimensional data over time provides invaluable insight into the contents of information—and helps in moving toward corrective action.

Once used in business and industry mainly for marketing purposes, animation software is now employed by analysts and designers to breath life into their artifacts.

Animating product designs enable one not only to see how a product or process will look, but also to evaluate how it will work.

- Animations are used for product design reviews to reveal how the market reaction may go, by means of a simulated market response.

- This permits one to bypass the fact that new financial products are currently limited by human perception capabilities.

By testing concepts and designs that analysts have only dreamed about, even in the recent past, we can see how far traders can push the market. We can also test responses and realistically evaluate risks before we commit to building a new financial product.

An example of what can be achieved in banking by the method outlined can be taken from computer graphics applications in the automotive industry. The ultimate in cruise control not only brakes and accelerates but also steers a vehicle.

- From a TV camera on the dash, digitized images of the road are fed into a computer system that is able to read and evaluate the road's midline and curb curvature.

- Motor vehicle developers envision this system serving as an autopilot for drivers on city streets and autoroutes, beyond the concept of a testing ground.

Pressing the accelerator gives the driver of the simulator the sound and movement of the car speeding up, taking a sharp curve, or entering 130 km/h traffic. The entire dome with car, screen, and projectors can rapidly swing and tilt, to add real-life sensations to starting, cruising, and stopping.

Rocket scientists with experience in the aerospace, nuclear, and motor vehicle industries appreciate that there is a major difference between two-dimensional graphics and three-dimensional graphics. What makes appreciating and moving around within a scene possible is the introduction of the third, or depth, dimension. This permits one to fly through a scene or change viewpoints in three dimensions and makes feasible ingenious exploitation of the what-if concept.

Capitalizing on the computer's capacity to analyze a variety of solutions to every problem is what makes computer graphics a powerful design tool. Product designers and end users can actually experience the sensation of dealing with instruments that have not yet been built merely by manipulating the product's and market's parameters. In finance, for instance,

- Rocket scientists[4] can experiment with limitless options before stabilizing a product.

- Clients can examine computer graphics images of their exposure from different angles and in different light long before commitment.

Because of the computer's unique ability to change the point of view on the screen, a solution can be examined from ground level up, in accordance with an impressive number of criteria. Many of these criteria could be personalized.

Among other major advantages, this permits concurrent development of processes and products. One of the major benefits offered by concurrent development is improved quality: Better product definitions result from the involvement of all parts of the organization in the initial stages of such a definition. And the process used to handle the product is practically developed at the same time as the product itself.

15.9   High Performance in Business and Real World Computing

Leading-edge organizations commented in the course of my research that concurrent development has allowed them to build processes and products interactively. This reduces the probability of miscoordination by different professionals, or that the development teams will produce orphans that have little chance of being produced in time, therefore of surviving in a very competitive market.

But while the visual programming of sophisticated models and three-dimensional color graphics foster a climate for cultural change, they also impose significant number-crunching requirements. Successful projects invigorate the organization as the knowledge, and hence effectiveness, of the team members increases. At the same time they challenge the current information technology resources from contents to machinery. Therefore, solutions have to be found which support significant increases in computer power, database bandwidth, and communications channel capacity at low cost. Such solutions must promote the approaches we are discussing because they constitute an integrative mechanism which, in all likelihood, will be the wave of the future.

It is therefore no wonder that from the United States to Europe and Japan, the goal of advanced projects is to support and enhance flexible autonomous control. Such efforts include the methodology to integrate sensing, perception, planning, and action from the viewpoint of adaptation and learning, which are attainable goals.

Real World Computing, a project financed by the Japanese government to the tune of 85 billion yen, aims at realizing integrated adaptable autonomous systems which work interactively in real time. The intelligent and sophisticated resolution of combinatorial problems is pursued for integrating individual novel functions.

- These functions are projected to be able to cooperate with others, in order to create newer functions, contributing to the robustness and openness of the system.

- Emphasis is placed on the discovery and development of new algorithms which will stimulate real-life conditions for creating new implementation paradigms.

What the Japanese target with the effort behind the second item above is breaking the current *algorithmic inefficiency.* In their judgment, we have practically reached the limits of what can be done with presently available algorithms and the models based on them. As the complexity of business increases, new and much more powerful mathematical tools will be needed. Every scientist should be aware of this fact.

It is the aim of the Real World Computing project to ensure that new ideas for flexible inference and problem solving are applied to multimedia information databases. These will incorporate not only voice, text, data, graphics, and video but also new types of algorithms designed for solving inference problems and constraint satisfaction.

Another milestone is expected to be the methodology for self-organization of a large number of databases and knowledge banks. This will go well beyond the services of object-oriented database management systems today and will make use of a significant number of agents.

Forward-looking research and development activities seek an autonomous information processing system which actively and adaptively grasps incomplete, uncertain, and changeable information in the real world—and learns from it. Then it works according to what it has learned by instigating the cooperation of various autonomous agents.

There are many applications in the financial industry which can benefit from the Real World Computing effort at large and from solutions described in the preceding paragraphs in particular. To take just two of them, from the day-in and day-out, year-in and year-out work in any bank, successful implementations can be in

- The *dealing room* which represents roughly two-thirds of the total exposure in any of the leading financial institutions

- *Credits and loans* which are typically under the commercial division and concern the other one-third of global risk

"In politics you judge the value of a service by the amount you put in. In business you judge it by the amount you get out," suggests Margaret Thatcher,[5] and she is right. But to get out profits, and therefore results, companies have to put in lots of energy and a superior organization.

As I never tire of repeating, it is hard to make gains without innovation in products and services as well as in the way to approach the market. Our epoch is one of altering the corporate culture, restructuring, right-sizing, and seeking new alliances to escape the dual traps of gigantism and inertia.

References

1. *To Our Authors,* Winter 1995/96.
2. See also D. N. Chorafas and H. Steinmann, *Database Mining,* Lafferty Publications, London, 1994.
3. See D. N. Chorafas, *Managing Derivatives Risk,* Irwin Professional Publishing, Burr Ridge, IL, 1996.
4. See D. N. Chorafas, *Rocket Scientists in Banking,* Lafferty Publications, London, 1996.
5. *The Downing Street Years,* Harper Collins, London, 1993.

Acknowledgments

The following organizations, their senior executives, and their system specialists participated in the 1992 and 1993 research projects which led to the contents of this book and its documentation.

United States

Bankers Trust

- Dr. Carmine Vona, Executive Vice President for Worldwide Technology
- Shalom Brinsy, Senior Vice President, Distributed Networks
- Dan W. Muecke, Vice President, Technology Strategic Planning
- Bob Graham, Vice President, Database Manager

One Bankers Trust Plaza, New York, NY 10006

Citibank

- Colin Crook, Chairman, Corporate Technology Committee
- David Schultzer, Senior Vice President, Information Technology
- Jim Caldarella, Manager, Business Architecture for Global Finance
- Nicholas P. Richards, Database Administrator
- William Brindley, Technology Officer
- Michael R. Veale, Network Connectivity
- Harriet Schabes, Corporate Standards
- Leigh Reeve, Technology for Global Finance

399 Park Avenue, New York, NY 10043

Morgan Stanley

- Gary T. Goehrke, Managing Director, Information Services
- Guy Chiarello, Vice President, Databases

- Robert F. De Young, Principal, Information Technology

1933 Broadway, New York, NY 10019

- Eileen S. Wallace, Vice President, Treasury Department
- Jacqueline T. Brody, Treasury Department

1251 Avenue of the Americas, New York, NY 10020

Goldman Sachs

- Vincent L. Amatulli, Information Technology, Treasury Department

85 Broad Street, New York, NY 10004

J. J. Kenny Services Inc.

- Thomas E. Zielinski, Chief Information Officer
- Ira Kirschner, Database Administrator, Director of System Programming and the Data Center

65 Broadway, New York, NY 10006

Merrill Lynch

- Kevin Sawyer, Director of Distributed Computing Services and Executive in Charge of the Mainframe to Client-Server Conversion Process
- Raymond M. Disco, Treasury/Bank Relations Manager

World Financial Center, South Tower, New York, NY 10080-6107

Teachers Insurance and Annuity Association/College Retirement Equities Fund (TIAA/CREF)

- Charles S. Dvorkin, Vice President and Chief Technology Officer
- Harry D. Perrin, Assistant Vice President, Information Technology

730 Third Avenue, New York, NY 10017-3206

Financial Accounting Standards Board

- Halsey G. Bullen, Project Manager
- Jeannot Blanchet, Project Manager
- Teri L. List, Practice Fellow

401 Merritt, Norwalk, CT 06856

Teknekron Software Systems, Inc.

- Vivek Ranadive, President and CEO
- Robert Rector, Senior Vice President, Client Technical Services
- Martin Luthi, Senior Director, Client Technical Services
- Gerard D. Buggy, Vice President, Global Financial Sales and Marketing
- Norman Cheung, Director, Quantum Leap Group
- Bradley C. Rhode, Vice President, Core Technology Engineering
- Tugrul Firatli, Director, Network Consulting Services
- John E. McDowall, Systems Specialist
- Tom Jasek, Director, Market Sheet
- Glenn A. McComb, Senior Member of Technical Staff, New Technologies
- Murat K. Sönmez, Member of Technical Staff
- Murray D. Rode, Member of Technical Staff

530 Lytton Avenue, Suite 301, Palo Alto, CA 94301

Evans and Sutherland

- Les Horwood, Director, New Business Development
- Mike Walterman, Systems Engineer, Virtual Reality Applications
- Lisa B. Huber, Software Engineer, Three-Dimensional Programming

600 Komas Drive, P.O. Box 58700, Salt Lake City, UT 84158

nCube

- Michael Meirer, President and Chief Executive Officer
- Craig D. Ramsey, Senior Vice President, Worldwide Sales
- Ronald J. Buck, Vice President, Marketing
- Matthew Hall, Director of Software Development

919 E. Hillside Boulevard, Foster City, CA 94404

Taligent

- Dr. Jack Grimes, Manager, Technology Evaluation
- Catherine Jaeger, Manager, Market Development

10201 N. De Anza Boulevard, Cupertino, CA 95014-2233

Visual Numerics

- Don Kainer, Vice President and General Manager
- Joe Weaver, Vice President, OEM/VAR Sales
- Jim Phillips, Director, Product Development
- Dr. Shawn Javid, Senior Product Manager
- Dan Clark, Manager, WAVE Family Products
- Thomas L. Welch, Marketing Product Manager
- Margaret Journey, Director, Administration
- John Bee, Technical Sales Engineer
- Adam Asnes, VDA Sales Executive
- William Potts, Sales Manager

6230 Lookout Road, Boulder, CO 80301

Massachusetts Institute of Technology

- Dr. Stuart E. Madnick, Professor, Information Technology and Management Science
- Patricia M. McGinnis, Executive Director, International Financial Services
- Peter J. Kempthorne, Professor, Project on Nontraditional Methods in Financial Analysis
- Dr. Alexander M. Samarov, Project on Nontraditional Methods in Financial Analysis
- Robert R. Halperin, Executive Director, Center for Coordination Science

292 Main Street, Cambridge, MA 02139

- Dr. Michael Siegel, Professor, Information Technology
- Amar Gupta, Professor, Sloan School of Management
- Jean-Luc Vila, Professor, Finance Department
- Bin Zhou, Professor, Management Science
- Eric B. Sundin, Industrial Liaison Officer
- David L. Verrill, Senior Liaison Officer, Industrial Liaison Program

Sloan School of Management, 50 Memorial Drive, Cambridge, MA 02139

- Henry H. Houh, Desk Area Network and ViewStation Project, Electrical Engineering and Computer Science
- Dr. Henry A. Lieberman, Media Laboratory

- Valerie A. Eames, Media Laboratory
- Dr. Kenneth B. Haase, Professor, Media Arts and Sciences
- Dr. David Zeltzer, Virtual Reality Project

Ames Street, Cambridge, MA 02139

University of Michigan

- Professor John H. Holland, Electrical Engineering and Computer Science
- Dr. Rick L. Riolo, Systems Researcher, Department of Psychology

Ann Arbor, MI 48109-2103

Santa Fe Institute

- Dr. Edward A. Knapp, President
- Dr. L. Mike Simmons, Jr., Vice President
- Dr. Bruce Abell, Vice President, Finance
- Dr. Murray Gell-Mann, Professor, Theory of Complexity
- Dr. Stuart Kauffman, Professor, Models in Biology
- Dr. Chris Langton, Artificial Life
- Dr. John Miller, Adaptive Computation in Economics
- Dr. Blake Le Baron, Nontraditional Methods in Economics
- Bruce Sawhill, Virtual Reality

1660 Old Pecos Trail, Santa Fe, NM 87501

School of Engineering and Applied Science, University of California, Los Angeles

- Dean A. R. Frank Wazzan, School of Engineering and Applied Science
- Professor Richard Muntz, Chair, Computer Science Department
- Dr. Leonard Kleinrock, Professor, Telecommunications and Networks
- Professor Nicolaos G. Alexopoulos, Electrical Engineering
- Dr. Judea Pearl, Professor, Cognitive Systems Laboratory
- Dr. Walter Karplus, Professor, Computer Science Department
- Dr. Michael G. Dyer, Professor, Artificial Intelligence Laboratory
- Susan Cruse, Director of Development and Alumni Affairs
- Joel Short, Ph.D. Candidate

- David Chickering, Ph.D. Candidate

Westwood Village, Los Angeles, CA 90024

School of Business Administration, University of Southern California

- Dr. Bert M. Steece, Dean of Faculty
- Dr. Alan Rowe, Professor of Management

Los Angeles, CA 90089-1421

Prediction Company

- Dr. J. Doyne Farmer, Director of Development
- Dr. Norman H. Packard, Director of Research
- Jim McGill, Managing Director

234 Griffin Street, Santa Fe, NM 87501

Simgraphics Engineering Corp.

- Steve Tice, President
- David J. Verso, Chief Operating Officer

1137 Huntington Drive, South Pasadena, CA 91030-4563

NYNEX Science and Technology, Inc.

- Thomas M. Super, Vice President, Research and Development
- Steven Cross, NYNEX Shuttle Project
- Valerie R. Tingle, System Analyst
- Melinda Crews, Public Liaison, NYNEX Labs

500 Westchester Avenue, White Plains, NY 10604

- John C. Falco, Sales Manager, NYNEX Systems Marketing
- David J. Annino, Account Executive, NYNEX Systems Marketing

100 Church Street, New York, NY 10007

Microsoft

- Mike McGeehan, Database Specialist
- Andrew Elliott, Marketing Manager

825 Eighth Avenue, New York, NY 10019

Reuters America

- Robert Russel, Senior Vice President
- William A. S. Kennedy, Vice President
- Buford Smith, President, Reuters Information Technology
- Richard A. Willis, Manager, International Systems Design
- M. A. Sayers, Technical Manager, Central Systems Development
- Alexander Faust, Manager, Financial Products USA (Instantlink and Blend)

40 E. 52nd Street, New York, NY 10022

Oracle Corporation

- Scott Matthews, National Account Manager
- Robert T. Funk, Senior Systems Specialist
- Joseph M. Di Bartolomeo, Systems Specialist
- Dick Dawson, Systems Specialist

885 Third Avenue, New York, NY 10022

Digital Equipment Corporation

- Mike Fishbein, Product Manager, Massively Parallel Systems (MAS-PAR Supercomputer)
- Marco Emrich, Technology Manager, NAS
- Robert Passmore, Technical Manager, Storage Systems
- Mark S. Dresdner, DEC Marketing Operations

146 Main Street, Maynard, MA 01754 (Meeting held at UBS New York)

Unisys Corporation

- Harvey J. Chiat, Director, Impact Programs
- Manuel Lavin, Director, Databases
- David A. Goiffon, Software Engineer

P.O. Box 64942, MS 4463, Saint Paul, MN 55164-0942 (Meeting held at UBS in New York)

Hewlett-Packard

- Brad Wilson, Product Manager, Commercial Systems
- Vish Krishnan, Manager, R&D Laboratory
- Samir Mathur, Open ODB Manager
- Michael Gupta, Transarc, Tuxedo, Encina Transaction Processing
- Dave Williams, Industry Account Manager

1911 Pruneridge Avenue, Cupertino, CA 95014

IBM Corporation

- Terry Liffick, Software Strategies, Client-Server Architecture
- Paula Cappello, Information Warehouse Framework
- Ed Cobbs, Transaction Processing Systems
- Dr. Paul Wilms, Connectivity and Interoperability
- Helen Arzu, IBM Santa Teresa Representative
- Dana L. Stetson, Advisory Marketing, IBM New York

Santa Teresa Laboratory, 555 Bailey Avenue, San José, CA 95141

UBS Securities

- A. Ramy Goldstein, Managing Director, Equity Derivative Products

299 Park Avenue, New York, NY 10171-0026

Union Bank of Switzerland

- Dr. H. Baumann, Director of Logistics, North American Operations
- Dr. Ch. Gabathuler, Director, Information Technology
- Hossur Srikantan, Vice President, Information Technology Department

- Roy M. Darhin, Assistant Vice President

299 Park Avenue, New York, NY 10171-0026

United Kingdom

Barclays Bank

- Peter Golden, Chief Information Officer, Barclays Capital Markets, Treasury, BZW
- Brandon Davies, Treasurer, UK Banking Group
- David J. Parsons, Director Advanced Technology
- Christine E. Irwin, Group Information Systems Technology

Murray House, 1 Royal Mint Court, London EC3N 4HH

Bank of England

- Mark Laycock, Banking Supervision Division

Threadneedle Street, London EC2R 8AH

Association for Payment Clearing Services (APACS)

- J. Michael Williamson, Deputy Chief Executive

14 Finsbury Square, London EC2A 1BR

Abbey National Bank

- Mac Millington, Director of Information Technology

Chalkdell Drive, Shenley Wood, Milton Keynes MK6 6LA

- Anthony W. Elliott, Director of Risk and Credit

Abbey House, Baker Street, London NW1 6XL

Natwest Securities

- Sam B. Gibb, Director of Information Technology
- Don F. Simpson, Director, Global Technology
- Richard E. Gibbs, Director, Equity Derivatives

135 Bishopsgate, London EC2M 3XT

Oracle Corporation

- Mr. Geoffrey W. Squire, Executive Vice President and Chief Executive Officer
- Mr. Richard Barker, Senior Vice President and Director British Research Laboratories
- Mr. Giles Godart-Brown, Senior Support Manager
- Mr. Paul A. Gould, Account Executive

Oracle Park, Bittams Lane, Guildford Road, Chertsey, Surrey KT16 9RG

Virtual Presence

- Stuart Cupit, Graphics Engineer

25 Corsham Street, London N1 6DR

VALBECC Object Technology

- Martin Fowler, Ptech Expert

115 Wilmslow Road, Handforth, Wilmslow, Cheshire SK9 3ER

Credit Swiss Financial Products

- Ross Salinger, Managing Director

1 Cabot Square, London E14 4QJ

Credit Swiss First Boston

- Geoff J. R. Doubleday, Executive Director

1 Cabot Square, London E14 4QJ

E.D.&F. MAN International

- Brian Fudge, Funds Division

Sugar Quay, Lower Thames Street, London EC3R 6DU

Scandinavia

Vaerdipapircentralen (VP)

- Mr. Jens Bache, General Manager
- Mrs. Aase Blume, Assistant to the General Manager

61 Helgeshoj Allé, Postbox 20, 2630 Taastrup, Denmark

Swedish Bankers' Association

- Bo Gunnarsson, Manager, Bank Automation Department
- Gösta Fischer, Manager, Bank-Owned Financial Companies Department
- Göran Ahlberg, Manager, Credit Market Affairs Department

P.O. Box 7603, 10394 Stockholm, Sweden

Skandinaviska Enskilda Banken

- Lars Isacsson, Treasurer
- Urban Janeld, Executive Vice President, Finance and IT
- Mats Andersson, Director of Computers and Communications
- Gösta Olavi, Manager, SEB Data/Koncern Data

2 Sergels Torg, 10640 Stockholm, Sweden

Securum AB

- Anders Nyren, Director of Finance and Accounting
- John Lundgren, Manager of IT

38 Regeringsg, 5 tr., 10398 Stockholm, Sweden

Sveatornet AB of the Swedish Savings Banks

- Gunar M. Carlsson, General Manager

(Meeting at Swedish Bankers' Association)

Mandamus AB of the Swedish Agricultural Banks

- Marie Martinsson, Credit Department

(Meeting at Swedish Bankers' Association)

Handelsbanken

- Mr. Janeric Sundin, Manager, Securities Department
- Mr. Jan Aronson, Assistant Manager, Securities Department

(Meeting at Swedish Bankers' Association)

Gota Banken

- Johannsson, Credit Department

(Meeting at Swedish Bankers' Association)

Irdem AB

- Gian Medri, Former Director of Research at Nordbanken

19 Flintlasvagen, 19154 Sollentuna, Sweden

Austria

Creditanstalt Bankverein

- Dr. Wolfgang G. Lichtl, Director of Foreign Exchange and Money Markets
- Dr. Johann Strobl, Manager, Financial Analysis for Treasury Operations

3, Julius Tandler-Platz, 1090 Vienna

Bank Austria

- Dr. Peter Fischer, Director of Treasury
- Peter Gabriel, Deputy General Manager, Trading
- Konrad Schcate, Manager, Financial Engineering

2, Am Hof, 1010 Vienna

Association of Austrian Banks and Bankers

- Dr. Fritz Diwok, Secretary General

11, Boersengasse, 1013 Vienna

Aktiengesellschaft fuer Bauwesen

- Dr. Josef Fritz, General Manager

2, Lothringenstrasse, 1041 Vienna

Management Data of Creditanstalt

- Ing. Guenther Reindl, Vice President, International Banking Software
- Ing. Franz Necas, Project Manager, RICOS
- Mag. Nikolas Goetz, Product Manager, RICOS

21-25 Althanstrasse, 1090 Vienna

Germany

Deutsche Bundesbank

- Eckhard Oechler, Director of Bank Supervision and Legal Matters

14, Wilhelm Epstein Strasse, D-6000 Frankfurt 50

Deutsche Bank

- Peter Gerard, Executive Vice President, Organization and Information Technology
- Hermann Seiler, Senior Vice President, Investment Banking and Foreign Exchange Systems
- Dr. Kuhn, Investment Banking and Foreign Exchange Systems
- Dr. Stefan Kolb, Organization and Technological Development

12, Koelner Strasse, D-6236 Eschborn

Dresdner Bank

- Dr. Karsten Wohlenberg, Project Leader Risk Management, Simulation and Analytics Task Force Financial Division
- Hans-Peter Leisten, Mathematician

- Susanne Loesken, Organization and IT Department

43, Mainzer Landstrasse, D-6000 Frankfurt

Commerzbank

- Helmut Hoppe, Director, Organization and Information Technology
- Hermann Lenz, Director Controllership, Internal Accounting and Management Accounting
- Harald Lux, Manager, Organization and Information Technology
- Waldemar Nickel, Manager, Systems Planning

155, Mainzer Landstrasse, D-60261 Frankfurt

Deutscher Sparkassen und Giroverband

- Manfred Krueger, Division Manager, Card Strategy

4, Simrockstrasse, D-5300 Bonn 1 (Telephone interview from Frankfurt)

ABN-AMRO (Holland)

- Mr. Schilder, Organization and Information Technology

(Telephone interview from Frankfurt)

Media Systems

- Bertram Anderer, Director

6, Goethestrasse, D-7500 Karlsruhe

Fraunhofer Institute for Computer Graphics

- Dr. Ing. Martin Goebel, Director, 3-D Graphics
- Wolfgang Felber, Systems Specialist

7, Wilhelminerstrasse, D-6100 Darmstadt

GMD First—Research Institute for Computer Architecture, Software Technology and Graphics

- Dr. Ing. Wolfgang K. Giloi, Professor, General Manager
- Dr. Behr, Administrative Director

- Dr. Ulrich Bruening, Chief Designer
- Dr. Joerg Nolte, Designer of Parallel Operating Systems Software
- Dr. Matthias Kessler, Parallel Languages and Parallel Compilers
- Dr. Friedrich W. Schroer, New Programming Paradigms
- Dr. Thomas Lux, Fluid Dynamics, Weather Prediction and Pollution Control Project

5, Rudower Chaussee, D-1199 Berlin

Siemens Nixdorf

- Wolfgang Weiss, Director of Banking Industry Office
- Bert Kirschbaum, Manager, Dresdner Bank Project
- Mark Miller, Manager, Neural Networks Project for UBS and German banks
- Andrea Vonerden, Business Management Department

27, Lyoner Strasse, D-6000 Frankfurt 71

UBS Germany

- H.-H. v. Scheliha, Director, Organization and Information Technology
- Georg Sudhaus, Manager IT for Trading Systems
- Marco Bracco, Trader
- Jaap van Harten, Trader

52, Bleichstrasse, D-6000 Frankfurt 1

Switzerland

Bank for International Settlements

- Frederik C. Musch, Secretary General, Basel Committee on Banking Supervision
- Claude Sivy, Director, Controllership and Operational Security

2 Centralbankplatz, Basel

BZ Bank Zurich

- Martin Ebner, President
- Peter Sjostrand, Finance

- Olivier Willi, Analyst
- Roger Jenny, Analyst

50 Sihlstrasse, 8021 Zurich

BZ Trust Aktiengesellschaft

- Dr. Stefan Holzer, Financial Analyst

24 Eglirain, 8832 Wilen

CIBA-GEIGY AG

- Stefan Janovjak, Divisional Information Manager
- Natalie Papezik, Information Architect

R-1045, 5.19, 4002 Basel

Ecole Polytechnique Federal de Lausanne

- Dr. Jean-Daniel Nicoud, Professor, Director, Microinformatics Laboratory
- Dr. Boi Faltings, Professor, Artificial Intelligence
- Dr. Martin J. Hasler, Professor, Circuits and Systems
- Dr. Ing. Roman Boulic, Computer Graphics

1015 Lausanne

Eurodis

- Albert Mueller, Director
- Beat Erzer, Marketing Manager
- B. Pedrazzini, Systems Engineer
- Reto Albertini, Sales Engineer

Bahnhofstrasse 58/60, CH-8105 Regensdorf

Olsen and Associates

- Dr. Richard Olsen, President

232 Seefeldstrasse, 8008 Zurich

Swiss Bank Corporation

- Dr. Marcel Rohner, Director, IFD Controlling

Swiss Bank Center, 8010 Zurich

Japan

Bank of Japan

- Harry Toyama, Counsel and Chief Manager, Credit and Market Management Department
- Akira Ieda, Credit and Market Management Department

2-1-1, Kongoku-Cho, Nihonbashi, Chuo-ku, Tokyo 103

Dai-Ichi Kangyo Bank

- Shunsuke Nakasuji, General Manager and Director, Information Technology Division
- Seiichi Hasegawa, Manager, International Systems Group
- Takahiro Sekizawa, International Systems Group
- Yukio Hisatomi, Manager Systems Planning Group
- Shigeaki Togawa, Systems Planning Group

13-3, Shibuya, 2-Chome, Shibuya-ku, Tokyo 150

Fuji Bank

- Hideo Tanaka, General Manager, Systems Planning Division
- Toshihiko Uzaki, Manager, Systems Planning Division
- Takakazu Imai, Systems Planning Division

Otemachi Financial Center, 1-5-4 Otemachi, Chiyoda-ku, Tokyo

Mitsubishi Bank

- Akira Watanabe, General Manager, Derivative Products
- Akira Towatari, Manager, Strategic Planning and Administration, Derivative Products
- Takehito Nemoto, Chief Manager, Systems Development Division

- Nobuyuki Yamada, Systems Development Division
- Haruhiko Suzuki, Systems Development Division

7-1, Marunouchi, 2-Chome, Chiyoda-ku, Tokyo 100

Nomura Research Institute

- Tomio Arai, Director, Systems Science Department
- Tomoyuki Ohta, Director, Financial Engineering Group
- Tomohiko Hiruta, Manager, I-STAR Systems Services

9-1, Nihonbashi, 1-Chome, Chuo-ku, Tokyo 103

Mitsubishi Trust and Banking

- Nobuyuki Tanaka, General Manager, Systems Planning Division
- Terufumi Kage, Consultant Systems Planning Division

9-8 Kohnan, 2-Chome, Minato-ku, Tokyo 108

Sakura Bank

- Nobuo Ihara, Senior Vice President and General Manager, Systems Development Office VIII
- Hisao Katayama, Senior Vice President and General Manager, System Development Office VII
- Toshihiko Eda, Senior Systems Engineer, Systems Development Division

4-2, Kami-Osahi, 4-Chome, Shinagawa-ku, Tokyo 141

Sanyo Securities

- Yuji Ozawa, Director, Systems Planning Department
- K. Toyama, Systems Planning Department

1-8-1, Nihonbashi, Kayabacho, Chuo-ku, Tokyo 103

Center for Financial Industry Information Systems (FISC)

- Shighehisa Hattori, Executive Director
- Kiyoshi Kumata, Manager, Research Division II

16th Floor, Ark Mori Building, 12-32, 1-Chome Akasaka, Minato-ku, Tokyo 107

Laboratory for International Fuzzy Engineering Research (LIFE)

- Dr. Toshiro Terano, Professor, Executive Director
- Dr. Anca L. Ralescu, Assistant Director
- Shunichi Tani, Fuzzy Control Project Leader

Siber Hegner Building, 89-1 Yamashita-Cho, Naka-ku, Yokohama-shi 231

Real World Computing Partnership (RWC)

- Dr. Junichi Shumada, General Manager of RWC
- Hajime Irisawa, Executive Director

Tsukuba Mitsui Building, 1-6-1 Takezono, Tsukuba-shi, Ibarahi 305

Tokyo University

- Dr. Michitaka Hirose, Professor, Department of Mechano-Informatics, Faculty of Engineering
- Dr. Kensuke Yokoyama, Virtual Reality Project

3-1, 7-Chome, Hongo Bunkyo-ku, Tokyo 113

Tokyo International University

- Dr. Yoshiro Kuratani, Professor

9-1-7-528, Akasaka, Minato-ku, Tokyo 107

Japan Electronic Directory Research Institute

- Dr. Toshio Yokoi, General Manager

Mita-Kokusai Building—Annex, 4-28 Mita, 1-Chome, Minato-ku, Tokyo 108

Mitsubishi Research Institute (MRI)

- Masayuki Fujita, Manager, Strategic Information Systems Department
- Hideyuki Morita, Senior Research Associate, Information Science Department
- Akio Sato, Research Associate, Information Science Department

ARCO Tower, 8-1 Shimomeguro, 1-Chome, Meguro-ku, Tokyo 153

NTT Software

- Dr. Fukuya Ishino, Senior Vice President

223-1 Yamashita-Cho, Naka-ku, Yokohama 231

Ryoshin Systems (Systems Developer Fully Owned by Mitsubishi Trust)

- Takewo Yuwi, Vice President, Technical Research and Development

9-8 Kohman, 2-Chome, Minato-ku, Tokyo 108

Sanyo Software Services

- Fumio Sato, General Manager, Sales Department 2

Kanayama Building, 1-2-12 Shinkawa, Chuo-ku, Tokyo 104

Fujitsu Research Institute

- Dr. Masuteru Sekiguchi, Member of the Board and Director of R&D
- Takao Saito, Director of the Parallel Computing Research Center
- Dr. Hiroyasu Itoh, R&D Department
- Katsuto Kondo, R&D Department
- Satoshi Hamaya, Information Systems and Economics

9-3 Nakase, 1-Chome, Mihama-ku, Chiba-City 261

NEC

- Kotaro Namba, Senior Researcher, NEC Planning Research
- Dr. Toshiyuki Nakata, Manager, Computer System Research Laboratory
- Asao Kaneko, Computer System Research Laboratory

3-13-12 Mita, Minato-ku, Tokyo 108

Toshiba

- Dr. Makoto Ihara, Manager, Workstation Product Planning and Technical Support Department
- Emi Nakamura, Analyst Financial Applications Department
- Joshikiyo Nakamura, Financial Sales Manager

- Minami Arai, Deputy Manager, Workstation Systems Division

1-1, Shibaura, 1-Chome, Minato-ku, Tokyo 105

Microsoft

- James Lalonde, Multinational Account Manager, Large Accounts Sales Department

Sasazuka NA Building, 50-1 Sasazuka, 1-Chome, Shibuya-ku, Tokyo 151

Apple Technology

- Dr. Tsutomu Kobayashi, President

25 Mori Building, 1-4-30 Roppongi, Minato-ku, Tokyo 106

Digital Equipment Japan

- Roshio Ishii, Account Manager, Financial Sales Unit 1

2-1 Kamiogi, 1-Chome, Suginamiku, Tokyo 167

UBS Japan

- Dr. Peter Brutsche, Executive Vice President and Chief Manager
- Gary P. Eidam, First Vice President, Regional Head of Technology
- Charles Underwood, Vice President, Head of Technical Architecture and Strategy
- Masaki Utsunomiya, Manager, IT Production Facilities

Yurakucho Building 2F, 1-10-1 Yurakucho, Chiyoda-ku, Tokyo 100

Index

ABOUT THE AUTHOR

Dimitris N. Chorafas, Ph.D., is an internationally known consultant, author, and lecturer specializing in strategic planning and design of information systems. He has written 107 books on management and computer topics, and is a well-known expert on computer systems design, operations research, simulation, expert systems, distributed data processing, database organization, and network systems design. Dr. Chorafas has been an independent consultant since 1961, working for companies such as Union Bank of Switzerland, Von Tobel Bank, Bank Austria, First Austrian Bank, Dresdner Bank, Commerzbank, Istituto Bancario Italiano, Credito Commerciale, Banca Provinciale Lombarda, Digital Equipment Corporation, General Electric, Olivetti, UNIVAC, and many others in the United States and Europe. He has also taught at the university level in Europe and at seven universities in the United States. Dr. Chorafas lives in Saint Laurent d'Eze, France, and in Switzerland.